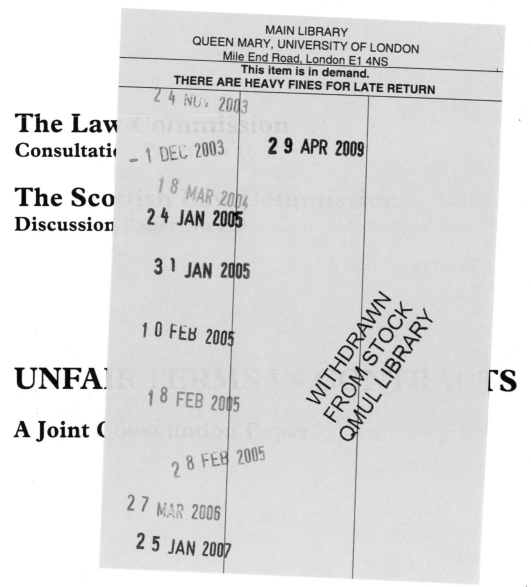

The Law Commission
Consultation

The Scottish
Discussion

UNFAIR TERMS IN CONTRACTS

A Joint Consultation Paper

London: TSO

Published by TSO (The Stationery Office) and available from:

Online
www.tso.co.uk/bookshop

Mail, Telephone, Fax & E-mail
TSO
PO Box 29, Norwich, NR3 1GN
Telephone orders/General enquiries 0870 600 5522
Fax orders 0870 600 5533
E-mail book.orders@tso.co.uk
Textphone 0870 240 3701

TSO Shops
123 Kingsway, London WC2B 6PQ
020 7242 6393 Fax 020 7242 6394
68-69 Bull Street, Birmingham B4 6AD
0121 236 9696 Fax 0121 236 9699
9-21 Princess Street, Manchester M60 8AS
0161 834 7201 Fax 0161 833 0634
16 Arthur Street, Belfast BT1 4GD
028 9023 8451 Fax 028 9023 5401
18-19 High Street, Cardiff CF1 2BZ
029 2039 5548 Fax 029 2038 4347
71 Lothian Road, Edinburgh EH3 9AZ
0870 606 5566 Fax 0870 606 5588

TSO Accredited Agents
(See Yellow Pages)

and through good booksellers

© Crown Copyright 2002
Published with the permission of the Law Commission on behalf
of the Controller of Her Majesty's Stationery Office

Applications for reproduction should be made in writing to
The Copyright Unit, Her Majesty's Stationery Office,
St. Clements House, 2-16 Colegate, Norwich NR3 1BQ

ISBN 0 11 730252 X

Printed in the United Kingdom by The Stationery Office
ID106189 C12 8/02 19585 761459

THE LAW COMMISSION

THE SCOTTISH LAW COMMISSION

UNFAIR TERMS IN CONTRACTS

CONTENTS

PART V: EXTENDING THE PROTECTION AGAINST UNFAIR TERMS TO BUSINESSES

vii

PART VIII: PUTTING THE NEW LEGISLATION INTO CLEAR, ACCESSIBLE TERMS

PART IX: PROVISIONAL PROPOSALS AND QUESTIONS FOR CONSULTEES

APPENDIX A: PROTECTION FROM UNFAIR TERMS AFFORDED TO BUSINESSES IN OTHER JURISDICTIONS

EXECUTIVE SUMMARY

THE BACKGROUND TO THE CONSULTATION PAPER

S.1 Without adequate legal controls, there is a risk that the terms of contracts will be unfair to one of the parties. This applies to both contracts between a business and a consumer ("consumer contracts") and business-to-business contracts, and is particularly the case where the terms of the contract have been drawn up by one party in advance. Although the other party may "agree" to the contract, he may not be aware of the term in question, or may not understand its implications. Even if he does realise what the term means, he may find that the other party is unwilling to change its "standard terms" just for him. Both Parliament and the courts have been concerned about unfair contract terms for many years.

S.2 Legislation to combat unfair terms was first passed in the 19th century. Until 1994 the controls centred on clauses which exclude or limit liability; the principal Act is now the Unfair Contract Terms Act 1977 (UCTA). However, in 1993 the European Council of Ministers passed a Directive on Unfair Terms on Consumer Contracts[1] which applies (with limited exceptions) to unfair terms of any type in consumer contracts. The Directive was implemented in the UK by Regulations made under the European Communities Act 1972; these have now been superseded by the Unfair Terms in Consumer Contracts Regulations 1999 (UTCCR).[2] The Regulations did not amend or repeal UCTA; they provide an additional set of controls. Thus potentially unfair terms in contracts are at present subject to one or both of two quite separate legal regimes.

S.3 If the term in question is one that purports to exclude or restrict the liability of one of the parties, it is likely to be subject to UCTA. UCTA applies both to consumer contracts and to contracts between businesses.[3] It may have the effect that the exclusion or restriction of liability is completely ineffective; or it may invalidate the term unless it "satisfies the requirement of reasonableness".

S.4 If the term is in a consumer contract it will normally be subject to UTCCR. UTCCR can apply to almost any type of term that has not been "individually negotiated", and will invalidate the term if it is "unfair". However, UTCCR do not apply to "core" terms involving the subject matter or the price of the goods or services.

S.5 The principal differences between UCTA and UTCCR are as follows:

---

[1] Council Directive 93/13/EEC on Unfair Terms in Consumer Contracts (OJ L95, 21.4.93, p 29).

[2] SI 1999 No 2083. See also Unfair Terms in Consumer Contracts (Amendment) Regulations 2001 (SI 2001 No 1186).

[3] UCTA also applies to notices that purport to exclude or restrict liability in tort [delict] for negligence [breach of duty] and to some exclusions and restrictions in contracts even where neither party is acting in the course of a business.

S.6   UCTA:

(1)   applies to both consumer and business-to-business contracts, and also to terms and notices excluding certain liabilities in tort [or, in Scotland, delict];

(2)   applies only to exclusion and limitation of liability clauses (and indemnity clauses in consumer contracts);

(3)   makes certain exclusions or restrictions of no effect at all;

(4)   subjects others to a "reasonableness" test;

(5)   contains guidelines for the application of the reasonableness test; *Sch 2.*

(6)   puts the burden of proving that a term within its scope is reasonable on the party seeking to rely on the clause;

(7)   applies for the most part whether the terms were negotiated or were in a "standard form";

(8)   does not apply to certain types of contract, even when they are consumer contracts; *ie E–E*

(9)   has effect only between the immediate parties; and

(10)   has separate provisions for Scotland.

S.7   In contrast, UTCCR:

(1)   apply only to consumer contracts;

(2)   apply to any kind of term other than the definition of the main subject matter of the contract and the price;

(3)   do not make any particular type of term of no effect at all;

(4)   subject the terms to a "fairness" test;

(5)   do not contain detailed guidelines as to how that test should be applied, but contain a list of terms which "may be regarded" as unfair;

(6)   leave the burden of proof that the clause is unfair on the consumer;

(7)   apply only to terms that have not been "individually negotiated";

(8)   apply to consumer contracts of all kinds;

(9)   are not only effective between the parties but empower various bodies to take action to prevent the use of unfair terms; and

(10)   apply to the UK as a whole.

S.8   Thus the two regimes have different scopes of application; to some extent they overlap; and they have different effects. In addition they use different concepts and terminology. The resulting complexity and inconsistency have been severely criticised.

THE THREE PARTS OF THE PROJECT

S.9   The project has three parts. The first part is to consider the feasibility of a single, unified regime to replace UCTA and UTCCR. (The new regime will replace both

New regime will replace both..

the controls over consumer contracts and the non-consumer aspects of UCTA.) This part of the project is primarily an exercise in simplification, though it also examines the impact on exclusion clauses of the recent European Directive on certain aspects of consumer sales (SCGD).[4] Except as required by that Directive, *No increase* it is not proposed that there should be any significant increase in the extent of controls over terms in consumer contracts, nor any great reduction in consumer protection.

S.10 The second part of the project considers extending the scope of the legislation to cover the kinds of unfair term in a "business-to-business" contract that are presently outside the scope of UCTA but that, had they been in a consumer contract, would have been within UTCCR.

S.11 The third part of the project is to produce draft legislation that will be clearer and more accessible to the reader than either UCTA or UTCCR. UCTA is a complex piece of legislation that it is hard to understand without very careful reading. UTCCR are in a much simpler style. However, because they largely "copy out" the Directive, UTCCR sometimes use terminology that is alien to readers in the UK, lawyers and non-lawyers alike; and in order to interpret them in what we *FLEXIBLE* believe to be the correct way, it is frequently necessary to "read into" phrases a good deal that is not apparent on the face of the language. We think that the use of simpler language and clearer structures could make the new legislation much easier to understand. This consultation paper includes some draft legislation prepared by Parliamentary Counsel, to give consultees an idea of how we think the new legislation might look.

S.12 This summary does not cover every point in the consultation paper, and in some cases the proposals are stated in a simplified version. References are to the provisional proposal (or, where we make no proposal, the question on which we invite views) in the body of the consultation paper itself. A full list of proposals and questions will be found in Part IX of the consultation paper.

COMBINING THE REGIMES FOR CONSUMERS

Restraints and policies

S.13 Any new legislation combining the regimes must implement fully the Directive on Unfair Terms and SCGD. We also consider that there should be no substantial reduction in the protection currently provided to consumers or businesses.[5] However, we see no need to have different provisions for England and Wales on the one hand and Scotland on the other.[6]

S.14 As far as consumers are concerned, our provisional proposals are as follows:

---

[4] Council Directive 99/44/EC on Certain Aspects of the Sale of Consumer Goods and Associated Guarantees (OJ L171, 7.7.99, p 12).

[5] Para 4.29.

[6] Para 4.17.

(1)   Certain terms that under UCTA are of no effect in any circumstances, should continue to be so.[7]   s2(1)

(2)   All other terms that are not specifically exempted should be valid only if they are "fair and reasonable".[8]

(3)   The requirement that the term be fair and reasonable should apply whether or not the term was individually negotiated. (This is already the case for terms that are within UCTA. In addition, we think that consumers are unlikely to have a sufficiently full understanding of the implications of other terms, except "core terms", that a term can be said to be "fair" simply because there was a degree of negotiation over it.)[9]

(4)   The "definition of the main subject matter" of the contract should be exempt from challenge (as under UTCCR), but it should be made clear that the exemption applies only so far as the subject matter is not substantially different to what the consumer should reasonably expect. The definition must also be in plain language (transparent).[10]   *Provided*

(5)   Similarly the "adequacy of the price" should be exempt from review provided that having to make the payment is not substantially different to what the consumer should reasonably expect and is not under a subsidiary term. The price must also be stated in plain language (transparent).[11]

(6)   Terms that merely reproduce what would be the law in the absence of contrary agreement should be exempt, but only if the terms are in plain language (transparent).[12]   *T with merely repro what would be the law in the absence of contrary arg exempt*

(7)   The new legislation should provide detailed guidelines on the application of the "fair and reasonable" test.[13]

(8)   The list of relevant factors should include not just whether the term is in "plain and intelligible language" (as under UTCCR) but whether the term is "transparent" in the sense that, for example, it is reasonably easy to follow and to read.[14] (Transparency should also replace "plain language" as a requirement of the exemptions referred to at (4)–(6) above.)

---

[7]   With the exception of UCTA s 5, which we believe to be redundant.

[8]   See para 4.40.

[9]   Para 4.52.

[10]   Para 4.58.

[11]   Para 4.66.

[12]   Para 4.71.

[13]   Para 4.99.

[14]   Para 4.102.

(9)   The legislation should contain a list of terms that will be unfair unless the business shows otherwise. The list should not follow the list in the Annex to the Directive word for word, but rather should refer to the types of clause found in the UK, and use UK terminology.[15] It should give examples of each type of clause, and it should list common types of unfair term that are not in the Annex to the Directive.[16]

(10)   A term which is unfair should be of no effect except to the extent that it is beneficial to the consumer.[17]

(11)   The existing powers given to the Director-General of Fair Trading and various listed bodies to act to prevent the use of unfair terms should continue. We ask who should bear the burden of proof in these cases, and whether there should be powers to prevent practices of negotiating terms that are unfair.[18]

S.15   We invite views on whether the burden of proving that a term is fair should *always* rest on the business, or whether the consumer should have to show that the term is unfair unless the term in question is on the list referred to in (9) above.[19]

BUSINESS-TO-BUSINESS CONTRACTS

S.16   As far as individual business-to-business contracts are concerned, we think that the somewhat wider range of terms that (for consumer contracts) are subject to UTCCR should equally be subject to control in business-to-business contracts.[20] Terms that, for instance, make it hard for a business to cancel a long-term contract, or that commit it to paying price increases, have just as much potential for unfairness as many of the clauses already covered by UCTA. Protection should not depend on the size of the business affected by the term, though relative size should be a factor in determining whether the term is fair and reasonable.[21] Some of the existing, more stringent controls of UCTA should be maintained. Thus:

(1)   Terms of a business-to-business contract that, under UCTA, are of no effect in any circumstances, should continue to be so.

(2)   Other terms in business-to-business contracts that are "standard" or have not been "individually negotiated" should be subject to a "fair and

---

[15]   Para 4.120.

[16]   Para 4.138.

[17]   Para 4.184.

[18]   Para 4.195.

[19]   Para 4.145.

[20]   Para 5.24.

[21]   Para 5.39.

reasonable test"[22] (with similar exceptions for the main definition of the subject matter, the adequacy of the price and terms that reflect the general "default" law as for consumer contracts[23]).

(3) Individually negotiated terms which, under UCTA, are subject to the requirement of reasonableness should no longer be controlled. (We think that businesses can be expected to understand the implications of individually negotiated terms and to take steps to safeguard their position.)[24]

(4) The question should be whether the term has been "individually negotiated" rather than whether it is "standard".[25]

(5) The existing exemptions from UCTA (for example, contracts of insurance) should continue, though we invite views on whether international business-to-business contracts, and contracts subject to the law of a part of the UK only by choice of the parties, should be exempt from the controls proposed for domestic contracts.[26]

(6) The same basic test of "fairness and reasonableness" as for consumer contracts should apply in business-to-business contracts;[27] and "transparency" should be incorporated into the list of factors for business-to-business contracts.[28]

(7) The legislation should contain the same list of factors as that for consumer contracts.[29]

(8) There should also be a list of terms that will be treated as unfair and unreasonable unless the contrary has been shown. The list should be limited to clauses excluding and restricting liability for breach of contract or for negligence [breach of duty], but there should be power to add to the list by Ministerial Order.[30]

---

[22] Para 5.43.

[23] Para 5.60.

[24] Para 5.46.

[25] Para 5.58.

[26] Paras 5.65, 5.69 and 5.71.

[27] Para 5.74.

[28] Para 5.78.

[29] Para 5.82.

[30] Para 5.87.

(9) Where a term is not on the list, the burden of proving that it is not fair and reasonable should be on the party disputing it.[31]

S.17 We invite consultees to comment on the desirability and the practicability of extending the preventive controls over unfair terms to business-to-business contracts.[32]

SALE OR SUPPLY OF GOODS NOT RELATED TO BUSINESS

S.18 The existing controls over clauses excluding or restricting implied obligations as to title, etc in contracts for the sale or supply of goods should be replicated in the new legislation.[33]

S.19 Clauses which exclude or restrict liability for breach of the obligations as to correspondence with description or sample should remain subject to a "fair and reasonable" test when the sale is between private parties or is by a consumer to a business, irrespective of whether the clause has been negotiated.[34]

NON-CONTRACTUAL NOTICES EXCLUDING BUSINESS LIABILITY FOR NEGLIGENCE OR BREACH OF DUTY

S.20 The existing controls over notices which might otherwise exclude a business's liability in tort [delict] to persons with whom it does not have a contractual relationship and who are killed, injured or harmed by its negligence [breach of duty] should be maintained.[35]

S.21 The preventive powers should be extended to cover non-contractual notices that purport to exclude or restrict a business's liability in tort [delict].[36]

---

[31] Para 5.89.

[32] Para 5.109.

[33] Para 6.5.

[34] Para 6.12.

[35] Para 7.3.

[36] Para 7.8.

ABBREVIATIONS USED IN THIS CONSULTATION PAPER

1979 Report	The Law Commission's 1979 report: Implied Terms in Contracts for the Supply of Goods, Law Com No 95
1994 Regulations	Unfair Terms in Consumer Contracts Regulations 1994
Anson	J Beatson (ed), *Anson's Law of Contract* (27th ed 1998)
Butterworths	M P Furmston (ed), *The Law of Contract* (Butterworths Common Law Series, 1999)
Cheshire, Fifoot & Furmston	M P Furmston (ed), *Cheshire, Fifoot & Furmston's Law of Contract* (14th ed 2001)
Chitty	*Chitty on Contracts* (28th ed 1999)
CISG	United Nations Convention on Contracts for the International Sale of Goods (Vienna, 1980)
DGFT	Director General of Fair Trading
Dicey and Morris	*Dicey and Morris, The Conflict of Laws* (13th ed 2000)
Directive	Directive 93/13/EEC of 5 April 1993 on Unfair Terms in Consumer Contracts
DTI	Department of Trade and Industry
ECJ	European Court of Justice
England	England, Wales and Northern Ireland
First Report	The Law Commissions' 1969 Report: Exemption Clauses in Contracts, First Report: Amendments to the Sale of Goods Act 1893 (Law Com No 24; Scot Law Com No 12)
indicative list	indicative and non-exhaustive list of terms which may be regarded as unfair, UTCCR Schedule 2
McBryde	W W McBryde, *The Law of Contract in Scotland* (2nd ed 2001)
Molony Report	Final Report of the Committee on Consumer Protection (1962) Cmnd 1781
OFT	Office of Fair Trading

OFT Guidance	Unfair Contract Terms Guidance (OFT 311, February 2001)
Rome Convention	The EC Convention on the Law Applicable to Contractual Obligations (Rome, 1980)
RRA	Regulatory Reform Act 2001
SCGD	Directive 99/44/EC of 25 May 1999 on Certain Aspects of the Sale of Consumer Goods and Associated Guarantees
Second Report	The Law Commissions' 1975 Report: Exemption Clauses: Second Report (Law Com No 69; Scot Law Com No 39)
SGA	Sale of Goods Act
SOGITA	Supply of Goods (Implied Terms) Act 1973
SSGCR	draft Sale and Supply of Goods to Consumers Regulations 2002 (DTI, Sale Of Consumer Goods Directive, Second Consultation Paper, URN 02/538, No CA 004/02)
Treitel	G H Treitel, *The Law of Contract* (10th ed 1999)
UCTA	Unfair Contract Terms Act 1977
UTCCR	Unfair Terms in Consumer Contracts Regulations 1999

PART I
INTRODUCTION

1. TERMS OF REFERENCE

1.1 In January 2001 the Law Commission and the Scottish Law Commission received from the Parliamentary Under Secretary of State for Consumers and Corporate Affairs a joint reference in the following terms:

> ... to consider the desirability and feasibility of:
>
> (1) Replacing the Unfair Contract Terms Act 1977 and the Unfair Terms in Consumer Contracts Regulations 1999 with a unified regime which would be consistent with Council Directive 93/13/EEC on Unfair Terms in Consumer Contracts;
>
> (2) Extending the scope of the Unfair Terms in Consumer Contracts Regulations (or the equivalent in any legislation recommended to replace those Regulations in accordance with (1) above) to protect businesses, in particular small enterprises; and
>
> (3) Making any replacement legislation clearer and more accessible to the reader, so far as is possible without making the law significantly less certain, by using language which is non-technical with simple sentences, by setting out the law in a simple structure following a clear logic and by using presentation which is easy to follow.

2. OUTLINE OF THE PROJECT

1.2 As the first paragraph of the terms of reference indicates, potentially unfair terms in contracts are at present subject to one or both of two quite separate legal regimes. If the term in question is one that purports to exclude or restrict the liability of one of the parties,[1] it is likely to be subject to the Unfair Contract Terms Act 1977 ("UCTA"). UCTA applies both to consumer contracts and to contracts between businesses.[2] It may have the effect that the exclusion or restriction of liability is completely ineffective; or it may invalidate the term unless it is fair and reasonable. If the term is in a consumer contract it will normally be subject to the Unfair Terms in Consumer Contracts Regulations 1999 ("UTCCR"),[3] which implement the European Directive of the same name ("the

---

[1] For more detail see para 3.12 below. UCTA also applies to indemnity clauses in consumer contracts: see para 3.12, n 28 below.

[2] UCTA also applies to notices that purport to exclude or restrict liability in tort [or, in Scotland, delict] for negligence [breach of duty] (see para 3.12 and Part VII below); and to some exclusions and restrictions in contracts even where neither party is acting in the course of a business (see para 3.8 below).

[3] As amended by the Unfair Terms in Consumer Contracts (Amendment) Regulations 2001, SI 2001 No 1186 (on this amendment see para 3.121 below).

Directive").[4] UTCCR can apply to almost any type of term[5] and will invalidate the term if it is unfair. Thus the two regimes have different scopes of application; to some extent they overlap; and they have different effects. In addition they use different concepts and terminology. The resulting complexity and inconsistency has been severely criticised.[6] The project covered by this consultation paper falls into three principal parts.

(1) A unified regime on unfair terms in consumer contracts

1.3　The first part is to consider the feasibility of a single, unified regime to apply to consumer contracts. As we explain in more detail in Part II, this part of the project is primarily an exercise in simplification. It is not proposed that there should be any significant increase in the extent of controls over terms in consumer contracts, nor any significant reduction in consumer protection. It is true that if the two regimes were to be unified into a simpler form, there would inevitably be some changes in the controls over potentially unfair terms in consumer contracts. This does require some consideration of underlying policy issues, but the changes proposed would be marginal.

1.4　This part of the project also examines the impact on exclusion clauses of the European Directive on certain aspects of consumer sales ("SCGD").[7] The main aim of SCGD is to ensure that consumers buying goods in any Member State have minimum rights as to the quality of the goods and their conformity to the contract, and have at least specified remedies if the goods do not conform. These points are not within the scope of this consultation paper. However, SCGD also requires Member States to ensure that certain types of limitation and exclusion clauses in consumer contracts are invalid. The consultation paper considers how the requirements of SCGD in relation to limitation and exclusion clauses can best be incorporated into the new legislation in such a way as to reduce the overall complexity of the law.

(2) Extending the controls

1.5　UCTA affects contracts between businesses but applies only to terms that, broadly speaking, purport to limit one party's liability or obligations under the contract. Although the statutory definition of the terms caught by UCTA is wide, it does not apply to all types of term that are potentially unfair. In particular, terms that increase the obligations or liability of the other party are outside UCTA. This has sometimes resulted in businesses, and in particular small businesses, being faced with terms that are widely regarded as unfair but having no means of challenging

---

[4]　Council Directive 93/13/EEC on Unfair Terms in Consumer Contracts (OJ L95, 21.4.93, p 29).

[5]　There are certain exclusions: in particular, terms setting out the main subject matter of the contract are not subject to review, nor is the adequacy of the price: see paras 3.19 – 3.34 below.

[6]　See para 2.22 below.

[7]　Council Directive 99/44/EC on Certain Aspects of the Sale of Consumer Goods and Associated Guarantees (OJ L171, 7.7.99, p 12).

their validity. Had the term in question been in a consumer contract, it would have been subject to the control of UTCCR, as these cover a wider range of terms. The second part of the project therefore considers extending the scope of the legislation to cover the kinds of unfair term in a "business-to-business" contract that are presently outside the scope of UCTA but that, had they been in a consumer contract, would have been within UTCCR. It also considers how any new legislation should incorporate the existing controls over business-to-business contracts.

(3) Making the new legislation "clearer and more accessible to the reader"

1.6 UCTA is a complex piece of legislation. As we know from our own experience, it is hard to understand fully without very careful reading. UCTA is structured in a way which, given its complexity, is economical but which is not easy to grasp. Frequently, a single provision will apply to a number of different types of contract and to a variety of different situations in a way that makes it difficult to see how UCTA applies, particularly for a reader without legal training. It sometimes uses words and phrases that are unlikely to be familiar to non-lawyers.

1.7 For the most part UTCCR are in a much simpler style. In this they reflect the Directive that they implement and which they follow very closely indeed. However, parts of UTCCR, in particular the "indicative and non-exhaustive list of terms which may be regarded as unfair" contained in Schedule 2 (the "indicative list"), use terminology that is alien to English and Scots readers, lawyers and non-lawyers alike. As will be seen from Part IV, we have had considerable difficulty in identifying the kinds of clause which are intended to be included in the list. Moreover, although the main regulations are apparently clear, we have found that in order to interpret them in what we believe to be the correct way, it is frequently necessary to construe their words in ways that are not obvious; on occasions it is necessary to "read into" phrases a good deal that is not apparent on the face of the language.

1.8 The third part of the project is therefore to produce draft legislation that will be clearer and more accessible to the reader. Unusually for the Law Commissions, this consultation paper includes draft legislation prepared by Parliamentary Counsel.[8]

3. STRUCTURE OF THE PAPER

1.9 In Part II of the consultation paper we explain why the law has come to be in the complex and confusing form that it is, and describe the general scope of each part of the project in greater detail. In Part III we examine the precise differences between UCTA and UTCCR. In Part IV we consider how the two regimes might best be combined into a single regime, setting out various issues of general policy before looking at each relevant point in turn. In Part V we consider whether the wider controls of UTCCR should apply to contracts between businesses and, if so,

---

[8] See further para 2.37 below.

whether they should apply only when the party disadvantaged by the term is a small business or an "occasional business customer" (in the sense that the transaction is not one that the business enters as a regular part of its business), or should apply to businesses in general. We also consider whether any extension should be restricted to the individual parties to the particular contract or whether the preventive controls of UTCCR should also be widened to include some, if not all, business-to-business contracts. This Part draws to some extent on comparative studies of other legal systems, which are described in more detail in Appendix A. "Private" sales, where neither party makes the contract in the course of a business, and sales by consumers to businesses are considered in Part VI. In Part VII, which is very short, we deal with non-contractual notices that purport to exclude business liability in tort [delict] for death or personal injury, or other loss or damage, caused by negligence. In Part VIII we give a more detailed explanation of the major issues raised by the attempt to draft the provisional version of the new legislation in a way that is "clear and more accessible". The draft itself forms Appendix B. Part IX is a list of our provisional proposals and questions for consultees. The text of UCTA is reproduced in Appendix C, that of UTCCR in Appendix D, and the body of the Directive in Appendix E. Appendix F is a table summarising the differences between the two regimes and our proposals.

4. ACKNOWLEDGEMENTS

1.10 An initial research project on the first two parts of the project was carried out for the Department of Trade and Industry by Dr Simon Whittaker of St John's College, Oxford. Dr Whittaker's report demonstrated that while consolidation would not be straightforward, it was feasible. It highlighted a number of issues that would need detailed consideration. The matter was then referred to the Law Commissions. This consultation paper draws on Dr. Whittaker's report, and we would like to acknowledge the considerable help that we derived from it. We would also like to acknowledge the help that has been given us by colleagues from the Unfair Contract Terms Unit of the Office of Fair Trading, the Financial Services Authority, OFGEM and OFTEL. We are also most grateful for assistance we have received from Professor Michael Bridge of University College, London; Susan Bright of Oxford University; Professor Andrew Burrows of Oxford University; Professor Peter Butt of the University of New South Wales; Dr Gerhard Dannemann of Oxford University; Professor Nick Gaskell of Southampton University; Professor Johnny Herre of the Stockholm School of Economics; Professor Martijn Hesselink of the University of Amsterdam; Professor Elizabeth Macdonald of the University of Wales, Aberystwyth; Richard Mawrey QC; Professor Dr Hans–W Micklitz of the University of Bamberg; Professor Robin Morse of King's College, London; Professor Christina Hultmark Ramberg of Gothenburg University; and Mr R G A Youard. It would, of course, be entirely unfair and unreasonable not to include the usual disclaimer to the effect that responsibility for this consultation paper is ours alone.

5. OVERVIEW OF OUR PROVISIONAL PROPOSALS

1.11 In Part IV we provisionally propose that the provisions of UTCCR and those of UCTA that apply to consumer contracts should be combined into a single regime. This would not follow the model of either existing piece of legislation; instead it should be put into clearer and more accessible form.[9] Terms which currently are automatically of no effect under UCTA should, with one exception, remain so under the new legislation.[10] All other terms except "core" terms (that is the definition of the main subject matter and the adequacy of the price, insofar as they are set out in a transparent way), terms required by law[11] and terms that merely set out what is, in substance, the general law anyway,[12] would be subject to a "fair and reasonable" test.[13] This would include both negotiated and non-negotiated terms.[14] The definitions of the main subject matter of the contract and of the exemption for the adequacy of the price would be clarified to reflect what we believe to be the existing position.[15] There would be clearer definitions of which terms are exempt because they are required by industry regulators. The legislation would contain detailed guidelines on the application of the "fair and reasonable" test.[16] It would also include a list of terms which would be presumed to be unfair unless the business showed otherwise.[17] This list would reflect the indicative list contained in the Annex to the Directive, but would contain examples of unfair terms found in the UK instead of, or in addition to, those listed in the Directive. (We ask consultees whether the business should also have to show that any other term which is to the detriment of the consumer is nonetheless fair and reasonable, or whether the burden should be on the consumer to show that a term not listed is unfair.[18]) The bodies currently authorised under UTCCR to take action to prevent the use of unfair terms would continue to be so authorised.[19] We ask whether their powers should be extended to allow them to prevent businesses repeating practices of negotiating terms which are nonetheless unfair.[20] Certain sections of UCTA that no longer seem to perform a useful function would not be reproduced in the legislation.[21]

1.12 In Part V we provisionally propose that the controls over terms in individual business-to-business contracts should be widened to include all terms that have not been negotiated, rather than merely exclusions and restrictions of liability as under UCTA.[22] (We ask consultees whether it is necessary to retain the existing

---

[9]   Para 4.19 below.

[10]   Paras 4.34 – 4.35 below.

[11]   Para 4.69 below.

[12]   Para 4.73 below.

[13]   Para 4.94 below.

[14]   Para 4.54 below.

[15]   Paras 4.55 – 4.68 below.

[16]   Paras 4.95 – 4.103 below.

[17]   Paras 4.112 – 4.145 below.

[18]   Paras 4.146 – 4.150 below.

[19]   Para 4.195 below.

[20]   Para 4.202 below.

[21]   Paras 4.205 – 4.211 below.

[22]   Para 5.44 below.

controls over some exemption clauses even when they have been negotiated.[23])
The control would be in the form of a "fair and reasonable" test, as for consumer
contracts.[24] It would not be limited to protecting small businesses, or those making
contracts which are not part of their ordinary course of business; as under UCTA,
those would be factors to be taken into account in deciding whether or not the
term is fair and reasonable.[25] There would be a shorter list of terms presumed to
be unfair unless shown otherwise; in any other case a party alleging that a term is
unfair would have the burden of showing that.[26] There would be exemptions for
"core terms" and those required by law or setting out what is the general law. The
contracts which are exempt from UCTA would remain exempt from the new
controls[27] (with the possible exception of "cross-border" contracts on which we
seek views from consultees[28]). (We ask whether there is a case for extending the
preventive controls over unfair terms in consumer contracts to cover unfair terms
in business-to-business contracts.[29])

1.13   In Part VI we consider the existing controls that apply to contracts for the sale or
supply of goods when the seller or supplier is not acting in the course of a
business. We ask whether consultees agree with us that these controls should be
retained. In Part VII we provisionally propose that the existing controls over non-
contractual notices purporting to exclude or restrict business liability in tort
[delict] for negligence be reproduced in the new legislation;[30] and that the
authorised bodies be empowered to prevent the use of such notices.[31]

---

[23]   Para 5.47 below.

[24]   Para 5.75 below.

[25]   Para 5.40 below.

[26]   Paras 5.88 and 5.90 below.

[27]   Para 5.66 below.

[28]   Para 5.70 below.

[29]   Para 5.111 below.

[30]   Para 7.3 below.

[31]   Para 7.8 below.

PART II
AN OVERVIEW OF THE LEGISLATION ON UNFAIR TERMS AND OUR PROPOSALS

1. THE NEED FOR LEGISLATION ON UNFAIR TERMS

2.1 The laws of contract of all the UK jurisdictions accept the basic principle of freedom of contract: the parties should be free to agree on any terms that they like provided that their agreement is not illegal or otherwise contrary to public policy because it infringes some public interest.[1] In practice, however, there have been restrictions on the principle of freedom of contract for hundreds of years.[2] In general terms the restrictions are justified by the fact that parties are not always sufficiently well-informed, or may not have sufficient bargaining power, to look after their own interests. In England, the common law and, more particularly, various equitable doctrines allow the courts to intervene in certain cases in which the process by which the "agreement" had been reached was unfair. Thus contracts may be avoided on grounds such as fraud, non-fraudulent misrepresentation, duress, undue influence and "unconscionability".[3] The position in Scots law is similar.[4] These doctrines do not, however, apply to many cases in which one party seems to have agreed to a contractual term that is very much against his own interests; and they do not apply at all if there has not been some "procedural unfairness" in the way the contract was made.[5] It is true that at common law certain types of contractual term are invalid irrespective of whether or not there was procedural unfairness; penalty clauses are an example.[6] Others, such as clauses in restraint of trade,[7] will be valid only if they are shown to be

---

[1] Contracts which are illegal or contrary to public policy are unenforceable: for an account of the law of illegality and public policy see, for example, *Chitty on Contracts* (28th ed 1999) ("Chitty") ch 17 or G H Treitel, *The Law of Contract* (10th ed 1999) ("Treitel") ch 11; for Scots law see W W McBryde, *The Law of Contract in Scotland* (2nd ed 2001) ("McBryde") ch 19. Contracts may be contrary to public policy not only because they are contrary to the interests of the public but because they are unreasonable as between the parties: see n 7 below.

[2] The history of interference with freedom of contract in England and Wales is charted in P S Atiyah, *The Rise and Fall of Freedom of Contract* (1979).

[3] For accounts of these doctrines see Chitty, chs 6 and 7; Treitel, chs 9 and 10. On unconscionability, see further para 4.65 below.

[4] See McBryde, chs 14–17.

[5] This is obvious for fraud, non-fraudulent misrepresentation, duress and undue influence. Unconscionability also requires procedural unfairness such as one party deliberately taking advantage of the other's ignorance or weakness: *Hart v O'Connor* [1985] AC 1000 (PC). See Chitty, para 7-081.

[6] The classic statement of the rules on penalty clauses is to be found in the speech of Lord Dunedin in *Dunlop Pneumatic Tyre Co Ltd v New Garage & Motor Co Ltd* [1915] AC 79, 87–88. In Scotland, the law on penalty clauses is the same as the law in England.

[7] The leading modern case is probably *Esso Petroleum Co Ltd v Harper's Garage (Stourport) Ltd* [1968] AC 269. Other cases, such as *A Schroeder Music Publishing Co Ltd v Macaulay* [1974]

reasonable. However, only a very narrow range of terms is affected by such common law rules and no general doctrine against unfair terms has ever been developed.[8]

2.2 In particular, the doctrines of common law and the courts of equity were inadequate to deal with the problems that emerged with the development in the 19th century of standard form contracts (essentially, pre-printed contracts drawn up in advance by one party for use on more than the particular occasion). Standard form contracts can be extremely beneficial to both the parties provided that the standard terms strike a fair balance between them. Their use enables the parties to make complex contracts with a minimum of time and trouble in negotiating the terms; to standardise the risks they face, since each contract will be on similar terms; and to delegate the making of the contract to relatively unskilled personnel, as the legal complexities will have been sorted out in advance, leaving only such matters as the description of the goods or services, the price and the time for performance to be filled in.[9]

2.3 The proviso, that the standard terms strike a fair balance, is, however, a significant one. Before legislative controls were introduced many standard terms, particularly in consumer contracts but also in business-to-business contracts, were not fair. Since this consultation paper is not proposing any fundamental change in the way that terms should be controlled, it is not necessary to give a full account of the underlying problems, but a brief summary may help the reader. Some of the points that will be made here will turn out to be relevant to particular issues of detail which we have to consider later.

2.4 In the *Suisse Atlantique* case Lord Reid said of standard conditions:

> In the ordinary way the customer has no time to read them, and if he did read them he would probably not understand them. And if he did understand and object to any of them, he would generally be told he could take it or leave it. And if he then went to another supplier the result would be the same. Freedom to contract must surely imply some choice or room for bargaining.[10]

Lord Reid's statement highlights two different problems.

---

1 WLR 1308 (HL), may be better illustrations of how the doctrine operates to protect one of the parties to the contract from unreasonable terms favouring the other party. The restraint of trade doctrine also applies in Scots law.

[8] Lord Denning MR's attempt to create a general principle of relief against harsh bargains on the ground of inequality of bargaining power (see *Lloyds Bank Ltd v Bundy* [1975] QB 326) was rejected by the House of Lords in *National Westminster Bank plc v Morgan* [1985] AC 686, 708, *per* Lord Scarman. Similarly, no general doctrine has been developed in Scots law: see J Thomson, "Unfair Contract Terms" in Reid and Zimmermann, *A History of Private Law in Scotland*, vol 2 (2000) ch 6.

[9] See F Kessler, "Contracts of Adhesion – Some Thoughts about Freedom of Contract" (1943) 43 Columbia LR 629, 631–632.

[10] *Suisse Atlantique Societe d'Armement Maritime SA v Rotterdamsche Kolen Centrale* [1967] 1 AC 361, 406.

2.5   First, because the customer is simply shown or asked to sign the standard form, she may well not have the chance to read the terms, let alone understand them. Because the customer may not know of the terms, or may not understand their meaning or how they might impact on her, she may be taken by "unfair surprise".

2.6   Secondly, even if the customer is aware of the term, he may find that the business is unwilling to remove (or alter) it. It has sometimes been suggested that this attitude on the part of business, and indeed the existence of unfair terms, is the result of "the concentration of particular kinds of business in relatively few hands".[11] In fact there seems little evidence of this. Harsh terms are found even in relatively competitive markets.[12] This may happen although many customers would be willing to pay the additional amount that the business would have to charge were it to eliminate the term from all its contracts and accept the risk which the clause places on the customer. It may also happen that a business will refuse to change the terms for a customer who asks for more favourable terms. The business is unlikely to be willing to incur the cost of altering its conditions for a single customer.

2.7   The presence of harsh terms is more likely to be the result of customers in general being unaware of the existence or meaning of the non-negotiated terms. It may be that, even in a market in which there is competition over prices, if only a few customers ask for "better" terms, businesses will not offer them. Rather, the majority of customers will simply seek low prices and, to remain competitive, businesses will shift more and more costs onto customers through harsher and harsher terms. Customers, being largely unaware of the terms until it is too late, will not complain. As a result there will be a trend towards "low cost, harsh term" contracts.[13] Thus the market is inefficient in that many of the customers would have preferred better terms even if that would have meant them having to pay somewhat higher prices. It is only if a substantial margin of customers begin to seek better terms, or if some businesses decide to compete over terms (as, for example, car manufacturers have by offering longer warranties) that businesses generally will start to compete over these terms.

2.8   This may explain why our law, like every Western system of law,[14] has found it necessary to provide some controls over unfair terms, at least in standard form consumer contracts. In fact the controls extend beyond both consumer contracts and standard form contracts. These extensions have been justified in a number of

---

[11]   Lord Diplock in *A Schroeder Music Publishing Co Ltd v Macaulay* [1974] 1 WLR 1308, 1316; also F Kessler "Contracts of Adhesion – Some Thoughts about Freedom of Contract" (1943) 43 Columbia LR 629, 631–632.

[12]   See Trebilcock, in Reiter and Swan (eds) *Studies in Contract Law* (1980) p 398; G Priest, "A Theory of the Consumer Product Warranty" (1980–81) 90 Yale LJ 1297.

[13]   See V Goldberg, "Institutional Change and the Quasi-invisible Hand" (1974) 17 J Law & Economics 461, 483 ff.

[14]   Some picture of the controls over clauses in consumer contracts found in other legal systems emerges from Appendix A, though that concentrates on controls over clauses in business-to-business contracts. The Directive (see paras 1.2 above and 2.14 below) of course requires that all Member States have controls over terms in consumer contracts.

different ways: on the grounds that business parties do not always realise what it is that they are agreeing to, or have the bargaining power to demand better terms; on the ground that problems of lack of understanding or of bargaining power can apply equally to clauses that were not drafted in advance by the other party;[15] or on the ground that the general law intends parties to have certain obligations and that these should not be reduced or limited.[16]

2.9 The courts in the UK developed some controls over unfair standard terms. First, they are sometimes able to hold that the clause has not become part of the contract if, for example, the term was printed on a sign or ticket and the party affected was not given reasonable notice of its existence.[17] This, however, will not protect a party who has signed a contract containing a harsh term; signature is taken to show agreement to the term.[18] Secondly, the courts can sometimes interpret the unfair term in such a way that it does not apply to what has happened.[19] However, this approach is always vulnerable in the sense that it will not work against a well-drafted clause.

2. A BRIEF HISTORY OF LEGISLATIVE CONTROLS OVER UNFAIR TERMS IN THE UK

2.10 The principal control over unfair terms has been legislative. Until 1994 these controls centred on exclusion and limitation of liability clauses.

2.11 The first statute invalidating such clauses in contracts is said to have been the Canals and Railways Act of 1854.[20] Over the years various other controls were also put in place, for example by the Hire Purchase Act 1938. Wider controls, even of exclusion and limitation of liability clauses, did not come until the 1970s. In 1962 the Final Report of the Committee on Consumer Protection (the Molony Committee) had recommended a prohibition on sellers in consumer contracts "contracting out" of their implied obligations under the Sale of Goods Act 1893 ("SGA 1893").[21] In 1966 the matter was referred to the Law Commissions, which in 1969 published the First Report.[22] This recommended a number of changes to

---

[15] See further paras 4.50 – 4.51 below.

[16] See Exemption Clauses in Contracts: First Report: Amendments to the Sale of Goods Act 1893 (1969) Law Com No 24; Scot Law Com No 12 ("The First Report") para 68, referring to the Final Report of the Committee on Consumer Protection (1962) Cmnd 1781, paras 431–435; and para 4.49 below.

[17] See, eg, *Parker v South Eastern Railway* (1877) LR 2 CPD 416 (CA); *McCutcheon v David MacBrayne Ltd* 1964 SC(HL) 28; *Interfoto Picture Library Ltd v Stiletto Visual Programmes Ltd* [1989] QB 433 (CA).

[18] In the absence of fraud or misrepresentation: *L'Estrange v F Graucob Ltd* [1934] 2 KB 394 (CA).

[19] See the rules of construction described in Chitty, paras 14-005 – 14-019; Treitel, pp 201–221; H MacQueen and J Thomson, *Contract Law in Scotland* (2000) p 110.

[20] See J H Baker, *Introduction to English Legal History* (3rd ed 1990) pp 405–406.

[21] Contracting out would be permitted if the goods were second hand, or were sold as shop-soiled or imperfect: para 445.

[22] See para 2.8, n 16 above.

the SGA 1893, including amendments to section 55 to prevent contracting out. The recommendations were put into effect by the Supply of Goods (Implied Terms) Act 1973 ("SOGITA"). SOGITA prevented any sellers from excluding or restricting liability under section 12 of the SGA 1893 (seller's implied obligation as to title). In consumer sales sellers were prevented from excluding or restricting their liability under sections 13–15 of the SGA 1893 (merchantability, fitness for particular purpose and correspondence with description or sample); in other sales those liabilities could be excluded or restricted, but only to the extent that it could be shown to be fair and reasonable to allow reliance on the exclusion or restriction.[23]

2.12 In 1975 the Law Commissions published Exemption Clauses: Second Report ("Second Report"),[24] which recommended wider controls over exclusion and limitation of liability clauses. This resulted in UCTA, which incorporated, in slightly modified form, the controls in SOGITA.[25] It also imposed wider controls over exclusions and limitations of "business" liability both for breach of contract and for negligence in tort [delict]. Certain exclusions or restrictions are made absolutely ineffective and others are subjected to a test of reasonableness. The protection of UCTA applies both to transactions between a business and a consumer and to many business-to-business transactions, particularly where a business deals on its own written standard terms. Despite its title, UCTA applies only to exclusion and limitation of liability clauses, broadly defined, and to indemnity clauses in consumer contracts. Thus other types of term were not subject to any statutory control. Some types of contract, for example contracts of insurance, were exempted from the operation of UCTA.[26]

2.13 UCTA contains separate provisions for England, Wales and Northern Ireland on the one hand and Scotland on the other. Part I of UCTA applies to England, Wales and Northern Ireland. (For brevity, in this paper we use "England" to include all three jurisdictions.) Part II applies to Scotland. Part III contains provisions which apply in all the jurisdictions. In this consultation paper, the relevant Scottish provisions of UCTA are cited in square brackets after the parallel provision for the remainder of the UK.

2.14 In 1993 the European Council of Ministers passed the Directive. This was implemented in the UK by the Unfair Terms in Consumer Contracts Regulations 1994 ("the 1994 Regulations"),[27] now superseded by UTCCR.[28] UTCCR apply a test of fairness to terms of any type (with limited exceptions for clauses defining the "main subject matter" and the price), provided that the term was not

---

[23] SOGITA s 4, amending SGA 1893, s 55.

[24] Law Com No 69; Scot Law Com No 39.

[25] UCTA, s 6. The provisions were modified, in particular, in respect of the "reasonableness" test: see para 3.54, n 124 below.

[26] Further details will be found in Part III below.

[27] SI 1994 No 3159.

[28] SI 1999 No 2083. UTCCR were amended by Unfair Terms in Consumer Contracts (Amendment) Regulations 2001 (SI 2001 No 1186): see para 3.121 below.

"individually negotiated" between the parties. UTCCR apply to all kinds of consumer contract. They also give powers to the Office of Fair Trading ("OFT") and other bodies to prevent the use of such unfair terms in consumer contracts.[29]

2.15 The 1994 Regulations were made under section 2(2) of the European Communities Act 1972. Rather than attempt to amend UCTA to comply with the requirements of the Directive, it was decided to keep the implementing legislation separate and to follow closely the wording of the Directive. This approach has become known as "copy out". In UTCCR, which were made in 1999 principally to give preventive powers to bodies other than the OFT, the opportunity was taken to follow the wording of the Directive even more closely than in 1994.

2.16 It is possible that the Council of Ministers may, in time, revise the Directive. Article 9 provides that the European Commission shall present a report to the European Parliament and the Council concerning the application of the Directive by the end of 1999. The Commission's report is mainly in the form of a consultation paper on the working of the Directive and its possible reform.[30] Our paper assumes that the Directive remains in its present form.

3. A SUMMARY OF THE PRINCIPAL DIFFERENCES BETWEEN UCTA AND UTCCR

2.17 The outcome of the legislative history is two separate regimes dealing with unfair terms, UCTA and UTCCR. The differences between them will be explored in more detail in Part III, but it may be useful to summarise the principal differences at this point.

2.18 UCTA:

    (1) applies to both consumer and business-to-business contracts, and also to terms and notices excluding certain liabilities in tort [delict];

    (2) applies only to exclusion and limitation of liability clauses (and indemnity clauses in consumer contracts);

    (3) makes certain exclusions or restrictions of no effect at all;

    (4) subjects others to a reasonableness test;

    (5) contains guidelines for the application of the reasonableness test;

    (6) puts the burden of proving that a term within its scope is reasonable on the party seeking to rely on the clause;

    (7) applies for the most part whether the terms were negotiated or were in a "standard form";

---

[29] Further details will be found in paras 3.119 – 3.123 below.

[30] Report from the Commission on the Implementation of Council Directive 93/13/EEC of 5 April 1993 on unfair terms in consumer contracts, COM(2000) 248 final of 27 April 2000. In turn DTI issued a consultation paper (Commission Review of Directive 93/13/EEC on unfair terms in consumer contracts, July 2000; URN 00/1033) and has made available copies of its response to the European Commission, on behalf of the UK.

(8)   does not apply to certain types of contract, even when they are consumer contracts;

(9)   has effect only between the immediate parties; and

(10)   has separate provisions for Scotland.

2.19   In contrast, UTCCR:

(1)   apply only to consumer contracts;

(2)   apply to any kind of term other than the definition of the main subject matter of the contract and the price;

(3)   do not make any particular type of term of no effect at all;

(4)   subject the terms to a "fairness" test;

(5)   do not contain detailed guidelines as to how that test should be applied, but contain a so-called "grey" list of terms which "may be regarded" as unfair;

(6)   leave the burden of proof that the clause is unfair on the consumer;

(7)   apply only to "non-negotiated" terms;

(8)   apply to consumer contracts of all kinds;

(9)   are not only effective between the parties but empower various bodies to take action to prevent the use of unfair terms; and

(10)   apply to the UK as a whole.

4. REPLACING UCTA AND UTCCR WITH A UNIFIED REGIME

2.20   The first limb of the project, as set out in the first paragraph of our terms of reference, is a direct result of the legislative history described earlier.

2.21   The legislative approach of implementing the Directive via free-standing Regulations that "copy out" the Directive has some advantages. It is easier to ensure that the Directive has been implemented correctly if the implementing legislation is free-standing and largely follows the exact wording of the Directive, rather than being a series of amendments to UCTA. However, the approach means that there are two overlapping pieces of legislation, as UTCCR apply to exclusion and limitation of liability clauses as much as to other terms; and the way in which the two pieces of legislation operate, their concepts, definitions and terminology differ. For example, some clauses which would appear to be valid under UTCCR provided they are "fair" are in fact of no effect at all as a consequence of UCTA; others are subject to the "reasonableness test" under UCTA, but will be valid only if they satisfy both that test and the test of "fairness" under UTCCR.

2.22   The result is considerable complexity. This led to criticism as soon as the 1994 Regulations were made. The Editor of the Law Quarterly Review suggested that the UK may be in breach of its Treaty obligations because the law was not accessible to consumers.[31] The Department of Trade and Industry received complaints from businesses and consumer groups about the difficulties caused by the existence of the two regimes. In its Consumer White Paper published in July 1999,[32] the DTI announced that research would be carried out into how the law might be improved. It recognised that it would be a complex task because the replacement regime must continue fully to implement the EC Directive. After preliminary research had been carried out for the DTI by Dr Simon Whittaker of St John's College, Oxford,[33] the matter was referred to the Law Commissions.

2.23 The first limb of the project is therefore to consider the desirability and feasibility of combining the two pieces of legislation into a unified regime that must, of course, comply with the Directive. We consider that a single regime must in principle be preferable if it can be achieved without compromising the various policy objectives which we set out in Part IV. That Part is principally concerned with how the regimes might be combined. Consultees may then see what we believe would have to be done and will thus be able to comment on whether they think a unified regime is desirable.

2.24 Control over terms in consumer contracts obviously involves striking a balance between the interests of the consumer, or the body of consumers, who might buy the particular product or service, and the interests of the business. In some situations it can be argued that there is in fact no conflict: what consumers want and what businesses would be happy to provide is in fact the same, but information problems of the kind described earlier[34] may prevent the parties reaching an efficient outcome. In other situations, interests may diverge. The individual consumer may find a term unfair while the business may feel that the particular consumer should not have greater rights than provided for in the contract, given the consumer's agreement to the contract and the price that the consumer was charged. Even for future contracts, the business may feel that the "better terms" being demanded by the consumer may cost the business more than it will be able to make up through any increased sales.

2.25 To invalidate a particular type of clause in all circumstances can only be justified if a clear case can be made that it will almost always be unfair to the consumer. Under UCTA only certain types of clause are invalid in all circumstances. More usually, in deciding whether the term was fair and reasonable, the question of the appropriate balance is left to the court to determine. Under UTCCR the question is always left to the court to decide. But the choice of what types of clause should be subject to the courts' control also involves striking a balance. Should, for instance, only exclusions and limitations of liability be subject to control, or should the controls apply to any type of unfair clause? Should the controls only

---

[31] F M B Reynolds, "Unfair Contract Terms" (1994) 110 LQR 1, 2–3. See also E Hondius, "Unfair Contract Terms: Towards a European Law Introduction" (1997) 5 ERPL 121, 122.

[32] The Government's Consumer White Paper – Modern Markets: Confident Consumers (1999) Cm 4410 – particularly para 6.15.

[33] See para 1.10 above.

[34] See paras 2.5 – 2.7 above.

apply to clauses which were part of a standard form contract and not negotiated, or should the consumer have the possibility of challenging a clause even if there was some degree of negotiation over it when the contract was made?

2.26 There is also a question of balance in a second, different sense: a balance between fairness and certainty. The wider the powers of the court to declare a clause invalid because it is unfair, the greater the uncertainty faced by the business.[35]

2.27 The principal issues of balance of both types were decided by Parliament when UCTA was passed in 1977 and by the Council of Ministers when the Directive and SCGD were issued in 1993 and 1999 respectively. It is not part of this project to change this balance in a major way. The Directive imposes minimum requirements of consumer protection. These must be maintained. Within its limited field of application, UCTA goes somewhat beyond the Directive. We will argue later that there should be no significant reduction in the protection which UCTA currently gives consumers. Conversely, it is not part of the provisional proposals of this consultation paper to increase consumer protection significantly. What is being considered is essentially the simplification of the legislation so that it will be easier for businesses to comply with it and easier for consumers and their advisers to discover the consumer's rights.

2.28 However, if the legislation is to be made less complex, there will probably have to be slight changes in the balance between business and consumer, and between fairness and certainty, on particular points. This is simply because the two pieces of legislation adopt different techniques of control; unifying them will produce somewhat different results in some cases. To that extent "consumer policy" (other than the need to simplify in itself) will occasionally be in issue. The issues will be addressed in detail at the relevant points of the paper. It is our provisional view that none of them raises major questions of balance between business and consumer.

2.29 Although we do not propose any major changes in the degree of protection from unfair terms afforded to consumers, it is our provisional view that the changes we propose would go a long way to meeting a very real need for simplification of the law. They would make the law simpler for both businesses and consumer advisers to understand and apply, and would reduce the burden on businesses that deal with consumers in having to comply with two overlapping and different regimes.[36]

---

[35] It may be that the stronger control of invalidating a clause in all circumstances produces less uncertainty than the weaker control of subjecting it to a fairness test: see para 4.28, n 29 below.

[36] To this extent the measure provisionally proposed would be one of de-regulation. At one time it was hoped that it might be possible to implement the changes proposed (in relation to consumer contracts and, except for Scotland, business-to-business contracts) under the Regulatory Reform Act 2001 ("RRA") (the project was listed in the Explanatory Notes as a candidate for RRA treatment). Whether this will in fact be possible depends partly on our final recommendations. This is because s 1(3) of the RRA (a provision inserted at a late stage) requires that any Order under the Act include provisions removing and reducing burdens. While repealing UTCCR and replacing UCTA with a single piece of legislation would undoubtedly reduce the burdens on business overall, the repeal of UTCCR could not

15

5. EXTENDING THE SCOPE OF UTCCR TO PROTECT BUSINESSES

2.30 As we indicated above, UCTA applies to terms in contracts between one business and another as well as to terms in consumer contracts, in most cases providing that the relevant terms will be valid only if they satisfy the requirement of reasonableness.[37] However, UCTA applies only to various kinds of exclusion and limitation of liability clause.[38] UTCCR apply to a significantly wider range of terms, but only when those terms are in a consumer contract. Many of the terms to which UTCCR apply but UCTA does not, may be unfair not only in a consumer contract but also in a business-to-business contract, especially where the business against whose interests the term operates is small. The DTI received various complaints from business;[39] it is these which led to the second limb of the reference to the Law Commissions.

2.31 This part of the project is covered in Part V of this consultation paper. At this stage we note that to extend the controls in the way that we are asked to consider would involve a somewhat greater change in balance than would our provisional proposals for consumer contracts. The change would not be of balance in the same sense that we discussed in the previous section. Since by definition we are dealing not with consumer contracts but with business-to-business contracts, the balance between business and consumer would not be affected. Rather, the change in balance might be of two other kinds. First, were the extension to be in favour of small businesses only, there would be a change as between small businesses and larger concerns. Secondly, there would again be a change in balance between fairness and certainty.[40] Each of these points is discussed in more detail in Part V.

2.32 When we examine UCTA in more detail we will see that its definitions of the various kinds of exclusion and limitation clauses to which it applies, particularly

---

be done by an Order under the RRA and therefore the RRA Order itself might not contain the necessary "reduction of burdens".

[37] In a few cases the terms are of no effect in any circumstances: see para 3.9 below.

[38] And, for consumer contracts only, to indemnity clauses.

[39] For example, over clauses in contracts for the lease of photocopiers, and in agreements for the supply of motor fuel for retail sale. In relation to leases of photocopiers, in *Eurocopy Rentals Ltd v Tayside Health Board* 1996 SLT 224 there is discussion of whether the provisions of a condition of the agreement were penal as they purported to provide for termination and payment calculated thereunder for any breach of contract, whether material or otherwise. Whether or not such a clause is a penalty, it would fall within UTCCR were it to be included in a consumer contract, but it is outside the scope of UCTA. Photocopier rental agreements have been the subject of litigation under UCTA: *Danka Rentals Ltd v Xi Software Ltd* (1998) 17 Tr LR 74. We have received anecdotal evidence of problems with small businesses being locked into long-term agreements at escalating prices. The terms of petrol supply agreements may also be rather one-sided. We have been shown a contract that permits the supplier to terminate the agreement forthwith for any breach by the buyer, whereas the buyer has no right to terminate for any breach unless it has given the supplier 21 days notice and the supplier has failed to cure the breach within that time. It also gives the supplier complete discretion as to whether to give the buyer "price support": cf *Shell UK Ltd v Lostock Garage Ltd* [1976] 1 WLR 1187 (CA).

[40] See paras 2.26 – 2.28 above.

the clauses that fall within section 3(2)(b) [s 17(1)(b)], are wide: the latter covers any clause which purports to allow a business to perform in a way that the other party will not reasonably expect, or not to perform at all. Thus clauses allowing a change in the goods to be delivered, or the services to be provided, are potentially within UCTA. So are clauses allowing the business to cancel the contract or any part of it. What are not covered are clauses which impose on the other party greater obligations than it might reasonably have expected; for example, to pay an increased price or to be bound to the contract for longer than it expected. It is our provisional view that, with UCTA covering so much already, to bring these clauses within the controls also would not be a major change.

2.33 Further, as part of our consideration of how the existing controls should be incorporated into the proposed new legislation, we raise the possibility of removing some of the controls that at present UCTA imposes over exclusions and limitations of liability in business-to-business contracts. We argue that the real problems in business-to-business contracts lie with terms that have not been negotiated and that the UCTA controls over terms of business-to-business contracts that have been negotiated might be removed. This would counterbalance any extension of control.

2.34 As with the first part of the project, it is our provisional conclusion that even though the changes we suggest would not be major, they would deal with types of unfair term that have caused very real problems to a number of businesses.

6. MAKING THE NEW LEGISLATION "CLEARER AND MORE ACCESSIBLE TO THE READER"

2.35 The Law Commissions are under a statutory duty to keep the law under review for a number of purposes, including its simplification.[41] We believe that an important aspect of our duty is to try to make the law more accessible. This means accessible not only to lawyers but, particularly where the law has an impact on the day to day life of individuals or the day to day operation of businesses, to the individuals or businesses concerned. Legislation on unfair terms is an example. It is relevant to businesses and consumers when contracts are being made, not just when a dispute has arisen and litigation is contemplated. That the legislation should be comprehensible to the business people and to the consumers affected is almost certainly unattainable in practice. However, we think that the legislation should at least be capable of being understood by consumer advisers, many of whom are not legally qualified, and by any person in business who has some knowledge of contracting.

2.36 The Law Commissions seek to make any draft legislation for which they are responsible as clear as possible. However, often there is a trade-off to be made between transparency of structure or language and conciseness. In this project we have provisionally decided to try to produce legislation that can readily be understood by consumer advisers and business people, even if this means that the new enactment is somewhat longer than the statute it is designed to replace. We

---

[41] Law Commissions Act 1965, s 3.

have been inspired by the example of the Tax Law Rewrite project.[42] The third limb of the terms of the current reference:

> Making any replacement legislation clearer and more accessible to the reader, so far as is possible without making the law significantly less certain, by using language which is non-technical with simple sentences, by setting out the law in a simple structure following a clear logic and by using presentation which is easy to follow

is taken from the published aims of that project. We refer to this part of our project as making the legislation "clearer and more accessible".

2.37   This has called for a procedure which is different from our usual practice of appending draft legislation only to the final report. It is difficult to argue against the abstract idea of making legislation more easily understandable. The real question is whether it can be achieved without undue length and loss of precision. We know of no way of discovering this, and of allowing consultees to judge our efforts, other than to include some examples of the draft in the consultation paper. Therefore this consultation paper contains draft legislation prepared by Parliamentary Counsel. It is not a complete draft; it seemed sensible to do only part of the work and offer that as a sample, so that if consultees consider the new approach to be unacceptable or not worth pursuing, too much time and effort will not have been wasted. We have therefore drafted provisions dealing with the main points which arise in relation to consumer contracts and contracts between private persons (that is, where neither party is acting in the course of a business), and in relation to terms and notices excluding liability for negligence. Only part of the indicative list is covered,[43] and the draft does not deal with the powers of the OFT and others to prevent businesses using unfair terms.[44] Equally, the clauses dealing with terms in business-to-business contracts and various ancillary provisions have not been included, though obviously Counsel has kept in mind what would be needed as this affects the drafting of the clauses which are included.

2.38   In order to draft these clauses it was necessary to make assumptions about what the substance of the law should be. For this purpose, and this purpose only, we have treated our provisional proposals as if they were final. **We must stress that this is completely without prejudice to our final recommendations.** Inclusion of a particular approach or decision in the draft does not create any presumption that, at the end of the day, it will be adopted in the report. Moreover the inclusion of the "clear and accessible" draft does not create any presumption that our final recommendation will be to adopt this drafting technique.

2.39   As will be explained in more detail in Part VII, the principal change between the new draft and UCTA is in structure. The language used is changed less, if only because the legislation has to deal with technical legal terms. We have of course

---

[42]   See Inland Revenue report The Path to Tax Simplification (December 1995) and The Path to Tax Simplification: A Background Paper.

[43]   See UTCCR, Sched 2.

[44]   See regs 10–15 and Sched 1.

endeavoured to provide explanations. The draft also attempts to set out explicitly some of the hidden complexities of the existing legislation, particularly of UTCCR. As will be seen, we are sufficiently convinced that the draft is a significant improvement over both UCTA and UTCCR that we provisionally propose that the new approach should be adopted. We believe that improving the accessibility of the law in this way would enable businesses to comply with their obligations more easily and make it more straightforward for both consumers and businesses to understand and obtain recognition of their rights.

7. THE IMPACT OF OUR PROPOSALS

2.40   We have indicated our provisional view that, in each of the three parts of this project, the changes we propose would (in terms of the substance of the law) be marginal or, in the case of the extension of controls in business-to-business contracts, modest; but that each part would produce changes that would satisfy real needs. In order to assist us in evaluating our provisional proposals before we make final recommendations, it would be very helpful to have, from consultees who are in a position to supply it, evidence about the costs and benefits of the proposals.

2.41   **We invite comments on the practical and economic impact that our proposals would have on both consumers and businesses.**

PART III
OVERLAPS AND DIFFERENCES BETWEEN UCTA AND UTCCR

1. INTRODUCTION

3.1 In this Part we consider in more detail the extent to which there are overlaps and differences between UCTA and UTCCR.[1] As we shall see, the number of differences is significant, both in the broad scope of application, concepts and terminology and in more detailed matters, such as definitions.

3.2 We also note the impact of Council Directive 99/44/EC of 25 May 1999 on Certain Aspects of the Sale of Consumer Goods and Associated Guarantees ("SCGD").[2] This is principally concerned with providing certain minimum rights and remedies for consumers in sales contracts. In essence, Member States must ensure that consumers have certain specified remedies if the goods do not conform to the contract,[3] and conformity is defined in terms that are broadly similar to sections 13–15 of the United Kingdom's Sale of Goods Act 1979 ("SGA 1979").[4] The rights and remedies are to be made inalienable by the consumer. Article 7(1) of SCGD states:

> *Binding nature*
>
> 1. Any contractual terms or agreements concluded with the seller before the lack of conformity is brought to the seller's attention which directly or indirectly waive or restrict the rights resulting from this Directive shall, as provided for by national law, not be binding on the consumer.
>
> Member States may provide that, in the case of second-hand goods, the seller and consumer may agree contractual terms or agreements which have a shorter time period for the liability of the seller than that set down in Article 5(1). Such period may not be less than one year.

---

[1] As amended by Unfair Terms in Consumer Contracts (Amendment) Regulations 2001, SI 2001 No 1186 (on this amendment see para 3.121 below).

[2] This was due to be implemented by 1 January 2002. Draft regulations have been circulated for consultation (see n 5 below) and regulations will be brought into effect later this year.

[3] These are set out in Arts 3 and 5.

[4] Art 2(2). Art 2(2)(d) is rather wider than SGA 1979 in that "public statements" by the producer or his representative have to be taken into account. It appears that the Directive does not cover conformity with an express term of the contract, as Art 2(2) appears to treat "conformity" within the meaning of the Directive as being confined to the matters listed. (Equally, UCTA ss 6 and 7 [ss 20, 21] do not affect clauses restricting liability for express undertakings: *Border Harvesters Ltd v Edwards Engineering (Perth) Ltd* 1985 SLT 128 (OH); *British Fermentation Products v Compair Reavell* [1999] 2 All ER (Comm) 389.)

Implementation of the positive aspects of SCGD will be carried out by regulations to be made under the European Communities Act 1972, section 2(2).[5] Any changes necessary to implement Article 7(1) will, in the first instance, be included in those regulations[6] but the relevant parts of the regulations may later be superseded by the legislation proposed in this project.

3.3 A list of the most obvious differences between the existing regimes was given in Part II.[7] In this Part we set out the significant differences point by point. In Parts IV and V respectively we consider how the regimes for consumer contracts might best be combined and how the controls over consumer contracts might be extended to protect business, taking the points in roughly the same order.

3.4 Because there are so many differences between the regimes, we have found it useful to summarise them in the form of a table. This is in Appendix F. Its first two columns show the position under UCTA and UTCCR respectively. The third column summarises our provisional proposals.

2. SEPARATE PROVISIONS FOR SCOTLAND

3.5 We have already noted that UCTA contains separate provisions for England, Wales and Northern Ireland on the one hand and Scotland on the other.[8] UTCCR apply to the UK as a whole.

3. CONSUMER CONTRACTS, BUSINESS-TO-BUSINESS CONTRACTS AND OTHER CONTRACTS

3.6 An obvious difference between UCTA and UTCCR is that UTCCR apply only to unfair terms in contracts between a seller or a supplier and a consumer,[9] whereas all but two of the various controls under UCTA apply to both consumer[10] and business-to-business contracts.[11]

---

[5] An initial Consultation Document was circulated by DTI on 4 January 2001 (DTI, EC Directive 1999/44/EC on Certain Aspects of the Sale of Consumer Goods and Associated Guarantees: First Consultation of 2001, URN 00/1471); a further Consultation Document and draft Sale and Supply of Goods to Consumers Regulations 2002 ("SSGCR") were circulated on 26 February 2002 (DTI, Second Consultation Paper on EC Directive 1999/44/EC on Certain Aspects of the Sale of Consumer Goods and Associated Guarantees, URN 02/538, No CA 004/02).

[6] The changes proposed in the draft SSGCR of 26 February 2002 are described at para 4.153, n 187 and 4.163, n 196 below.

[7] Paras 2.18 – 2.19 above.

[8] See para 2.13 above. There are few substantive differences between the two regimes: see para 4.16 below.

[9] Whether this distinction should be maintained, or the protection of UTCCR extended to some businesses, is discussed in Part V below.

[10] In addition, what amounts to a consumer contract differs under the two pieces of legislation: see in particular paras 3.81 – 3.88 below.

[11] The two exceptions are s 4 [s 18] (unreasonable indemnity clauses) and s 5 [s 19] ("guarantee" of consumer goods).

3.7 However, the sections of UCTA that apply to both kinds of contract operate differently depending on whether or not the contract is a consumer contract. Exclusions and restrictions of liability that fall within sections 6 and 7 [ss 20 and 21] are simply of no effect against a party who deals as a consumer,[12] whereas as against a non-consumer they may be valid if they satisfy the requirement of reasonableness.[13] Section 3 [s 17] applies to both negotiated and non-negotiated terms in consumer contracts, but in non-consumer contracts only to terms that are part of the business's written standard terms.[14]

3.8 Most of the controls of UCTA apply only to consumer contracts (that is, where one party makes the contract in the course of business but the other does not) and to contracts between businesses.[15] However, there is also limited control in relation to other contracts. This is provided by section 6. No seller or supplier under a hire-purchase contract, whether or not acting in the course of a business, may exclude his obligations as to title,[16] and non-business sellers may exclude or restrict their liability for breach of the implied terms as to correspondence with description or sample but only if the term is reasonable.[17] These controls will "bite" in two further types of contract: where neither party is making the contract in the course of a business and where a consumer sells goods, or lets them on hire-purchase,[18] to a business.[19]

4. TERMS OF NO EFFECT

3.9 Under UCTA, attempts to exclude or restrict certain types of liability are simply of no effect.[20] These are:

(1) business liability for death or personal injury caused by negligence or breach of duty;[21]

---

[12] Sections 6(2) and 7(2) [ss 20(2)(i), 21(1)(a)(i) and 21(3)(a)]. The terms to which these provisions apply are explained in para 3.9 below.

[13] Sections 6(3) and 7(3) [ss 20(2)(ii), 21(1)(a)(ii) and 21(3)(a)].

[14] For Scotland, though s 17(1) does not seem to require that the standard terms be in writing, the effect of the definition of "customer" in s 17(2) is that for non-consumer contracts to be covered by the section the standard terms will need to be written. Section 3 [s 17] has the broadest application of any section of UCTA; see para 3.13 below.

[15] This is because ss 2–7 apply only to "business liability": s 1(3). For Scotland a similar result is obtained as a result of ss 16(1), 17(2), 18(2) and 21(3).

[16] Under SGA 1979, s 12, or SOGITA, s 8; see UCTA, s 6(1) [s 20(1)].

[17] Under SGA 1979, ss 13 and 15, or SOGITA, ss 9 and 11; see UCTA, ss 6(3) and (4) [s 20(2)(ii)]. SGA 1979, s 14 and SOGITA, s 10 do not affect sellers or suppliers who are not acting in the course of a business.

[18] This seems an unlikely situation.

[19] See Part VI below.

[20] The position in Scotland is similar to that in England, but differences between the wording of the relevant provisions may have consequential effects on terms which contain wider exclusions or restrictions than those listed in this paragraph. See paras 3.108 – 3.113 and 4.179 below.

[21] Section 2(1) [s 16].

(2) liability for breach of the implied terms as to title in contracts for sale, hire-purchase or (except for Scotland) other transfer of property in goods;[22]

(3) liability for breach of the implied terms as to description, quality etc in contracts for the supply of goods to a person dealing as a consumer;[23] and

(4) a manufacturer's or distributor's liability in tort [delict] to a person injured by goods proving defective while in consumer use (where the exclusion or restriction is by means of a term or notice in a "guarantee" of the goods).[24]

3.10 All other terms caught by UCTA may be valid if they satisfy the requirement of reasonableness.[25] It is for the party claiming that a term satisfies the requirement of reasonableness to show that it does.[26]

3.11 In contrast, under UTCCR no terms are automatically of no effect; the terms to which UTCCR apply must simply not be unfair.

5. RANGE OF TERMS CONTROLLED

3.12 UCTA applies to only a limited range of potentially unfair terms. Despite its broad title,[27] nearly all its provisions[28] are aimed at clauses which in one way or another exclude or restrict the liability of a party.[29] Some sections of UCTA are aimed at the exclusion or restriction of particular kinds of liability in particular types of contract: thus sections 6 and 7 [ss 20 and 21] apply to exclusion or restriction of various implied terms in contracts of sale, hire-purchase, barter, hire,

---

[22] Sections 6(1) and 7(3A) [s 20(1); there is no equivalent of s 7(3A) for Scots law].

[23] Sections 6(2) and 7(2) [ss 20(2), 21(1)(a)(i) and 21(3)(a)].

[24] Section 5 [s 19].

[25] Section 2(2) [s 16(1)] (other loss or damage caused by negligence); s 3 [s 17]; s 4 [s 18] (indemnities in consumer contracts); s 6(3) [s 20(2)] and s 7(3) [s 21(1)(a)(ii), (3)(a)] (description, quality, etc in non-consumer contracts for supply of goods); s 7(4) [s 21(1)(b), (3)(b)] (right to transfer possession, etc in contracts of hire, etc).

[26] Section 11(5) [s 24(4)]. See further para 3.79 below.

[27] The draft Bills contained in the Second Report were entitled the Exemption Clauses (England and Wales) Bill and the Exemption Clauses (Scotland) Bill. The wider title was given to the combined (and rather differently drafted) Bill during its passage through Parliament. See *Hansard* (HC) 6 May 1977, vol 931, col 819.

[28] The exception is s 4 [s 18], which covers clauses requiring a consumer to indemnify either the other party or a third person (eg an employee of the other party) for liability incurred to another (eg to a neighbour or member of the public who has been injured in the course of performance). It also applies to clauses requiring the consumer to indemnify a third person for liability to the consumer herself. (A clause requiring the consumer to indemnify the other party for liability which the other party had incurred to the consumer would in effect be an exclusion clause and would be caught by other sections of the Act: *Phillips Products Ltd v Hyland* [1987] 1 WLR 659 (CA).)

[29] Section 13 defines this widely, including (but only for the purposes of ss 2 and 5–7: s 3 has its own provision on this point, see below) terms which would prevent the relevant obligation arising (eg "There is no implied obligation that the goods sold shall be of satisfactory quality" or, more simply, "sold as seen"). The parallel provisions for Scotland are s 25(3) and (5): while the wording differs slightly the substantive effect is the same.

and work and materials.[30] Section 2 [s 16] is not limited to particular types of contract but applies only to exclusions or restrictions of a certain kind, namely of business liability[31] for negligence[32] (in England) and breach of duty (in Scotland).[33]

3.13   The section of UCTA with the broadest application is section 3 [s 17]. This applies to clauses that are used by a business in its written standard terms or in a contract with a consumer and that either purport to exclude or restrict the business's liability for breach of contract,[34] or fall within section 3(2)(b) [s 17(1)(b)]. This paragraph is designed to catch certain types of clause which

> are expressed not as excluding or restricting liability for the breach of subsisting obligations but as preventing the obligations to which they relate from arising or as providing that such obligations are to arise only in restricted or qualified form.[35]

It applies to clauses which purport to permit the business party

   (i)   to render a contractual performance substantially different from that which was reasonably expected of him, or

   (ii) in respect of the whole or any part of his contractual obligation, to render no performance at all …,

and subjects such clauses to the requirement of reasonableness.[36]

---

[30]   Section 6 [s 20] applies to sale and hire-purchase contracts, covering clauses which exclude or restrict liability for breach of the implied terms as to title, etc, and conformity with description or sample, quality or fitness for a particular purpose; s 7 [s 21] does the equivalent for other types of contract "under or in pursuance" of which possession or ownership of goods passes.

[31]   Section 1(3) [s 16(1)].

[32]   Similarly, s 8 (which amends Misrepresentation Act 1967, s 3) applies to any kind of contract but only to clauses excluding or restricting liability, or the remedies available, for misrepresentation. There is no parallel Scottish provision as the Misrepresentation Act 1967 does not apply to Scotland.

[33]   Breach of duty means (a) a breach of a contractual obligation to take reasonable care; (b) a breach of a delictual duty to take reasonable care; and (c) a breach of the duty of reasonable care imposed by s 2(1) of the Occupiers' Liability (Scotland) Act 1960: s 25(1).

[34]   Section 3(2)(a) [s 17(1)(a)].

[35]   Second Report, para 143. The Law Commissions gave the example of the clause in *Anglo-Continental Holidays Ltd v Typaldos Lines (London) Ltd* [1967] 2 Lloyd's Rep 61. This allowed the defendant travel agent to change steamers, sailing dates, rates and itineraries without prior notice. The contract was between two travel agents, but clauses of this general type are to be found in some package holiday contracts (albeit heavily qualified and of less severity). Package holiday contracts are now subject to Package Travel, Package Holidays and Package Tours Regulations 1992, SI 1992 No 3288 (implementing Council Directive 90/314/EEC on Package Travel, Package Holidays and Package Tours (OJ L158, 23.6.90, p 59) but these regulations seem not to affect this point, merely providing that "where the organiser is constrained before the departure to alter significantly an essential term of the contract" the consumer must be given the right to withdraw from the contract without penalty (reg 12(a)). The Code of Conduct of the Association of British Travel Agents reiterates this requirement (s 2.2).

[36]   The Scottish provision, s 17(1)(b), is worded as follows:

3.14 These provisions are capable of applying to clauses which allow the business to alter the substance of its own performance, for example by changing the hotel accommodation or the means of transport in a holiday contract,[37] changing the specification of goods in a contract of sale,[38] or cancelling the contract in certain circumstances.[39] They do not apply to clauses allowing the supplier to increase the price payable by the consumer since that is not a question of the supplier's contractual performance.[40]

3.15 In contrast to UCTA, UTCCR are capable of applying to a term of any kind in a consumer contract of any type, so long as the term was not individually negotiated[41] and was unfair.[42] (The question of fairness does not apply to either the adequacy of the price or the definition of the main subject matter of the

> ... in respect of a contractual obligation, to render no performance, or to render a performance substantially different from that which the consumer or customer reasonably expected from the contract;
>
> if it was not fair and reasonable to incorporate the term in the contract.
>
> It is submitted that this is substantially the same as s 3(2)(b).

[37] Cf *Williams v Travel Promotions Ltd*, *The Times* 9 March 1998 (CA); *P & O Steam Navigation Co v Youell* [1997] 2 Lloyd's Rep 136 (CA).

[38] These three examples would fall within s 3(2)(b)(i) [s 17(1)(b)]; it would also be necessary for the consumer to show that the change was substantially different from what was reasonably expected.

[39] This would fall within s 3(2)(b)(ii) [s 17(1)(b)]. See *Timeload Ltd v British Telecommunications plc* [1995] EMLR 459 (CA). A well-known pre-Act case in which the clause seems to fall within the words of s 3(2)(b)(ii) [s 17(1)(b)] is *Sze Hai Tong Bank Ltd v Rambler Cycle Co Ltd* [1959] AC 576 (PC) (clause in bill of lading contract stating that the carrier's responsibility for the goods would "cease absolutely after the goods are discharged" from the ship). In all the four cases mentioned in the text it would be open to the business to show that the term in question satisfied the requirement of reasonableness. [In Scotland, the reasonableness test is contained in s 24(1).] There is considerable doubt about the scope of s 3(2)(b)(ii) [s 17(1)(b)]. Treitel (at pp 228 and 232) argues that it does not catch clauses which are drafted in such a way that the business has no obligation to perform in any circumstances at all, but does apply if there is a contractual obligation but the business is given a wide discretion whether to perform at all or in full. In the unusual case in which the clause seems to remove any obligations to perform in certain circumstances, we think that the section is to be interpreted as applying whenever, but for the term in question, there would be an obligation to perform. This would bring in clauses making time of the essence when it would not otherwise be so, though Treitel argues against such an interpretation on the ground that this was not what was intended. Obviously this unsatisfactory form of drafting must be avoided in any new legislation. For discussion of the difficulties from a Scottish perspective, see M G Clarke's notes to UCTA s 17 in *Scottish Current Law Statutes Annotated*.

[40] See *Paragon Finance v Nash* [2001] EWCA Civ 1466, [2002] 1 WLR 685. Treitel, p 224, gives the further example of clauses in a guarantee given on the creditor's standard form which strip the guarantor of the protection of the rules which would otherwise limit his obligation (such as that the guarantor will be released if the creditor gives the debtor extra time to pay). Again these do not affect the creditor's performance. At p 252, Treitel identifies also, and for essentially the same reason, terms within UTCCR, Sched 2, paras 1(h), (l), (o) (insofar as it goes beyond set-off) and (p).

[41] See para 3.16 below.

[42] See para 3.51 below.

contract, provided it is in plain intelligible language.)[43] Thus UTCCR apply equally to clauses affecting the performance of either party and appear to cover a significantly wider range of types of term than UCTA.

6. TERMS WHICH HAVE NOT BEEN INDIVIDUALLY NEGOTIATED

3.16   UTCCR apply only to terms which, in the words of regulation 5(1), have "not been individually negotiated". Regulation 5(3) makes it clear that if one party has put forward a pre-formulated standard contract, only the specific terms or those aspects of specific terms which have been individually negotiated will be exempt. It is for the business to show that the term was individually negotiated.[44]

3.17   Regulation 5(2) provides:

> A term shall always be regarded as not having been individually negotiated where it has been drafted in advance and the consumer has therefore not been able to influence the substance of the term.

This appears to mean that a term may be regarded as not individually negotiated even though it was drawn up by the business for the specific contract, rather than being a standard term, provided that it was drawn up before the negotiations[45] and was not negotiated.[46]

3.18   In contrast, the application of UCTA to terms in consumer contracts[47] does not depend on whether the term was negotiated (though that may be very relevant to the question of reasonableness). The same is true in relation to non-consumer contracts with the exception of section 3 [s 17].

7. TERMS NOT SUBJECT TO CONTROL

(1) "Definitional" and "core" terms

3.19   Because UCTA is dealing with particular types of clause (exclusion clauses and restrictions of liability and indemnity clauses) there is no need for a statement of the terms to which it does not apply. In contrast, under UTCCR certain terms are exempt from the requirement of fairness. Terms relating to the definition of the

---

[43]   Reg 6(2). See paras 3.19 – 3.34 below and, on plain intelligible language, para 3.73 below.

[44]   Reg 5(4).

[45]   This appears to be the meaning of "drawn up in advance": see Treitel, p 247.

[46]   M Furmston (ed), *The Law of Contract* (Butterworths Common Law Series, 1999) ("Butterworths") para 3.103 (referring to the 1994 Regulations). A further question is whether the term is still to be regarded as non-negotiated when the other party has tried to negotiate an improvement but has failed to obtain one. In *St Albans City and District Council v International Computers Ltd* [1996] 4 All ER 481, the Court of Appeal held that if the defendant's general conditions of contract remained untouched by the negotiations, then the final deal had indeed been made on the defendant's standard terms for the purposes of UCTA, s 3(1)[s 17(1)]. As Nourse LJ pointed out at p 491, "as a matter of plain English 'deals' means 'makes a deal', irrespective of any negotiations that may have preceded it". This decision has since been followed in *South West Water Services Ltd v International Computers Ltd* [1999] BLR 420 (QBD).

[47]   See para 3.7 above.

main subject matter of the contract, provided they are in plain intelligible language, are exempt.[48] The adequacy of the price or remuneration, as against the goods or services supplied in exchange, is also exempt from assessment for fairness, again provided that the price or remuneration is in plain intelligible language.[49] These are sometimes referred to as the "core" terms.[50]

3.20   In fact UCTA does contain something similar to the exemption for the main subject matter. Each piece of legislation attempts to exclude from review terms which merely define what the consumer should expect under the contract, but the methods used to achieve this, and possibly therefore the results, differ. The precise differences are hard to define because they depend on fine points of interpretation.

(a) Reasonable expectations and "definition of the main subject matter"

3.21   UCTA section 3(2)(b)(i) [s 17(1)(b)] is restricted in that it affects only clauses which purport to allow the business to perform in a way which is "substantially different" from what was "reasonably expected".[51] As Lord Bingham MR pointed out in *The Zockoll Group Ltd v Mercury Communications Ltd (No 2)*,[52] what was reasonably expected cannot be a question of relying on the proper construction of the contract because that would mean that there was no difference between the other party's expectation and what, by reference to a term, the business claimed to be entitled to render. It seems to refer to the other party's reasonable expectations derived from all the circumstances, including the way the contract was presented to him. This appears to mean that if it was made reasonably clear to a consumer that the business had the right to and might in fact perform in the way it is now seeking to do, the section will have no application.[53] Thus if a holidaymaker had been told that the hotel booked was still under construction and that, if completion was delayed, the holidaymaker would be put in another hotel of a

---

[48]   Reg 6(2). On plain intelligible language see para 3.73 below. In relation to the definition of the main subject matter it appears to be the term that is exempt from review. See also Recital 19 to the Directive, which reads:

> Whereas, for the purposes of this Directive, assessment of unfair character shall not be made of terms which describe the main subject matter of the contract ...

We shall see later that, in relation to price, it is the issue of adequacy rather than the price term that seems to be exempt: see para 3.27 below.

[49]   Reg 6(2).

[50]   Though in *DGFT v First National Bank plc* [2000] QB 672, 686, Peter Gibson LJ pointed out that the phrase does not appear in the regulations; the question is whether the term falls within what is now reg 6(2).

[51]   Curiously, s 3(2)(b)(ii) is not so qualified. Similarly, for Scotland, it seems that the reference in s 17(1)(b) to a term enabling a party to render no performance is not so qualified: see para 3.13, n 36 above.

[52]   [1999] EMLR 385, 395.

[53]   *P & O Steam Navigation Co v Youell* [1997] 2 Lloyd's Rep 136, 142, *per* Potter LJ; *W Photoprint v Forward Trust Group* (1993) 12 Tr LR 146; *Megaphone International Ltd v British Telecommunications plc*, *The Independent* 1 March 1989.

stated category, and this is what in fact happened, it seems that the section would not apply.[54]

3.22　UTCCR would also apply to the examples we considered earlier of terms allowing a holiday company to change the hotel accommodation or the means of transport in a holiday contract, or to change the specification of goods in a contract of sale, or to cancel the contract in certain circumstances, unless the term can be classified as relating to the definition of the main subject matter.[55] This can also be difficult to determine.

3.23　Terms which are to apply only in certain events, and which are separate from those describing the main features of the performance, do not seem to define the main subject matter.[56] However, a provision to the same legal effect in the description of the main features may do so. So in a contract for a "holiday with travel by air", a clause in the "small print" allowing the company, in the event of air traffic control strikes, to carry the consumer by rail and sea seems to be reviewable for fairness; but it can be argued that if the holiday is "with travel by air or, in the event of strikes, by rail and sea", the option of mode of travel *might* be part of the definition of the main subject matter. In other words, whether the term relates to the definition of the subject matter depends (at least in part) on how the "deal" was presented to the consumer. This seems to be the corollary of a point made by the OFT:

> In our view, it would be difficult to claim that any term was a core term unless it was central to how consumers perceived the bargain. A supplier would surely find it hard to sustain the argument that a contract's main subject matter was defined by a term which a consumer had been given no real chance to see and read before signing ...[57]

3.24　If it is correct that whether a term is part of the definition of the main subject matter depends in part on how the "deal" was presented to the consumer,[58] the

---

[54]　It has been argued that a similar test of what should reasonably have been expected should be used to decide, for the purposes of s 6 or 7 [s 20 or 21], whether the clause concerned was an attempt to exclude liability by excluding the relevant duty or was simply defining what the contract was about, eg that a painting was not being sold as the work of a particular artist: J Beatson (ed), *Anson's Law of Contract* (27th ed 1998 – "Anson") p 185. See also the discussion of the current interpretation of s 13 of UCTA: E Macdonald, "Exclusion Clauses: the Ambit of s 13(1) of the Unfair Contract Terms Act 1977" (1992) 12 LS 277, and "Mapping The Unfair Contract Terms Act 1977 and the Directive on Unfair Terms in Consumer Contracts" (1994) JBL 441.

[55]　See para 3.15 above.

[56]　See para 3.25 below.

[57]　Unfair Contract Terms Bulletin 2 (OFT 170, September 1996) para 2.26.

[58]　It has been pointed out (Butterworths, para 3.104) that this is not wholly consistent with Recital 19, which reads:

> ... whereas the main subject matter of the contract and the price/quality ratio may nevertheless be taken into account in assessing the fairness of other terms; whereas it follows, *inter alia*, that in insurance contracts, the terms which clearly define or circumscribe the insured risk and the insurer's liability shall not be subject to such

question of "definition of the main subject matter" under UTCCR may in this respect be similar to whether the clause purports to permit a performance "substantially different from that which was reasonably expected" under UCTA.[59]

(b) Contingencies and "definition of the main subject matter"

3.25 However, the tests under UCTA and UTCCR are not interchangeable. The "definition of the main subject matter" seems to involve a second dimension. A consumer might "reasonably expect" a particular term (because, for instance, she had been warned of it) but yet the condition might not be "part of the main subject matter" because it is only to apply in certain circumstances, rather than defining the main subject matter. In *DGFT v First National Bank plc*[60] the term in question was a clause in a contract of loan giving the bank, in the event of a default by the borrower, the right to demand payment of the outstanding balance and accrued interest and further interest at the contractual rate after judgment up to the date of actual payment. Both the Court of Appeal and the House of Lords rejected the argument that the provision for interest fell within either "the definition of the main subject matter" or "adequacy of the price". The courts agreed with the DGFT's argument that the exemption is limited to those terms "which define the parties' rights and obligations in the due performance of the contract".[61] Lord Bingham quoted Chitty to the effect that there is an important "distinction between the term or terms which express the substance of the bargain and 'incidental' (if important) terms which surround them".[62] Lord Steyn said that the offending term was not a "core term" because it was a "subsidiary term".[63]

3.26 That clause was one that applied when the borrower was in default and it is easy to see that it did not form part of the main subject matter in that sense. But equally it seems arguable that a term that is to apply in a contingency which is not the fault of either party but which the consumer would not anticipate as likely, and therefore would not give careful consideration, is not part of the definition of

assessment since these restrictions are taken into account in calculating the premium paid by the consumer ...

Unfortunately the Recital cannot be taken literally as almost any term, including for example exemption clauses which are clearly not core, may affect the price to be paid by the consumer.

[59] For the similar wording of the Scottish provisions [s 17(1)(b)], see para 3.13, n 36 above.

[60] [2000] QB 672 (CA); reversed on the point of whether the term itself was unfair, [2001] UKHL 52, [2002] 1 AC 481 (HL). The case was decided under the 1994 Regulations, but the differences between these and UTCCR do not seem relevant to the point at issue. See further para 2.15 above.

[61] [2000] QB 672, 685; [2001] UKHL 52, [2002] 1 AC 481 (HL), especially at [12], [34] and [43]. Chitty, para 15-026, gives another telling example: a clause giving the supplier the right to determine the price at the date for delivery or to increase the price without giving the consumer the right to cancel the contract is listed in Sched 2, para 1(l) as a term which may be unfair.

[62] [2001] UKHL 52 at [12], referring to Chitty, para 15-025.

[63] *Ibid*, at [34]. Lord Hope said at [43] that it was "a default provision".

the main subject matter. The clauses relating to the change of means of transport or accommodation, or to a right to cancel the holiday even in circumstances beyond the holiday company's control, would probably not form part of the main subject matter.[64]

(c) Adequacy of the price

3.27 There are also difficulties in interpreting the extent of control over "price" clauses under UTCCR. Regulation 6(2) states:

> In so far as it is in plain intelligible language, the assessment of fairness of a term shall not relate – ...
>
> (b) to the adequacy of the price or remuneration, as against the goods or services supplied in exchange.

In this case the meaning of the regulation seems to be not that the "price term" is exempt but that the issue of adequacy of the price is exempt.[65] The effect is that if the price payable is set out in clear language, the amount cannot be challenged. In contrast, a clause which allows the price to be increased in certain circumstances must be subject to review, as such clauses are referred to in the indicative list.[66] The distinction appears to be that, in the case of a price increase clause, it is not the adequacy of the price that is in question but the unfairness that may be caused to the consumer because the price may be changed.

3.28 The distinction is not always easy to apply, nor the extent of control clear. Take for example a "low cost" four-year loan which provides for a low level of interest to be payable for the first two years, and thereafter a higher rate; but which also provides that in the event of any default by the borrower within the first two years the rate of interest payable for the whole of the remaining period shall be at the higher rate. Thus a week's delay in making a single payment might result in a very

---

[64] This is not, of course, to say that the term applying in these situations would necessarily be unfair. That would depend on what it provided.

[65] See S Whittaker, "Judicial Interventionism and Consumer Contracts" (2001) 117 LQR 215, 219. This difference of treatment between "definition of the main subject matter" (where the term seems to be exempt: see para 3.19 above) and "adequacy of the price" seems to be reflected in the Directive at Recital 19. This reads:

> Whereas, for the purposes of this Directive, assessment of unfair character shall not be made of terms which describe the main subject matter of the contract nor the quality/price ratio of the goods or services supplied ...

The Recital makes sense only if the word "terms" qualifies only the words "which describe the main subject matter of the contract", because no term in a contract will describe the quality/price ratio of the goods or services supplied. It must be that ratio (ie the issue of adequacy) that is exempt. Admittedly this means interpreting the Recital as if it read "... nor *of* the quality/price ratio ...".

[66] Sched 2, para 1(l): terms which have the object or effect of

> providing for the price of goods to be determined at the time of delivery or allowing a seller of goods or supplier of services to increase their price without in both cases giving the consumer the corresponding right to cancel the contract if the final price is too high in relation to the price agreed when the contract was concluded.

substantial increase in the overall cost to the borrower. We believe that the provision for the increase after two years is exempt from review, even if the rate of interest after two years seems significantly higher than is necessary to compensate for the lower rate in the first two years, provided that the provision is in "plain, intelligible language" and that it forms part of "the deal" as it was put to the consumer,[67] the "price" of the loan. The rates of interest payable go to the adequacy of price. On the other hand, the provision for an increased rate in the event of default may be challenged.[68] This is no more a question of adequacy than the price increase clause that appears on the indicative list.

3.29   Further, it is our understanding that it is not just the existence of the provision for an increased rate in the event of default, or the conditions under which it is to come into play, that may be challenged. The challenge may go to the amount of the increase itself, so that even if it is fair that the defaulting consumer should pay a higher rate, the court could hold the term to be unfair because of the amount of the increase. It is only the adequacy of the price as against the goods or services supplied that is exempt from review, and the default rate is not the price.

3.30   Perhaps more controversially, we would say that the same *may* be true of a provision which allows the borrower to pay off the loan within the first two years but only at the price of having to make up the difference between the low rate paid and some higher rate over the period between the start of the loan and repayment. This depends, we believe, on whether at the time the contract was made the option of early repayment was presented to the consumer as a main feature of the contract.[69]

3.31   We have two bases for these arguments. The first rests on the *First National Bank* case.[70] It will be recalled that the clause in question in that case provided for the continuation of the contractual rate of interest after judgment. The Court of Appeal accepted two arguments made by the Solicitor-General on behalf of the DGFT: first, that since the term set out when the contractual rate would be payable, the question was not one of adequacy, and secondly that the relevant terms were

> default provisions dealing with the situation where there is a breach of contract; it is not there that one finds defined the main subject matter of the contract ... Terms concerned with the adequacy of the price or remuneration are ... those which define the parties' rights and obligations in the due performance of the contract.[71]

---

[67]   The reason for the second qualification will appear from para 3.33 below.

[68]   See *Falco Finance Ltd v Gough* (1999) 17 Tr LR 526 (Macclesfield Cty Ct).

[69]   A similar example might be a provision in a pension scheme allowing the subscriber to leave the scheme subject to an "exit fee" of 10% of the accumulated benefits; and the conclusions we give below would apply equally.

[70]   [2000] QB 672 (CA) and [2001] UKHL 52, [2002] 1 AC 481 (HL); para 3.25 above.

[71]   *Ibid* at p 685 (CA), [24]–[25] (HL).

This second argument covers our example of a higher rate of interest payable after a default: it is not part of the original price but a default rate. But the logic of the Solicitor-General's argument would also apply to a higher rate payable as a price of early repayment. This is not a "default" provision but nor is it part of the normal performance of the contract. We think that, as in the *First National Bank* case, a clause requiring a higher rate of interest as the price of early repayment could be described as "incidental" or "subsidiary".

3.32 Our second basis depends on the logic of the Directive's exemptions of the "definition of the main subject matter" and the "adequacy of the price as against the goods or services supplied in exchange". We think that the reason for not subjecting these to review is that consumers will generally be aware of the terms in question and (provided they are in plain, intelligible language) understand them. Therefore consumers are unlikely to be taken by surprise, and also the terms will be subject to "the discipline of the market". Consumers are much less likely to take into account terms which will only apply in certain circumstances (whether or not those circumstances involve a default) and accordingly these terms should be subject to review.

3.33 This suggests that whether an amount payable under the contract is subject to review may well depend on how the "deal" is presented to the consumer. If, for example, the consumer is told explicitly that the deal is "x% for two years and then y% for two years; you can pay off early but then you must make your payments up to z%", we think that the rates could not be challenged; they would then form part of the price the consumer knows he has to pay and the amounts go to the adequacy of the price.[72] In other words, the exemption for the "adequacy of the price" should be interpreted in a similar way to that for the "main subject matter of the contract". The adequacy of the price will be exempt from review only to the extent that the sum payable was part of how the consumer "perceived the bargain";[73] and what the consumer should reasonably have expected to pay during the normal operation of the contract.[74] This is in effect the approach taken by both the Court of Appeal and the House of Lords in the *First National Bank* case.

3.34 We have dwelt on the question of "price" at some length because we will recommend in Part IV that this difficult question be clarified in the new legislation. However, for present purposes we do not think it necessary to define further the precise differences in the kinds of term to which UCTA and UTCCR apply. It is clear that, on the one hand, there are many terms in consumer contracts which are subject to both regimes, though, as we shall see, the requirements of each regime may differ; on the other, that there are a number of

[72] This assumes that the rates are in "plain intelligible language".

[73] Cf Unfair Contract Terms Bulletin 2 (OFT 170, September 1996) para 2.26, quoted at para 3.23 above.

[74] Cf paras 3.25 – 3.26 above.

potentially unfair terms which are within UTCCR but outside the scope of UCTA. We return to these points in Parts IV and V below.[75]

(2) Mandatory and permitted terms

3.35 Each instrument contains provisions designed to exclude from its operation terms which conform to what is required or permitted by other legislation, international convention or the decision of a competent authority.[76]

3.36 As to terms that conform to what is required by statutory provisions, the regimes appear similar.[77] One difference is that UTCCR curiously refer to terms that reflect mandatory statutory or regulatory provisions of any Member State,[78] so that apparently a term used by a supplier in the UK will not be subject to control if the term reflects such provisions of some other Member State, even though the contract has no connection with that Member State and the term does not reflect provisions of the UK. The Directive itself makes no mention of this, referring only to "contractual terms which reflect mandatory statutory or regulatory provisions".[79] We are of the view that UTCCR are an incorrect incorporation of the Directive in this respect, and that terms reflecting mandatory statutory or regulatory provisions of some other Member State, but not of the relevant jurisdiction in the UK, should be subject to UTCCR.[80]

3.37 There is more difficulty over terms which are merely permitted by statute or other rules. These seem to be exempt from UCTA.[81] The position under UTCCR is far from clear. Regulation 4(2), like Article 1(2) of the Directive, exempts "contractual terms which reflect mandatory statutory or regulatory provisions". Recital 13 to the Directive states that the phrase "mandatory statutory or regulatory provisions" includes "rules which, according to the law, shall apply between the contracting parties provided that no other arrangements have been established". This makes the intention on "default" rules clear but is hard to fit with the words of Article 1(2) in the English text.[82] We believe that terms which are detrimental to the consumer but which in substance are not significantly

---

[75] See esp paras 5.2 – 5.6.

[76] UCTA, s 29; UTCCR, reg 4(2).

[77] UCTA, s 29(1)(a); UTCCR, reg 4(2)(a).

[78] Reg 4(2)(a).

[79] Art 1(2).

[80] Unless the term reflects principles of international conventions to which the UK or the Community are party. See para 3.38 below.

[81] UCTA, s 29(1)(a) exempts provisions which are "authorised or required" by legislation. This seems to cover both terms which are compulsory and those which are allowed even though not compulsory (eg the example given by Treitel, p 253, in the context of UTCCR, of the permitted 50% minimum payment clause in a regulated hire-purchase agreement). It seems likely that a term which merely restates the general "default" rule which applies in the absence of contrary agreement (eg if, in a contract for the sale of a used car to a car dealer, it were stated that time for payment by the dealer was not of the essence: see SGA 1979, s 10) would be treated as "authorised".

[82] Chitty, paras 15-028 – 15-029, asks whether "mandatory" adds anything.

different from the "default rule" that would otherwise apply under the general law are exempt, as suggested by Recital 13, though this has the consequence that such terms cannot be challenged even if they are not in "plain intelligible language".[83]

3.38 On terms reflecting international conventions, the instruments are to similar effect. However, there are two differences. First, UCTA refers to international agreements to which the UK is a party,[84] but UTCCR refer to international conventions "to which the Member States or the Community are party".[85] This may be significant, particularly as many Member States have ratified the United Nations Convention on Contracts for the International Sale of Goods (Vienna, 1980 – "CISG") but the UK has not. Secondly, UTCCR regulation 4(2)(b) refers to terms which "reflect the ... principles of international conventions". It has been argued that the effect of this is to exempt terms which follow the model of an international convention even though that convention is not applicable to the type of contract in question.[86] Thus the terms of a contract for domestic carriage which follow the model of a contract for international carriage under an international convention would be exempt. If this is correct it seems undesirable, as the convention will probably have been drawn up with international commercial transactions in mind, not domestic consumer ones, and its provisions may not be suitable for the latter. For this reason alone this interpretation seems doubtful.

3.39 It has been argued that any international supply contract governed by CISG will be exempt under the exception for terms reflecting international conventions, even if the contract contains exclusions or restrictions on liability, since the latter are permitted by CISG. It would seem to follow that a domestic contract modelled on CISG and containing exclusions would also have to be exempt.[87]

3.40 Terms required or approved by competent authorities, such as an industry regulator, acting in the course of any statutory jurisdiction or function are deemed to comply with the requirement of reasonableness (or to satisfy the fair and reasonable test) under UCTA.[88] There is some difficulty in interpreting UTCCR

---

[83] See para 3.73 below.

[84] Section 29(1).

[85] Reg 4(2)(b).

[86] Treitel, p 253; Chitty, para 15-031 is to the same effect.

[87] Treitel, p 254. We have difficulty with this argument, at least in so far as it is suggested that this would mean that consumer contracts for carriage on terms "reflecting" CISG would be exempt. However, it is doubtful whether a consumer contract would ever "reflect" the principles of CISG since it is clear from CISG Art 2(a) that consumer transactions are not meant to be covered, albeit that the test of what is a consumer contract under CISG depends on the nature of the goods rather than the purpose of the transaction.

[88] Section 29(2). We assume the regulator is a public authority and will be approving the terms in the exercise of a statutory function. In *Timeload Ltd v British Telecommunications plc* [1995] EMLR 459 the CA held that the DGFT, who had seen the terms and had not objected to the term in question, was a public authority, but Lord Bingham MR expressed grave doubts as to whether the DGFT approved them in the exercise of a statutory function. Section 29(2) does not apply if the authority itself is a party to the contract. Terms which are simply of no effect (see para 3.9 above) are not exempted under this provision.

on this point. Regulation 4(2) exempts terms which reflect "mandatory statutory or regulatory provisions". It appears that "regulatory" provisions means not rules imposed by a regulator but simply secondary legislation.[89] It is possible, however, that a term which a regulatory agency has required to be inserted in a consumer contract, or even one which the regulator has approved, is exempt on the ground that it "reflects" the statutory provisions empowering the terms to be set, or requiring that they be approved, by the regulator.[90] If such terms are not exempt, then UTCCR seem to operate more broadly than UCTA in this respect.

8. EXCLUDED CONTRACTS

(1) Domestic contracts

(a) Consumers as suppliers

3.41   Repeating the words of the Directive,[91] UTCCR apply to contracts "concluded between a seller or a supplier and a consumer".[92] This seems to cover all cases in which the business is the party providing the property[93] or service and the consumer is the recipient.[94] There is doubt, however, as to whether a sale by a consumer to a business (for example, the sale or trade-in of a used car to a dealer), or the provision of a service by a consumer to a business (for example, where a private person gives a guarantee of another person's debt to a bank)[95] is within UTCCR.[96] On the one hand, the business is not the seller; on the other, "seller or supplier" is defined as:

---

[89]   The French text refers to "dispositions ... réglementaires", which normally means secondary legislation.

[90]   Chitty, para 15-030, which points out that Recital 13 refers to "provisions which directly or indirectly determine the terms of consumer contracts".

[91]   Art 1(1).

[92]   Reg 4(1).

[93]   Under the 1994 Regulations the definitions of "seller" and "supplier" referred to sellers and suppliers "of goods" (reg 2(2)). This created doubts as to whether land transactions were caught by the 1994 Regulations and whether the Directive had been implemented correctly: see S Bright and C Bright, "Unfair Terms In Land Contracts: Copy Out or Cop Out?" (1995) 111 LQR 655.

[94]   Most academic commentators are now of the opinion that UTCCR and the Directive do apply to all consumer contracts: see S Bright, "Winning the Battle Against Unfair Contract Terms" (2000) 20 LS 331, 339–341; S Whittaker, "Unfair Contract Terms, Public Services and the Construction of a European Conception of Contract" (2000) 116 LQR 95, 99; Chitty, paras 15-004 ff. At the 1999 Brussels Conference, "The 'Unfair Terms' Directive, Five Years On", both Mario Tenreiro (Opening Comments) and Professor Wilhelmsson (Introduction to Workshop 1) adhered to this view. Bradgate, at the same conference (Experience in the UK), expressed the view that if the Directive is limited to contracts for the sale and supply of goods or services, then it may not apply to contracts for computer software as the legal status of computer software is still not definitively settled.

[95]   For a full discussion see Chitty, paras 15-018 and 44-120, where it is suggested that the ECJ might take an autonomous view of the question.

[96]   Again at the 1999 Brussels Conference both Mario Tenreiro and Professor Wilhelmsson asserted that these contracts are covered by the Directive. See also S Bright, "Winning the Battle Against Unfair Contract Terms" (2000) 20 LS 331, 341.

any natural or legal person who, in contracts covered by these Regulations, is acting for purposes relating to his trade, business or profession, whether publicly owned or privately owned ...[97]

The definition seems to suggest that it does not matter whether the business party was supplying or receiving. The question is whether this definition is taken to override the normal meaning of the words "seller or supplier". Although UTCCR are following the English text of the Directive, it appears that in other language versions the wording is not limited to consumers as recipients of goods or services, and so it may be that this is the correct interpretation to follow.[98]

3.42 In contrast, UCTA section 3 [s 17] applies whether the consumer is buyer or seller, supplier or recipient.

(b) Insurance, land, securities and guarantees

3.43 UCTA has much more serious restrictions on its application to certain types of consumer contract. For English law, certain consumer contracts are excluded from the operation of UCTA, as is set out in Schedule 1. They are:

(1) contracts of insurance,[99]

(2) any contract so far as it relates to[100] the creation or transfer of any interest in land, or the termination of such an interest, and

(3) any contract so far as it relates to the creation or transfer of securities or of any right or interest in securities.[101]

---

[97] Reg 3(1), repeating Art 2(c) of the Directive.

[98] Chitty correctly points out that this would cause difficulty in UTCCR because it would then seem that contracts of employment might be covered by the Regulations, whereas Recital 10 of the Directive states that contracts relating to employment are to be excluded. See para 3.45 below.

[99] The exclusion of the application of UTCCR to terms in insurance contracts which "clearly define or circumscribe the insured risk and the insurer's liability" (Recital 19 of the Directive; see para 3.27, n 65 above) is much narrower than the total exclusion of insurance contracts in UCTA. Hence as Treitel, p 250, points out, a clause requiring the consumer to give notice of insurance claims within an unreasonably short period could be unfair under UTCCR, but would not be affected by UCTA. See also H Collins, "Good Faith in European Contract Law" (1994) 14 OJLS 229, 242–243, who welcomes the inclusion of insurance contracts in the Regulations, saying that "consumer insurance contracts represent the abyss of exploitation permitted by free markets".

[100] In *Electricity Supply Nominees Ltd v IAF Group Ltd* [1993] 1 WLR 1059, 1063–1064, it was held that any covenant that is integral to a lease is exempt. This was followed in *Unchained Growth III plc v Granby Village (Manchester) Management Co Ltd* [2000] 1 WLR 739 (CA). Transactions of a different kind included in the same document as the lease would not be exempt. It may be that a clause which deals with an exempt subject matter but which forms merely a subsidiary part of a non-exempt contract will not make the main contract exempt, but will itself be exempt still: *Micklefield v SAC Technology Ltd* [1990] 1 WLR 1002 (Ch D), 1008 (share option within contract of employment).

[101] None of the other exemptions in Sched 1 appear to affect consumer contracts, either because there is an express saving in favour of persons dealing as consumer or because the nature of the contract (eg for the formation of a company: para 1(d)) makes it implausible that either party could be dealing as a consumer. Another exception is more problematic: that of any

For Scots law they are:

(1) contracts of insurance;[102]

(2) any contract which creates or transfers any interest in land;[103]

(3) any contract so far as it relates to the creation or transfer of securities or of any right or interest in securities;[104] and

(4) contracts of guarantee.[105]

3.44 There are no equivalent exclusions in UTCCR.

(c) Contracts of employment

3.45 UCTA applies to contracts of employment with the exception that section 2 does not apply "except in favour of the employee".[106] It has been held that a contract of employment may be a consumer contract within the meaning of section 3 [s 17].[107] It is clear from Recital 10 that the Directive is not intended to apply to employment contracts. The 1994 Regulations expressly excluded employment contracts from their ambit. UTCCR do not do so, apparently assuming that an employment contract is not a consumer contract.[108]

---

contract so far as it relates to the creation or transfer of any interest in various forms of intellectual property. Chitty, para 15-022, takes the view that this excludes from UCTA "contractual licences under which use of computer software is permitted". However, this argument was rejected in *The Salvage Association v CAP Financial Services Ltd* [1995] FSR 654 and does not appear to have been taken since; we understand that most intellectual property practitioners regard the point as definitively decided by the *Salvage Association* case. It was not raised in *St Albans City and District Council v International Computers Ltd* [1996] 4 All ER 481 (CA). Para 14-096 of Chitty, by contrast, is neutral on the point.

[102] Section 15(3)(a)(i).

[103] These are not listed in s 15(2) and are therefore excluded. The Act does apply to "a grant of any right or permission to enter upon or use land not amounting to an estate or interest in the land": s 15(2)(e).

[104] These are not listed in s 15(2) and are therefore excluded.

[105] These are not listed in s 15(2) and are therefore excluded.

[106] Sched 1, para 4. This appears to mean that the employee can limit her liability to the employer for negligence but not vice versa. In Scotland UCTA applies to contracts of employment: s 15(2)(b).

[107] In *Chapman v Aberdeen Construction Group plc* 1993 SLT 1205, 1209 the court took the view that an employee does not contract "in the course of a business" when she hires out her labour: consequently, the contract of employment is a consumer contract. There is some disagreement over how s 3 applies. It has been said that an employment contract can be the employer's "written standard terms of business": *Liberty Life Assurance Co Ltd v Sheikh, The Times* 25 June 1985 (CA). The contrary was said in *Brigden v American Express Bank Ltd* [2000] IRLR 94, but Morland J, partly relying on the Scottish case, held that the employee was dealing as a consumer so that s 3 applied for that reason.

[108] Chitty, para 15-021.

(2) International contracts

3.46 UCTA section 26[109] exempts from the operation of certain sections any contract for the supply of goods made by parties in different States and which involves carriage of the goods between States, offer and acceptance across State borders or delivery in a different State to that where the contract was made. The section does not draw any distinction between consumer and non-consumer contracts.[110]

3.47 UTCCR has no similar exemption.[111] Thus UTCCR will apply whenever the law of part of the UK applies. Under the Rome Convention,[112] as implemented by the Contracts (Applicable Law) Act 1990, the two general principles are that the parties are free to choose the law to govern their contract,[113] and that in the absence of choice the contract shall be governed by the law of the country to which the contract has the closest connection.[114] However, first, under Article 3(3), a party cannot be deprived of the protection of the mandatory rules of a system to which all the other elements of the contract relate. Secondly, under Article 5 a consumer cannot be deprived of the protection provided by the mandatory rules of the law of the country of his habitual residence if one of three conditions is met.[115] These are that the contract was preceded by a specific invitation to the consumer or advertising in his country; or that the other party or his agent received the order in that country; or, in the case of sale of goods, that the goods were bought in another country in the course of a trip organised for that purpose by the seller. The Rome Convention applies to disputes heard in the UK whether or not the other party resides in a State which has ratified the Convention.[116] Thus many consumer contracts which involve delivery across State borders and which would thus escape UCTA will be subject to UTCCR.[117]

(3) Choice of UK law

3.48 UCTA also exempts from its operation contracts in which English or Scots law applies only because the parties have chosen English or Scots law to govern their contract.[118] The aim of this exemption was to avoid discouraging "foreign

---

[109] As amended by Contracts (Applicable Law) Act 1990, s 5 and Sched 4.

[110] The form of s 26 can be confusing. Section 26(1) allows parties to international contracts to exclude or restrict liability. Section 26(2) then exempts terms which would otherwise be caught by s 3 or 4 (ie the English law controls) or Part II of UCTA (ie the Scots law controls).

[111] Nor does SCGD.

[112] EC Convention on the Law Applicable to Contractual Obligations (Rome 1980).

[113] Art 3.

[114] Art 4.

[115] See generally Chitty, para 31-087.

[116] See Chitty, para 31-022.

[117] And even if the contract does not meet one of the three conditions referred to, and thus is subject to the law of another State, it will of course be subject to the Directive if the State is a member of the EU.

[118] Section 27(1). The choice of law may be either express or implicit: see *Benjamin's Sale of Goods* (5th ed 1997) para 25-086.

businessmen from agreeing to arbitrate their disputes in England or Scotland".[119] There is no parallel provision in UTCCR or SCGD.

9. THE TEST OF VALIDITY

(1) "Fair and reasonable" versus "unfair"

3.49   When a term is subject to the control of UCTA and is not simply ineffective, in English law the test under UCTA is whether the clause "satisfies the requirement of reasonableness". This is defined in section 11 of UCTA:

> (1) In relation to a contract term, the requirement of reasonableness for the purposes of this Part of this Act ... is that the term shall have been a fair and reasonable one to be included having regard to the circumstances which were, or ought reasonably to have been, known to or in the contemplation of the parties when the contract was made.
>
> (2) In determining for the purposes of section 6 or 7 above whether a contract term satisfies the requirement of reasonableness, regard shall be had in particular to the matters specified in Schedule 2 to this Act; but this subsection does not prevent the court or arbitrator from holding, in accordance with any rule of law, that a term which purports to exclude or restrict any relevant liability is not a term of the contract. ...
>
> (4) Where by reference to a contract term or notice a person seeks to restrict liability to a specified sum of money, and the question arises (under this or any other Act) whether the term or notice satisfies the requirement of reasonableness, regard shall be had in particular (but without prejudice to subsection (2) above in the case of contract terms) to –
>
>> (a) the resources which he could expect to be available to him for the purpose of meeting the liability should it arise; and
>>
>> (b) how far it was open to him to cover himself by insurance.

In Scots law, the test under UCTA is whether it was "fair and reasonable" to incorporate the clause into the contract. This is defined in section 24:

> (1) In determining for the purposes of this Part of this Act whether it was fair and reasonable to incorporate a term in a contract, regard shall be had only to the circumstances which were, or ought reasonably to have been, known to or in the contemplation of the parties to the contract at the time the contract was made.
>
> (2) In determining for the purposes of section 20 or 21 of this Act whether it was fair and reasonable to incorporate a term in a contract, regard shall be had in particular to the matters specified in Schedule 2 to this Act; but this subsection shall not prevent a court or arbiter from holding, in accordance with any rule of law, that a term which purports to exclude or restrict any relevant liability is not a term of the contract.

---

[119] Second Report, para 232.

(2A) In determining for the purposes of this Part of this Act whether it is fair and reasonable to allow reliance on a provision of a notice (not being a notice having contractual effect), regard shall be had to all the circumstances obtaining when the liability arose or (but for the provision) would have arisen.

(3) Where a term in a contract or a provision of a notice purports to restrict liability to a specified sum of money, and the question arises for the purposes of this Part of this Act whether it was fair and reasonable to incorporate the term in the contract or whether it is fair and reasonable to allow reliance on the provision, then, without prejudice to subsection (2) above in the case of a term in a contract, regard shall be had in particular to –

>   (a) the resources which the party seeking to rely on that term or provision could expect to be available to him for the purpose of meeting the liability should it arise;

>   (b) how far it was open to that party to cover himself by insurance.

(4) The onus of proving that it was fair and reasonable to incorporate a term in a contract or that it is fair and reasonable to allow reliance on a provision of a notice shall lie on the party so contending.

It is submitted that the test is in substance the same in both jurisdictions.

3.50 Technically there appear to be no fewer than three slightly different tests of reasonableness under these provisions. The general test is that set out in section 11(1) [s 24(1)]. For cases falling within sections 6 and 7 [ss 20 and 21] only, the court is required to have regard to a list of "guidelines" specified in Schedule 2.[120] Thirdly, where the clause restricts liability to a specified sum, section 11(4) [s 24(3)] requires the court to have regard in particular to questions of the resources available to the party and insurance. However, in practice there is but a single reasonableness test, as the courts have said that they will take the factors referred to by the guidelines into account in all cases in which they appear relevant,[121] and questions of insurance are also treated as highly relevant in cases in which section 11(4) [s 24(3)] does not strictly apply.[122]

3.51 Under UTCCR regulation 5(1) the test is in very different words:

> A contractual term which has not been individually negotiated shall be regarded as unfair if, contrary to the requirement of good faith, it causes a significant imbalance in the parties' rights and obligations arising under the contract, to the detriment of the consumer.

3.52 Regulation 6(1) provides:

---

[120] This list survives from SOGITA, from which ss 6 and 7 [ss 20, 21] are derived (see para 2.12 above).

[121] Eg *Rees Hough Ltd v Redland Reinforced Plastics Ltd* (1984) 27 BLR 141, 151; *Stewart Gill Ltd v Horatio Myer & Co Ltd* [1992] QB 600, 608.

[122] Eg *Phillips Products Ltd v Hyland* [1987] 1 WLR 659.

> Without prejudice to regulation 12,[123] the unfairness of a contractual term shall be assessed, taking into account the nature of the goods or services for which the contract was concluded and by referring, at the time of conclusion of the contract, to all the circumstances attending the conclusion of the contract and to all the other terms of the contract or of another contract on which it is dependent.

3.53   Is there any difference in substance between the requirement of reasonableness under UCTA and the test of unfairness under UTCCR? Clearly there are close similarities on some points but on others the question is not easy to answer.

3.54   One similarity is that both tests require the court to take into account the circumstances in which the contract is made. A second is that fairness or reasonableness is to be judged by the circumstances, as UTCCR regulation 6(1) puts it, "at the time of conclusion of the contract". It appears from this that the relevant question under UTCCR is whether it was fair to include the clause in the contract, rather than whether the clause appears fair, or whether it is fair to rely on it, in the light of subsequent events. This is certainly the test under UCTA section 11(1) [s 24(1)]. SOGITA had applied a different test, namely, whether it would "be fair or reasonable to allow reliance on the term", but the test was altered in UCTA to whether the term "is a fair and reasonable one to be included ..." (England); whether it was "fair and reasonable to incorporate [the] term" (Scotland).[124]

3.55   There are certainly differences in the factors to which the two instruments specifically refer, but as neither limits the courts' consideration to these it is hard to see that this is a difference in substance.

3.56   Whether there are further differences depends on the meanings of the two different tests. Unfortunately these are not easy to pinpoint, particularly the meaning of the test under UTCCR.

---

[123]   This deals with the powers of certain bodies to seek injunctions [interdicts] to prevent the continued use of unfair terms (see para 3.119 below).

[124]   In their Second Report, the Law Commission recommended use of the SOGITA test (para 183), but Parliament preferred the Scottish Law Commission's recommendation (at para 177). Lord Elwyn-Jones, the then Lord Chancellor, stated that

> the Scottish approach, by limiting the importance of considerations attaching to a particular case, should facilitate the creation of case law and so help to reduce future uncertainty.

Hansard (HL) 23 May 1977, vol 383, col 1134.

The test of whether the term was a fair one to be included seems to have two consequences. On the one hand a party which puts into its contract terms a clause which is fair at the time can rest assured that the term cannot be rendered invalid by subsequent events. On the other hand, a party which might reasonably limit its liability to some extent, or might reasonably exclude certain liabilities, but which inserts a clause purporting to give it wider protection which would not be reasonable, will not be able to rely on the clause at all.

(a) "Contrary to the requirement of good faith" and "significant imbalance"

3.57 There has been considerable debate in the legal literature as to the correct interpretation of the words of regulation 5(1). One view is that "contrary to the requirement of good faith" and "significant imbalance" are two separate but equal requirements, the first addressing issues of procedural fairness and the other of substantive fairness. Thus a term would be unfair only if it is shown both that in substance the term produced an imbalance between the rights and obligations of the parties to the consumer's detriment; and that the process by which the contract was made was contrary to good faith.[125]

3.58 This approach would suggest a possible difference between UTCCR and UCTA. It suggests that a term will be unfair under UTCCR only if both substantive and procedural unfairness are present. In contrast, under UCTA it would appear permissible for the court to conclude that a clause is unreasonable simply because of its content ("substantive" unfairness) without there having been anything unreasonable in the way in which the contract was made or the term included in it ("procedural" unfairness).[126] For example, it seems open to a court to conclude that it was not reasonable for a business to exclude its liability for negligence causing loss or damage to property even though the business had taken care to point out the clause to the consumer and the consumer had not raised any protest.

3.59 A second view of UTCCR is that "significant imbalance ... to the detriment of the consumer" is in the nature of a threshold requirement: the clause cannot be regarded as unfair if any imbalance is either insignificant or is actually in the consumer's favour. This leaves the main test of whether or not a term is unfair resting on the concept of "contrary to ... good faith". The question then arises of

---

[125] The speech of Lord Bingham in *DGFT v First National Bank plc* [2001] UKHL 52, [2002] 1 AC 481 may appear to support this "double requirement" approach. Lord Bingham said, at [17]:

> A term falling within the scope of the Regulations is unfair if it causes a significant imbalance in the parties' rights and obligations under the contract to the detriment of the consumer in a manner or to an extent which is contrary to the requirement of good faith. The requirement of significant imbalance is met if a term is so weighted in favour of the supplier as to tilt the parties' rights and obligations under the contract significantly in his favour ... The requirement of good faith in this context is one of fair and open dealing.

However, his Lordship was not addressing directly the point whether both substantive and procedural unfairness is required.

[126] The distinction between "procedural" and "substantive" unfairness derives from a famous article by A A Leff, "Unconscionability and the Code – The Emperor's New Clause" (1967) 115 U Pa L Rev 485. The notion of "procedural unfairness" (as contrasted to "contractual imbalance") found its way into English law in the speech of Lord Brightman in *Hart v O'Connor* [1985] AC 1000 (PC) at p 1018.

the meaning of "good faith" in this context. Can it consist entirely of substantive elements, not requiring any procedural impropriety?[127]

3.60 A third and converse approach is to say that the reference to good faith is no more than a "bow in the direction of [the] origins" of the German law on unfair terms[128] which was so influential on the Directive, and which in turn was a development from the initial case law on the good faith article of the German Civil Code.[129] German law is said now to pay scant regard to good faith when dealing with unfair clauses.[130] On this view, the critical question is whether there is a significant imbalance to the detriment of the consumer. This view is supported by the fact that the French legislature decided not to incorporate the good faith criterion in its legislation implementing the Directive. It is also a view that seems to be supported by the European Commission.[131]

---

[127] R Brownsword, G Howells & T Wilhelmsson, "Between Market and Welfare: Some Reflections on Article 3 of the EC Directive on Unfair Terms in Consumer Contracts" in C Willett, *Aspects of Good Faith* (1995) pp 25–59, make a persuasive argument that "good faith" could and should be read as an entirely substantive test. They argue that because the 1994 Regulations allow for a pre-emptive challenge to the validity of contractual clauses, it is difficult to see how procedural conditions can apply to the test, unless there is a different test for pre-emptive and *ex casu* challenges. Further, reliance on questions of procedural impropriety does not effectively promote a fair European standard form, since it would be impossible to regulate unfair terms without getting entangled in secondary questions of procedural abuse, and enables dealers to evade the effects of the Directive. If good faith must be read as comprising a procedural element, they say that it should be a question of choice – whether the requirement of good faith is satisfied depends on whether a different reasonable standard form was realistically on offer to the consumer, which is indirectly a substantive test. See also H Collins, "Good Faith in European Contract Law" (1994) 14 OJLS 229, who points out that the Directive states that it is the term, as opposed to the negotiating procedures, which must be in bad faith and that it would therefore be wrong to confine the requirement of good faith to procedural matters.

[128] Chitty, para 15-034, referring to Gesetz zur Regelung des Rechts der Allegemeinen Geschaftsbedingunged (Act on Standard Contract Terms – "AGBG") of 1976.

[129] M Tenreiro, "The Community Directive on Unfair Terms and National Legal Systems" [1995] 3 ERPL 273, 277.

[130] See the discussion of s 9 of the AGBG 1976 (which contains a reference to the principle of good faith) in N Reich and H-W Micklitz, *Consumer Legislation in the Federal Republic of Germany* (1981) pp 270–272.

[131] The Head of the Legal Matters Unit in DG XXIV, Mário Tenreiro, writing in his personal capacity in "The Community Directive on Unfair Terms and National Legal Systems" (1995) 3 ERPL 273, 279 (having discussed the thinking that guided the Commission in drafting the Directive) has said:

Let us be clear: there is no way that a contractual term which causes "a significant imbalance in parties' rights and duties arising under the contract to the detriment of the consumer" can conform with the requirement of "good faith". Indeed, the opposite is true: a term is always regarded as contrary to the requirement of "good faith" when it causes such an imbalance.

By 1999, at least, this was the official Commission view – see proceedings of the Brussels Conference 1999, Introduction by M Tenreiro and E Ferioli ("Examen comparatif des législations nationales transposant la directive 93/13" in "L'intégration de la directive 93/13 dans les systèmes législatifs nationaux") and Professor V Roppo, Preliminary Document to Workshop 3, "The Definition of 'Unfairness': The Application of Art 3(1), 4(1) – and of the Annexes of the Directive".

3.61   However, the Recitals to the Directive seem to consider good faith to be an operative criterion, as they refer to the requirement of good faith being "satisfied by the seller or supplier where he deals fairly and equitably with the other party whose legitimate interests he has to take into account".[132] The omission from the French legislation is partly explicable by the facts that French law already has a general requirement of performance in good faith, and that it would regard a supplier who sought to enjoy a disproportionate advantage to the detriment of the consumer as not acting in good faith.[133]

3.62   A final approach is to say that there are two routes to unfairness within UTCCR. A term which in itself causes a significant imbalance will be contrary to "good faith" and hence unfair. A term which appears in its substance not to have such an effect may in fact also be unfair if there has been a lack of procedural good faith.[134] This approach allows for both procedure and substance to be considered, but allows certain terms to be ruled unfair per se.

UNFAIRNESS IN SUBSTANCE

3.63   It is submitted that, whichever approach is followed, it must be the case that substantive unfairness alone can make a term unfair under UTCCR. This is because the Director General of Fair Trading ("DGFT") and the bodies listed in Schedule 1 have power to prevent the use of unfair terms and this may be done "in the abstract", in the sense that the precise way in which the clause is presented to the consumer may not be known. If there had to be procedural unfairness this preventive power could only be used when the procedure was known to the DGFT or other body. Equally, the indicative list would lose much of its force. It is clearly aimed at terms which, for the most part, are thought to be unfair in substance. It makes separate provision for terms which have been incorporated by an unfair procedure, such as "irrevocably binding the consumer to terms with

---

[132]   Recital 16. In the Final Report to Workshop 3 of the Brussels Conference it is stated (para 3.3) that the main aim of the Commission's view above is clearly political, to avoid the risk of the criterion of good faith becoming a potentially harmful criterion for consumers and reducing the level of consumer protection. The Chairman (Professor Roppo) said that the DG's position is hardly compatible with the wording of the Article, that to assert otherwise would leave the reference to good faith with a purely literary, symbolic or rhetorical value, and that the criterion of good faith is positively incorporated into the additional criteria for judging fairness in Art 4(1) so that the criterion of good faith must affect the evaluation of unfairness.

[133]   Chitty, para 15-034.

[134]   S Bright, "Winning the Battle Against Unfair Contract Terms" (2000) 20 LS 331, 348. Bright argues that the decision in *DGFT v First National Bank plc*, especially at first instance, supports this approach. The approach may however be criticised by a similar argument to that raised by Brownsword, Howells and Wilhelmsson (see n 127 above) in that it creates two tests for unfairness, one a purely substantive one to be judged by the tests set out in UTCCR (ie essentially for pre-emptive challenge), and another to be judged by procedural criteria. However, in Bright's approach it is the nature of the term that decides whether procedural considerations will come into play (an unfair term will not be saved by good procedure) as opposed to the timing of the challenge.

which he had no real opportunity of becoming acquainted before the conclusion of the contract".[135]

3.64   In the major reported case under UTCCR, *DGFT v First National Bank plc*,[136] Peter Gibson LJ delivering the judgment of the Court of Appeal appeared to support the argument that procedural unfairness is not a necessary requirement and that some clauses may cause such an imbalance that they should always be treated as unfair.[137] He remarked:

> The element of significant imbalance would appear to overlap substantially with that of the absence of good faith. A term which gives a significant advantage to the seller or supplier without a countervailing benefit to the consumer (such as a price reduction) might fail to satisfy this part of the test of an unfair term.[138]

3.65   The Court of Appeal's decision in this case also supports the argument. It will be recalled that the term in question was a clause in a contract of loan giving the bank, in the event of a default by the borrower, the right to demand payment of the outstanding balance and accrued interest and further interest at the contractual rate up to the date of payment. The provision for continued interest can have the result that, if judgment for the debt is given or the consumer obtains a "time order" permitting him to pay in instalments which he can afford, he may find that he still has to pay further sums by way of interest. In practice this continuing liability is unlikely to be raised for the court's consideration, so that the court will not consider whether a time order might be needed or whether any time order being made should allow for this liability to further interest. Counsel for the bank accepted that the term in question could cause hardship but argued that it was not necessary to order the bank to amend the term; it would suffice to amend the forms given to the consumer so as to bring this to his attention. The Court of Appeal held that this would not be adequate to ensure that the problem would be dealt with, and indicated that unless the bank were to give a suitable undertaking it would issue an injunction requiring amendment of the term.[139]

3.66   In the House of Lords the decision was reversed on the question of whether the term was unfair; their Lordships considered that the term entitling the bank to interest at the contractual rate until the date of payment was not unfair. It was the procedures that could give rise to the consumer having to pay more than he had

---

[135]   Sched 2, para 1(i).

[136]   [2000] QB 672 (CA); reversed on the point of whether the term itself was unfair, [2001] UKHL 52, [2002] 1 AC 481. The case was decided under the 1994 Regulations but the differences between these and UTCCR do not seem relevant to the point at issue.

[137]   At pp 686–687. He read a passage to this effect from H Beale, "Legislative Control of Fairness: The Directive on Unfair Terms in Consumer Contracts" in Beatson and Friedmann (eds) *Good Faith and Fault in Contract Law* (1995) p 245.

[138]   [2000] QB 672, 687C.

[139]   The Court of Appeal's references to procedural measures as mere "palliatives", which could not prevent the term being unfair, show that the real problem with the term was its substantive unfairness: C Mitchell, "Unfair Terms in Consumer Contracts" (2000) 116 LQR 557.

anticipated which were problematic. However, in their Lordships' speeches there is no contradiction of the view that a term may be unfair purely as a matter of substance, and some explicit support for it. Lord Steyn said that the examples given in Schedule 3 to the 1994 Regulations

> convincingly demonstrate that the argument of the bank that good faith is predominantly concerned with procedural defects in negotiating procedures cannot be sustained. Any purely procedural or even predominantly procedural interpretation of the requirement of good faith must be rejected.[140]

This case therefore also suggests that under UTCCR, as under UCTA, a term may be invalid simply because of its substance, without the need for procedural unfairness.

UNFAIRNESS IN PROCEDURE

3.67   Conversely, we believe that a term may be unfair under UTCCR because the way in which it was incorporated into the agreement was unfair, even though the term is not necessarily unfair in substance and would therefore have passed the test had the process by which it was "agreed" been fair. This seems to follow from the inclusion in the indicative list of terms which have the object or effect of

> irrevocably binding the consumer to terms with which he had no real opportunity of becoming acquainted before the conclusion of the contract.[141]

This makes no reference to the substance of the term to which the consumer is bound. Suppose a consumer taking a film to be processed were asked to sign a contract which by reference incorporated the processor's standard conditions, and the conditions included a term to the effect that the processor's liability in case of loss of the film would be limited to providing the consumer with a new, unexposed film unless, when the contract was made, the consumer paid a higher price for a "guaranteed service". Such a clause might be perfectly fair in substance.[142] However, if the consumer were not told she had this choice and was not given an opportunity to read the processor's standard terms before the contract was made, it is submitted that the terms incorporated by reference would for that reason alone be unfair.[143]

---

[140]   [2001] UKHL 52, at [36].

[141]   Sched 2, para 1(i).

[142]   Cf *Woodman v Photo Trade Processing Ltd*, unreported, 7 May 1981 (cited in R Lawson, "The Unfair Contract Terms Act: A Progress Report" (1981) 131 NLJ 933, 935), a case under UCTA holding that a clause limiting liability to the cost of a new film was unreasonable when the consumer was not offered this choice.

[143]   Another example is a clause requiring notification of any defects within a specified time:

> If the consumer is not aware of such a term, it will work to cause significant imbalance to the detriment of the consumer even though the substance of the term is not unfair. This weaves together matters of substance and procedure.

3.68 It might be asked, how can a term that is fair in substance cause "a significant imbalance in the parties' rights and obligations arising under the contract, to the detriment of the consumer", as required by regulation 5(1)? We think that there is "a significant imbalance in the parties' rights and obligations arising under the contract" within the meaning of the Regulation if the consumer does not know what her rights and obligations are and, had she known, she would have been able to safeguard her interests or might not have entered the contract.[144]

CONCLUSIONS

3.69 Thus we reject the idea that a term cannot be unfair under UTCCR unless there is unfairness both in substance and procedure. Any of the other approaches to interpretation of UTCCR seems possible, though we do not think that the third approach is easy to reconcile with the wording of the Directive. Either the second or the fourth seems better. But the truth is probably that theories as to the exact roles to be played by "good faith" and "substantive imbalance" make very little difference in practice. The court should make, as Recital 16 to the Directive puts it, "an overall evaluation of the different interests involved" and consider whether the seller or supplier has dealt "fairly and equitably with the other party whose legitimate interests he has to take into account",[145] and it is clear that on any of theories two, three or four the court has considerable leeway to decide what is or is not fair. What matters is how UTCCR will actually be applied.

(b) Are the tests under UCTA and UTCCR different?

3.70 We have argued that the tests under UCTA and UTCCR are similar in that a term may be unfair in substance, or because of the way it was "agreed", or both. Some commentators have argued that the test of fairness under UTCCR and that of reasonableness under UCTA are different because the two pieces of legislation point to different factors to be taken into account. Thus regulation 6(1) requires the court to take into account "all the other terms of the contract", which is not

---

S Bright, "Winning the Battle Against Unfair Contract Terms" (2000) 20 LS 331, 348. A similar argument may be made about terms that are not in "plain intelligible language" (see para 3.73 below) or terms that purport to state the parties' rights and obligations in a misleading way. See also OFT, Unfair Contract Terms Bulletin 3, p 12, quoted at para 4.71 below.

[144] E Macdonald, "The Emperor's Old Clauses: Unincorporated Clauses, Misleading Terms and the Unfair Terms in Consumer Contracts Regulations" (1999) 58 CLJ 413; L Koffman and E Macdonald, *The Law of Contract* (4th ed 2001) p 235:

> It can be suggested that a purposive approach is required by the Directive and certainly in relation to the question of the creation of a "significant imbalance in the rights and obligations of the parties" the terms, or clauses, could be regarded as distorting the rights which the consumer believes he, or she, has and thus creating an imbalance in the rights and obligations which will be, effectively usable under the contract. It may be that that should be regarded as sufficient for the unfairness test.

[145] See L Koffman and E Macdonald, *The Law of Contract* (4th ed 2001) pp 233–234.

mentioned explicitly in UCTA.[146] However, as we pointed out earlier,[147] under either piece of legislation the court is free to take into account any relevant fact.

3.71 It is hard to resist the conclusion reached in Chitty:

> There is ... a profound similarity in the two tests ... . [T]his does not mean ... that the two tests will have the same significance, but their differences do not stem from use of the language, on the one hand, of "reasonableness" and, on the other, of "fairness" and "good faith." Instead, they flow from the differences in ambit of the two pieces of legislation, in particular as regards the types of term to be tested.[148]

(2) Factors

3.72 UCTA directs the court to take into account various factors. Thus we have noted that section 11(4) [s 24(3)] directs the court to consider the insurance position; and that Schedule 2 contains a list of guidelines for application of the reasonableness test. Technically the latter applies only to questions of reasonableness under sections 6(3), 7(3) and (4), 20 and 21, but in practice the guidelines are applied more widely.[149] Some of the words of these guidelines found their way into Recital 16 of the Directive, along with the instruction to take into account whether the seller or supplier dealt "fairly and equitably with the other party whose legitimate interests he has to take into account". These were repeated in Schedule 2 to the 1994 Regulations, but UTCCR follow the words of the Directive itself and do not instruct the court to have regard to any particular factors other than "all the circumstances attending the conclusion of the contract".[150]

(3) Plain and intelligible language

3.73 Regulation 7(1) of UTCCR, mirroring the Directive, states:

> A seller or supplier shall ensure that any written term of a contract is expressed in plain, intelligible language.

---

[146] Anson, p 197; Treitel, p 249. It has been said that the Directive makes it clear that it is the interaction of terms which is important in determining fairness (ie a term is unfair if it causes significant imbalance in the rights of the parties under the contract as a whole), whereas UCTA deals only with individual terms in isolation: M Dean, "Unfair Contract Terms: The European Approach" (1993) 56 MLR 581, 583.

[147] Para 3.54 above.

[148] Chitty, para 15-050. C Willett, "Directive on Unfair Terms in Consumer Contracts" (1994) 2 Consumer LJ 114, 120, suggests that the UK courts should take a broadly similar approach to unfairness under Art 3 of the Directive as is taken to unreasonableness under UCTA, looking at substantive risk allocations in the context of the bargaining environment and appreciating that both can influence the overall position. Treitel, p 258, says it is "possible to imagine" cases where the two tests might lead to different results, eg where one provision has guidelines on a particular point and the other does not.

[149] See para 3.50, n 121 above.

[150] Reg 6(1).

Curiously, no general sanction is stated other than that, if the meaning of a written term is in doubt, the interpretation most favourable to the consumer shall prevail.[151] The fact that the clause is not in plain, intelligible language is not even stated to be a factor to be taken into account in deciding whether the term is unfair, though no doubt a court could take it into account under its general assessment.

3.74 It has been argued that Article 5 (and by implication regulation 7(2), which is in the same terms) does contain a sanction beyond the normal common law rule that a clause should be interpreted against the interests of the party putting it forward,[152] in that it requires not just an interpretation in favour of the consumer but the interpretation *most* favourable to the consumer.[153] This may not be very different to the extreme way in which, before the advent of statutory controls over exemption clauses,[154] the courts sometimes applied the common law rule. However, regulation 7 may be somewhat stronger than the common law rule as it is applied in the UK courts today.[155] Even if it is correct that the regulation requires more than an application of the common law rule, it is, like all rules of construction, a weak weapon. Many clauses have only one possible meaning yet are in language which is neither plain nor intelligible to consumers.

3.75 There is a sanction when the term which is not in plain, intelligible language is a "core" term (the price or the definition of the main subject matter). In this case the term may be reviewed for fairness.[156]

3.76 UCTA has no equivalent requirement. The rule of interpretation against the party putting the clause forward will apply to any ambiguous term as a matter of common law. The court can take into account the intelligibility of a term, and

---

[151] This does not apply in proceedings brought under reg 12 (see para 3.119 below). It has been argued that even in proceedings by or against an individual consumer, the interpretation which is "most favourable to the consumer" should be that which is best for the consumer in the light of the fairness test, so that what would otherwise be the least favourable interpretation should be adopted if that would result in the clause being held unfair and therefore not binding: Butterworths, para 3.56.

[152] Often still referred to as the *contra proferentem* rule.

[153] M Tenreiro and E Ferioli, "Examen comparatif des législations nationales transposant la directive 93/13/" at the 1999 Brussels Conference "The 'Unfair Terms' Directive, Five Years On: Evaluation and Future Perspectives", p 9.

[154] Eg *Webster v Higgin* [1948] 2 All ER 127.

[155] See *Photo Production Ltd v Securicor Transport Ltd* [1980] AC 827, 851:

> ... any need for ... judicial distortion of the English language has been banished by Parliament's having made these kinds of contracts subject to the Unfair Contract Terms Act 1977.

[156] Reg 6(2). The DGFT interprets this, when read with Recital 20, as also requiring that the terms must be properly drawn to the consumer's "attention": OFT, Unfair Contract Terms Bulletin 4, pp 13–18.

other factors relating to "transparency", in assessing whether it satisfies the requirement of reasonableness.[157]

(4) Indicative list

3.77 UCTA defines closely some of the terms to which it applies.[158] However, its broadest control over terms in consumer contracts is that in section 3(2)(b) [s 17(1)(b)], whose scope is not easy to define. UCTA does not provide examples of what terms might fall within this subsection, and the Law Commissions' Second Report, on which UCTA is based, gives only one example.[159]

3.78 UTCCR contain an indicative list of terms which may be regarded as unfair.[160] This list is referred to in regulation 5(5), but there does not seem to be any presumption against a clause which appears on the list.[161]

(5) Burden of showing unfairness

3.79 Under UCTA the burden of showing that a term is fair and reasonable is on the party claiming that the term satisfies the requirement of reasonableness.[162] UTCCR, however, do not state which party bears the burden.[163] It seems that it is for the consumer to show that the term is unfair, as neither UTCCR nor the

---

[157] Cf *Stag Line Ltd v Tyne Shiprepair Group Ltd (The "Zinnia")* [1984] 2 Lloyd's Rep 211, 222, where Staughton J said:

> I would have been tempted to hold that all the conditions are unfair and unreasonable for two reasons: first, they are in such small print that one can barely read them; secondly, the draughtsmanship is so convoluted and prolix that one almost needs an LLB to understand them. However, neither of those arguments was advanced before me, so I say no more about them.

On "transparency" see paras 4.104 – 4.109 below.

[158] In particular see s 13(1) [s 25(3)], which gives a (non-exhaustive) list of clauses which, for the purpose of the Act, count as exclusions or restrictions of liability.

[159] Second Report, paras 143–146. The example is the clause in *Anglo-Continental Holidays Ltd v Typaldos Lines (London) Ltd* [1967] 2 Lloyd's Rep 61; see para 3.13, n 35 above. However the Law Commissions do refer to dicta in two other cases, the facts of which involve terms which give one party a wide discretion as to how to perform: *Glynn v Margetson & Co* [1893] AC 351 ("liberty to deviate" clause) and *Sze Hai Tong Bank Ltd v Rambler Cycle Co Ltd* [1959] AC 576 (PC) (see para 3.14, n 39 above).

[160] Sched 2. The list is copied from the Annex to the Directive. It is often termed a "grey" list.

[161] DTI, Implementation of the EC Directive on Unfair Terms in Consumer Contracts 93/13/EEC, A Consultation Document (October 1993) states that where a term in the Annex does not fall within the scope of UCTA "it will be for the consumer to demonstrate that the term is unfair according to the test in Art 3(1)".

[162] UCTA, s 11(5) [s 24(4)]. In *Sheffield v Pickfords Ltd* (1997) 16 Tr LR 337 the Court of Appeal said that, if the party relying on the term does not raise UCTA in its pleadings, then the implication is that it is arguing that the term is reasonable. Hence the issue becomes live and the other party will not be penalised for not raising the point. Lord Woolf MR continued that it would be preferable for the party seeking to rely on the term to state in its pleadings that it was entitled to rely on that term under UCTA, but it was not said that that party was required to do so. See also *Killick v PricewaterhouseCoopers (No 1)* [2001] 1 BCLC 65.

[163] Except to say that a seller or supplier who claims that a term was individually negotiated must show that it was: reg 5(4).

Directive make any provision to displace the normal burden of proof resting on the claimant.[164] If a clause appears in the "indicative and non-exhaustive list of terms which may be regarded as unfair" of Schedule 2 to UTCCR, then it has been said that this at least raises a inference that the term is unfair.[165] Nevertheless it is likely that the general common law rule in civil cases will still apply,[166] and the consumer who asserts that a term is unfair will have to prove that it is.[167]

3.80   It is not clear that this is affected by a decision of the European Court of Justice ("ECJ") that a domestic court has the power, and possibly the duty,[168] to raise the issue of fairness of its own motion when the consumer does not do so (in the case in question because the action was undefended).[169] This presumably applies only when the unfairness of the clause is clear on the face of the documents or from the way that the case was presented to the court.[170] It may be argued that the

---

[164]   Cf reg 5(4) (for the party claiming that a term was individually negotiated to show that it was). Chitty, para 15-047, contemplates that the ECJ may develop a European view on where the burden of proof under the Directive lies, and might hold that, since the purpose of the Directive is to protect consumers, the burden of proving fairness should be placed on the business. S Weatherill, "Prospects for the Development of European Private Law Through 'Europeanisation' in the European Court – the Case of the Directive on Unfair Terms in Consumer Contracts" (1995) 3 ERPL 307, 317, also argues that, as a consequence of the general aim of the Directive to protect consumers, the burden of proof must be taken to lie on the business. However, the European Commission's opinion is that there is no burden of proof at all, since it is an issue of law, and not a matter of fact to be substantiated by the parties: V Roppo, Introduction to Workshop 3, "The Definition of 'Unfairness': The Application of Art 3(1), 4(1) – and of the Annexes of the Directive", at the 1999 Brussels Conference, "The 'Unfair Terms' Directive, Five Years On". The Final Report on the Workshop disputes this apparent oversimplification, stating that those taking part in the discussion largely agreed with the proposition that if a term appears in the Annex the burden is on the supplier to prove it is fair, and otherwise the consumer must show it is unfair.

[165]   Cheshire, Fifoot & Furmston, p 218; Treitel refers to them as "prima facie unfair terms", p 251. M Dean, "Unfair Contract Terms: The European Approach" (1993) 56 MLR 581, 587, suggests that it would be "unlikely for them to be found fair".

[166]   Chitty, para 15-047, referring to *Cross & Tapper on Evidence* (8th ed 1995) pp 133–134.

[167]   See DTI, Implementation of the EC Directive on Unfair Terms in Consumer Contracts 93/13/EEC, A Consultation Document (October 1993). The result, criticised by C Willett, "Directive on Unfair Terms in Consumer Contracts" (1994) 2 Consumer LJ 114, 121, is that, even though all the terms in the Annex are indicatively unfair, if the term is an exemption clause under UCTA the business will have to prove it is reasonable, but if not, the consumer will have to prove it is unfair. See also R Brownsword, G Howells and T Wilhelmsson, "Between Market and Welfare: Some Reflections on Article 3 of the EC Directive on Unfair Terms in Consumer Contracts" in C Willett, *Aspects of Good Faith* (1995) p 34, who suggest that such a weak interpretation offers much less protection to the consumer than was intended in the Directive.

[168]   S Whittaker, "Judicial Interventionism and Consumer Contracts" (2001) 117 LQR 215, 218.

[169]   *Océano Grupo Editorial SA v Roció Murciano Quintero (C-240/98)* [2000] ECR I-4941. In this case it was the unfair nature of the clause which led to the actions being undefended. It gave the sellers of encyclopaedias on credit the right to sue consumers in the courts of a region in which they had their principal place of business, but far from where the consumers lived.

[170]   S Whittaker, "Judicial Interventionism and Consumer Contracts" (2001) 117 LQR 215, 217.

business is still entitled to have its clause enforced unless the court has been convinced (by the consumer or otherwise) that the term is unfair.

10. DEFINITIONS

(1) "Consumer"

3.81 The definitions of "consumer" in the two pieces of legislation differ. UCTA section 12 provides:

> (1) A party to a contract "deals as consumer" in relation to another party if –
>
> > (a) he neither makes the contract in the course of a business nor holds himself out as doing so; and
> >
> > (b) the other party does make the contract in the course of a business; and
> >
> > (c) in the case of a contract governed by the law of sale of goods or hire-purchase, or by section 7 of this Act, the goods passing under or in pursuance of the contract are of a type ordinarily supplied for private use or consumption.
>
> (2) But on a sale by auction or by competitive tender the buyer is not in any circumstances to be regarded as dealing as consumer.
>
> (3) Subject to this, it is for those claiming that a party does not deal as consumer to show that he does not.

The Scottish provisions refer to a "consumer contract". This is defined in section 25(1) as

> a contract (not being a contract of sale by auction or competitive tender) in which –
>
> > (a) one party to the contract deals, and the other party to the contract ("the consumer") does not deal or hold himself out as dealing, in the course of a business, and
> >
> > (b) in the case of a contract such as is mentioned in section 15(2)(a) of this Act [namely, one which relates to the transfer of the ownership or possession of goods from one person to another] the goods are of a type ordinarily supplied for private use or consumption;
>
> and for the purposes of this Part of this Act the onus of proving that a contract is not to be regarded as a consumer contract shall lie on the party so contending.

This definition is substantially the same as that in section 12.

3.82 Under UTCCR regulation 3(1),

"consumer" means any natural person who, in contracts covered by these Regulations, is acting for purposes which are outside his trade, business or profession.[171]

3.83 There are a number of differences between the two definitions. The first is that the UCTA definitions of contracting "as consumer" depend on the other party acting in the course of a business, and the definitions of business under UTCCR and UCTA differ somewhat. This is taken up in the next section.

3.84 A second difference is as to the "persons" who may be a consumer. The Court of Appeal has held that a company may "deal as consumer" within UCTA if it enters a transaction which is only incidental to its business activity and which is not of a kind it makes with any degree of regularity.[172] Under UTCCR only a natural person can be a consumer.[173]

3.85 Thirdly, UCTA uses the test of whether the contract is made (by either party) in the course of business, whereas UTCCR define a consumer as a person acting "outside his trade, business or profession". The latter formula appears to exclude from the application of UTCCR transactions that are related to a person's business even if they are not a central or regular part of it. Moreover, the ECJ has held in relation to another Directive that a trader cannot claim that because the transaction was not a normal part of his business (in the case concerned, a contract to advertise the sale of the business), he is entitled to the protection granted by the Directive to "consumers".[174] Following the *R & B Customs* case[175] it would seem that a sole trader who makes a contract which is only incidental to his business and not one he makes with any degree of regularity will be regarded as a consumer under UCTA.[176]

---

[171] SCGD uses a different definition again, defining a consumer as

> any natural person who, in the contracts covered by this Directive, is acting for purposes which are not related to his trade, business or profession.

We are not convinced that this formula is materially different.

[172] *R & B Customs Brokers Co Ltd v United Dominions Trust Ltd* [1988] 1 WLR 321 (purchase of car for personal and business use of directors).

[173] There is one exception. The Arbitration Act 1996, ss 89–91, provides that in a consumer contract an arbitration clause is unfair so far as it relates to a claim for a "modest" amount (currently fixed at £3,000), and for this purpose a legal person may be a consumer (s 90).

[174] *Criminal proceedings against Patrice Di Pinto*, Case C-361/89 [1991] ECR I-1189 (Directive 85/577/EEC). See also *Benincasa v Dentalkit Srl*, Case C-269/95 [1997] ECR I-3767 (on the Brussels Convention on Jurisdiction and Enforcement of Judgments in Civil and Commercial Matters (1968)).

[175] [1988] 1 WLR 321; see n 172 above.

[176] The Court of Appeal relied on the decision of the House of Lords in *Davies v Sumner* [1984] 1 WLR 1301, where s 1 of the Trade Descriptions Act 1968, which creates a criminal offence in respect of false or misleading trade descriptions made in the course of business, was considered. For criticism of this approach see S Jones and D Harland, "Some Problems Relating to Consumer Sales – *R & B Customs Brokers Ltd v United Dominions Trust Ltd*" (1989-90) 2 JCL 266, 272–275; R Kidner, "The Unfair Contract Terms Act 1977 – Who Deals as Consumer?" (1987) 38 NILQ 46; D Price, "When is a Consumer not a Consumer?" (1989) 52 MLR 245. See also *Chapman v Aberdeen Construction Group* 1993

3.86 A fourth difference is that under UCTA, where the contract is one for the sale or supply of goods, a party will only be "dealing as consumer" if the goods supplied are of a type ordinarily supplied for private use or consumption.[177] There is no equivalent limitation in UTCCR, nor in SCGD.[178]

3.87 Fifthly, sales by auction or competitive tender do not count as consumer sales under UCTA,[179] whereas they can under UTCCR. SCGD permits business sellers to exclude their liability only in auction sales of second-hand goods and then only if the buyer can be present.[180]

3.88 A final difference is that under UCTA, a party will not deal as a consumer if he "holds himself out as" making the contract in the course of a business.[181] There is no such restriction in UTCCR or SCGD.

SLT 1205 (distinguished on facts). In *Stevenson v Rogers* [1999] QB 1028 (sale by fisherman of his old working boat held to be made in course of business within SGA 1979, s14(2)) Potter LJ, delivering the leading judgment, also seems to cast some doubt on the *R & B* case. The legislative history of s 14(2) showed a clear intention to widen the scope to cover any sale made by a business and, had the CA in the *R & B* case considered s 14(2), instead of comparing s 12 to the criminal statute, the Trade Descriptions Act, it might have concluded that it was desirable to construe s 12 of UCTA in the same way. However, Potter LJ also points out that the decisions are in a sense consistent in that each interpretation has the effect of giving more protection to the buyer. See further H Collins, "Good Faith in European Contract Law" (1994) 14 OJLS 229, 240; E Macdonald, "Mapping The Unfair Contract Terms Act 1977 and the Directive on Unfair Terms in Consumer Contracts" (1994) JBL 441, 458; C Willett, "The Directive on Unfair Terms in Consumer Contracts and its Implementation in the United Kingdom" (1997) 2 ERPL 223, 229. Willett, for example, gives the example of a solicitor who buys a car for use in her business, arguing that the car will not have been bought "in the course of a business", and so the solicitor would be within the UCTA definition of "consumer", but that it will have been bought for business purposes, so that the transaction will not be protected by UTCCR. She will also fall outside SCGD: see n 171 above.

[177] Section 12(1)(c) [s 25(1)]. The restriction seems to derive from the Molony Report (see paras 465–469). Presumably the aim is to enable the business to decide more easily when it will be dealing with a consumer.

[178] See n 171 above.

[179] Section 12(2) [s 25(1)].

[180] Art 1(3).

[181] Section 12(1)(a) [s 25(1)]. The First Report (see paras 87, 92 and 95) recommended this qualification without giving an example of holding out, nor is there an example in the preceding Working Paper No 18, para 51. A possible example would be a person buying for private use or consumption who presents a card to claim a trade discount: Cheshire, Fifoot & Furmston, p 204. Another example may be a person asking for "trade terms" at a builder's merchant. However it has been argued that such behaviour implies nothing about carrying on a business but merely implies the buyer is entitled to the same discount as a trade buyer: R Kidner, "The Unfair Contract Terms Act 1977 – Who Deals as Consumer?" (1987) 38 NILQ 46. If the *R & B Customs* case is correct (see n 176 above), it would appear that the consumer would have to hold out that the transaction was one that he made regularly or as an integral part of his business.

(2) "Business"

3.89 As a general rule, UCTA applies only to terms affecting "business liability".[182] While this is an express provision of English law,[183] it is also true of Scots law.[184] There are two exceptions. The first are terms affecting liability for misrepresentation.[185] The second are clauses falling within section 6 [s 20] (sale and hire-purchase). This means that even a non-business seller[186] cannot exclude or restrict liability for breach of the implied terms under section 12 of the SGA 1979 (title), and can exclude or restrict her liability under section 13 (correspondence with description) or 15 (correspondence with sample)[187] only if the term satisfies the requirement of reasonableness.[188]

3.90 As we have seen, UTCCR applies only to contracts "concluded between a seller or a supplier and a consumer",[189] and "seller or supplier" is defined as a business.[190]

3.91 The definition of "business" under the two instruments is similar but not identical. UCTA section 14 [s 25(1)] provides that

> "business" includes a profession and the activities of any government department or local or public authority.

3.92 UTCCR regulation 3(1) provides that

> "seller or supplier" means any natural or legal person who, in contracts covered by these Regulations, is acting for purposes relating to his trade, business or profession, whether publicly owned or privately owned.

---

[182] Section 1(3).

[183] Section 1(3).

[184] Section 16 expressly stipulates that the controls are restricted to breach of duty in the course of a business. Since the other controls only apply to consumer or written standard form contracts which must involve at least one party who is dealing in the course of business, the Scottish provisions in effect only apply to business liability [ss 17–19, 21, 25].

[185] Section 8, amending Misrepresentation Act 1967, s 3. This provision does not apply to Scotland.

[186] Nor a hire-purchase supplier who is not acting in the course of a business, if such an animal exists. The relevant sections for hire-purchase are SOGITA, ss 8 and 9.

[187] There are no implied terms as to quality or fitness for purpose under s 14 if the seller is not selling in the course of a business (for hire-purchase the equivalent section is SOGITA, s 10).

[188] Since the seller is not acting in the course of a business, the other party cannot be "dealing as consumer" within the definition of s 12 [s 25(1)] even if she is in fact buying for private purposes.

[189] Reg 4(1).

[190] Reg 3(1).

3.93 There are obvious similarities between the two, but also some possible differences.[191]

(a) "Occasional sales"

3.94 UCTA applies only if the party is acting in the course of a business.[192] It is possible that this may exclude activities which are merely incidental to the business and are not carried out regularly. Thus we saw earlier that when the question is whether the other party is acting in the course of a business or is dealing as a consumer, the Court of Appeal has held that a company may "deal as consumer" within UCTA if it enters a transaction which is only incidental to its business activity and which is not of a kind it makes with any degree of regularity.[193] UTCCR's definition is broader in referring to purposes "relating" to a trade, business or profession. Curiously, SCGD's definition is closer to that of UCTA than of UTCCR: a "seller" is defined as a person who sells consumer goods in the course of his trade, business or profession.[194]

3.95 However, we do not believe that there is any practical difference between the definitions on this point. Although the Court of Appeal has held that a company may be a consumer within UCTA when buying, we doubt whether the courts would apply the same interpretation of UCTA when the question is whether the seller or supplier is acting in the course of a business, as the Court of Appeal has also held that the sale of an item which is not regularly sold by the seller is still within the course of business within the meaning of the SGA 1979.[195]

(b) Contracts with government departments or local or public authorities

3.96 UCTA's definition of business is not exhaustive but it expressly includes government departments and local or public authorities. UTCCR's definition is exhaustive. It includes businesses in public ownership.[196] It might be argued that it does not include a contract between, say, a local authority and a consumer, but

---

[191] A further difference relates to UCTA's exclusion of occupiers' liability to visitors allowed onto land for educational or recreational purposes not connected to the occupier's business, though this will not normally be under a contract and it is dealt with in Part VII below. This exception does not apply in Scots law.

[192] There are exceptions under s 6 [s 20]: see para 3.8 above.

[193] *R & B Customs Brokers Co Ltd v United Dominions Trust Ltd* [1988] 1 WLR 321 (purchase of car for personal and business use of directors).

[194] Art 1(2)(c).

[195] *Stevenson v Rogers* [1999] QB 1028: see n 176 above. The Second Report seemed to intend to exclude from control only supply in a "purely private" capacity: para 9.

[196] Thus it does not seem that UTCCR are limited to contracts between profit-making organisations and consumers, so that a contract between a pupil and an educational charity might be covered: Chitty, para 15-016. The same seems true of UCTA: Chitty, para 14-063; R Kidner, "The Unfair Contract Terms Act 1977 – Who Deals as Consumer?" (1987) 38 NILQ 46, 53.

this seems an unlikely interpretation,[197] and the OFT has secured the removal of unfair terms from a number of such contracts.[198]

(3) "Party" and third party beneficiaries

(a) UCTA: English law

3.97 A term in a contract may attempt to remove or limit the right of a third person to sue one of the parties to the contract in tort. There is no doubt that such a provision (as against the third party, it is a non-contractual notice rather than a contractual term) may be subject to UCTA.[199]

3.98 The Contracts (Rights of Third Parties) Act 1999 creates an exception to the doctrine of privity of contract. If a contract provides that a third party may enforce one of its terms, or if the term is expressed to be for the third party's benefit and on the construction of the contract it does not appear that the parties did not intend the term to be enforceable by the third party, the third party may enforce the term in her own name.[200]

3.99 Such enforcement is subject to any relevant terms,[201] which would include any clause limiting the liability of the promisor (the party who has undertaken the obligation to the third party). Even if the limitation is one which, were it to apply as between the original parties to the contract, would fall within UCTA, the third party cannot, with one exception, challenge its validity under UCTA.

3.100 This is principally because section 7(4) provides that the third party shall not be treated as a party to the contract for the purposes of any other Act (or any instrument made under any other Act). Thus even if the third party is (in lay terms) a consumer, or the contract is on the promisor's written standard terms of business, the third party does not count as a contracting party for the purposes of UCTA section 3. Nor will the third party be a consumer within sections 6(2) and 7(2), which operate in favour of those "dealing as consumer". Section 12 describes a person dealing as consumer as being "a party to a contract".

---

[197] Chitty, para 15-016, which says that the definition clearly does include a local authority but gives no argumentation. In "Unfair Contract Terms, Public Services and the Construction of a European Conception of Contract" (2000) 116 LQR 95, S Whittaker states that it is a fairly clear proposition that, according to the Directive, the *provider of the service* (as opposed to business) may be publicly or privately owned. See also "Rapport sur l'application de la Directive 93/13/1993 aux prestations de service public", a report by the National Consumer Council and L'Institut National de la Consommation to the European Commission in 1997 (eds Hall and Tixador) p 13, which states that the Directive's application to public authorities in principle is clearly confirmed by Art 2, and by Recitals 14 and 16 of the preamble.

[198] See Chitty, para 15-016, n 61.

[199] See *Smith v Eric S Bush* [1990] 1 AC 831 (HL); *Killick v PricewaterhouseCoopers (No 1)* [2001] 1 BCLC 65, 72; *Melrose v Davidson & Robertson* 1993 SLT 611 (1st Div); *Bank of Scotland v Fuller Peiser* 2002 SLT 574.

[200] Sections 1(1) and (2).

[201] Section 1(4).

3.101   The one exception is section 2(1) of UCTA , which refers simply to a person (in this situation, the promisor) being unable to exclude his liability for death or personal injury caused by negligence to other "persons", rather than to the other party. Section 2(2) would also have applied but it is expressly prevented from so doing by section 7(2) of the 1999 Act.

3.102   It appears that, if the other contracting party (the promisee) were to seek to enforce the contract term for the third party's benefit, the promisee could rely on section 3 or other provisions of UCTA to challenge the limitation of the promisor's liability on the grounds that, as against the promisee, the limitation is unreasonable.[202]

(b) UCTA: Scots law[203]

3.103   Scotland has known the *ius quaesitum tertio* for many years. It has been argued that section 17 of UCTA does not apply where a tertius has title to sue since the tertius is not a party to the contract.[204] The controls in sections 20 and 21 do not apply to a tertius for the same reason. However, both sections 16(1)(a) (death and personal injury caused by breach of duty) and 16(1)(b) (other loss or damage caused by breach of duty) seem to apply whether the pursuer is the original party to the contract or a third party claiming a right under it.[205]

(c) UTCCR

3.104   The position under UTCCR is less clear. These, like the Directive, refer to clauses which produce a significant imbalance in the rights and obligations of the parties,[206] in contracts concluded with a consumer by a seller, as not being "binding on the consumer".[207] This suggests that it is only the contracting consumer who will benefit from UTCCR, not a third party beneficiary. The Law Commission Report on Contracts for the Benefit of Third Parties expressed the view that the 1994 Regulations appear not to apply to limitations on the rights of

---

[202] See Contracts for the Benefit of Third Parties (1996) Law Com No 242, para 13.10 (vi). It is not completely clear whether the third party could argue that the clause is unreasonable as between the original parties and therefore of no effect, so that in effect the third party can enforce his or her rights irrespective of the clause, but it seems unlikely. In effect that would be to allow a non-party to challenge the clause, and that seems to be beyond the terms of UCTA.

[203] Section 17(1)(a) provides that an unfair term shall have no effect as against a consumer or customer. The latter is defined in terms of persons who are parties to the contract: s 17(2) [s 25]. It is submitted that s 17(1)(b) is similarly restricted.

[204] H MacQueen, "Third Party Rights in Contract: English Reform and Scottish Concerns" (1997) 1 Edin LR 488.

[205] It has been argued that the rule should be the same on either side of the border: *ibid*, p 493. See further para 4.176 below.

[206] Reg 5(1).

[207] Reg 8(1).

third parties.[208] We are not aware of any reason to take a different view of UTCCR, nor of any later authority on the point.

(d) SCGD

3.105 Whether SCGD applies to third party beneficiaries is an open question. The language used would not prevent a third party beneficiary being treated as "the consumer" under the Directive, but there is nothing to indicate that this was intended or that the ECJ would adopt this interpretation.

(4) "Contract"

3.106 Most of UCTA's provisions apply only where there is a contract of the relevant type between the parties (the exception is for clauses dealing with business liability for negligence or breach of duty[209]). Thus if there is some agreement between the parties but it does not amount to a legally enforceable contract (for example, in England, an agreement under which one party is to provide a gratuitous service[210] or an agreement for the supply of water to a consumer by a company acting under statutory duty[211]), only terms attempting to exclude the supplier's liability for negligence will be subject to UCTA's control. UTCCR also speak of "contracts" concluded between a seller or a supplier and a consumer, but it has been suggested that the ECJ may adopt an autonomous view of "contract" which would include such supply arrangements.[212]

11. APPLICATION OUTSIDE CONTRACT

3.107 UCTA applies not only to contract terms but also to notices which would exclude or restrict tortious [delictual] liability for negligence or breach of duty outside any

---

[208] (1996) Law Com No 242, para 13.10 (x).

[209] See Part VII below.

[210] This would be unenforceable as a contract under English law for want of consideration. In Scots law, the absence of consideration does not prevent an agreement operating as a gratuitous contract: that said, such contracts are rare. Because it refers to contracts, it is submitted that UCTA does not apply to voluntary unilateral obligations.

[211] Agreements for the supply of gas, electricity and telecommunications are all now considered contractual following the privatisation of the industries. The position for the water industry is unclear as the old statutory duty to supply (which has been removed from the regulation of the other three industries) appears to remain. See *Read v Croydon Corpn* [1938] 4 All ER 631 and the Water Industry Act 1991, which imposes on water undertakers a duty to supply domestic premises upon reasonable request (s 52). Furthermore there do not appear to be any proposals to remove or alter this duty. See DETR, Water Bill – Consultation on Draft Legislation (31 January 2001) and DEFRA, Water Bill – Consultation on Draft Legislation: Government Response (May 2002).

[212] Chitty, para 15-020; S Whittaker, "Unfair Contract Terms, Public Services and the Construction of a European Conception of Contract" (2000) 116 LQR 95. For UK law the question of reviewing the terms of supply of utilities is likely to be theoretical as the terms are regulated and will thus be exempt under reg 4(2): see para 3.40 above. However, if necessary the terms of the relevant supply licences could be used to require the use of fair terms even when there is no contract.

contract,[213] where the liability is "business liability".[214] There is no equivalent in UTCCR.[215] However, again it is possible that the ECJ might take an autonomous view of contract on this point also and hold that any agreement between the parties, such as that a person might enter another's land free of charge, amounts to a contract within the meaning of the Directive.[216] Were the entry in connection with the occupier's business and were the entrant there for private purposes, the Directive would then apply.

12. EFFECT OF INVALID EXCLUSION OR RESTRICTION

3.108   Part I of UCTA (which applies to England) does not contain a specific provision on the effect of an exclusion or restriction being held invalid.[217] Where an exclusion or restriction is invalid under Part I of UCTA (whether it is automatically invalid or fails the requirement of reasonableness), it is simply of no effect and the parties' relationship is as if the exclusion or restriction had not existed.[218] However, two issues arise (in relation to both Parts I and II). First, can a term of a contract which offends UCTA remain partly effective (to the extent that it also contains exclusions or restrictions which do not offend UCTA), or is the term invalid as a whole? Secondly, if in principle a term may remain partly effective, where part of a term would in itself be reasonable, can it still be reasonable even if another part of the same term is unreasonable or of no effect at all? Or does the inclusion of the unreasonable or void part render the clause as a whole unreasonable?

3.109   In respect of the first issue, in relation to England, Part I sets out those exclusions or restrictions which a person cannot achieve by way of a contractual term (or a notice).[219] Part I does not state the effect of an exclusion or restriction being held to be ineffective,[220] and does not state whether a term can be partly effective.[221]

---

[213]   Section 2 [s 16]. This includes both direct and vicarious liability: s 1(4) [s 25(2)].

[214]   Section 1(3) [s 16]. This includes liability arising from the occupation of land for business purposes except where the injured party was allowed access to the land for recreational or educational purposes not connected to the occupier's business. This exception does not apply under Scots law.

[215]   Unless the notice is part of an "agreement" which might fall within an autonomous definition of "contract": see para 3.106 above.

[216]   Such an agreement might already be recognised as a gratuitous contract in Scots law.

[217]   Part II of UCTA (which applies to Scotland) provides that offending terms are void, or shall be of no effect: see, for example, ss 16(1) and 17(1).

[218]   The limited range of terms to which UCTA applies (see para 3.12 above) means that in many cases the contract will still be workable without the offending term. Where for example a term restricting damages is invalid, the general rule applies, viz that the party in breach is liable for all damages which are not too remote and which could not have been avoided by taking reasonable steps in mitigation.

[219]   See, eg, s 2(1) and (2).

[220]   Part II contains specific provisions which address the status of such an exclusion or restriction: see para 3.110 below.

[221]   For example, a term which purports to limit a business's liability for any kind of loss or damage caused by its negligence to £1,000. Under section 2(1) liability for death or personal injury cannot be excluded. Can the limit in relation to other forms of loss or damage be relied upon (subject to the other provisions of UCTA)?

Treitel believes that terms may be "partly effective".[222] Chitty takes the same view in the case of a term which covers different types of injury.[223] To say that, where a term in a contract excludes liability for negligence in respect of all types of harm, the term may be partly effective, would be consistent with section 2(2). The few reported cases do not provide clear guidance.[224] On balance, we believe that a term of a contract which offends Part I of UCTA can remain partly effective, to the extent that it also contains exclusions or restrictions which do not offend UCTA.

3.110   In respect of the first issue, in relation to Scotland, Part II sets out those contractual terms (or notice provisions) which are ineffective. Part II provides that offending terms (or notice provisions) shall be void, or of no effect,[225] and does not state whether a term can be partly effective. There is no statutory definition of a "term". It is arguable that a single group of words (for example a single clause of a contract) may consist of more than one term. However, on balance, we believe that in view of the drafting of Part II it is more likely that a court would hold that a clause of a contract was a single term and was either wholly effective or wholly ineffective.[226] On balance, we therefore believe that a term of a contract which (wholly or partly) offends Part II of UCTA will be wholly ineffective.

3.111   In respect of the second issue, the "reasonableness test" in section 11 (of Part I) is applied to a "contract term" or "notice". UCTA does not define what is meant by a "term". The current approach of the English courts is to say that the offending part of a term cannot be severed.[227] The effect of this is that the term as a whole will be unreasonable and that the non-offending part cannot be relied upon.[228] In

---

[222]   Treitel, pp 235–236.

[223]   Chitty, para 14-093.

[224]   In *Stewart Gill Ltd v Horatio Myer & Co Ltd* [1992] QB 600, 605, Lord Donaldson MR stated that ss 3 and 7 of UCTA "would render ineffective any clause" which excluded or restricted liability. However, in *R W Green Ltd v Cade Bros Farms* [1978] 1 Lloyd's Rep 602 it was held that earlier legislation (which was consolidated and modified in UCTA) permitted a clause to be partly effective.

[225]   See, for example, ss 16(1)(a), (b).

[226]   This might depend upon whether the clause could be regarded as a single unit and whether the exclusion or limitation could therefore be regarded as a single limitation upon the rights of the other party.

[227]   See Chitty, para 14-091, and *Stewart Gill Ltd v Horatio Myer & Co Ltd* [1992] QB 600, 607, *per* Stuart-Smith LJ. However, a previous, unreported Court of Appeal case, *Trolex Products Ltd v Merrol Fire Protection Engineers Ltd*, 20 November 1991, seems to disagree to some extent. The court held that where a term purports to exclude liability which under UCTA cannot be excluded in any circumstances and also liability which can be excluded subject to the test of reasonableness, the term is ineffective to exclude the former liability but could be upheld as reasonable in respect of the latter exclusion. The court expressly left open the question of whether one can sever when only reasonableness is in issue (ie when no part is automatically unfair).

[228]   This is so even if in the actual event the liability he has incurred, and against which he seeks to rely on the clause, is of the kind which he could reasonably have excluded or limited. See *Thomas Witter Ltd v TBP Industries Ltd* [1996] 2 All ER 573 (exclusion of liability for misrepresentation); though cf *Skipskredittforeningen v Emperor Navigation* [1998] 1 Lloyd's Rep 66.

the previous paragraph we concluded that a term which offends Part II will be wholly ineffective. On that basis, the second issue does not arise in relation to Scotland.

3.112 Thus, under Part I, a term may be partly effective, but the non-offending part cannot be relied upon as the reasonableness of the term must be assessed as a whole. Under Part II a partly offending term will be wholly ineffective. The practical outcome is therefore the same under both Parts.

3.113 UTCCR cover a greater range of terms and, while in many cases the contract will be workable without the offending term, this may not always be the case.[229] For example, even a term which gives the definition of the main subject matter may be held unfair if it is not in plain, intelligible language.[230] It might be difficult to enforce a contract which no longer contains a definition of the subject matter. Regulation 8 therefore provides that the offending term shall not be binding on the consumer and the contract shall continue to bind the parties "if it is capable of continuing in existence without the unfair term".

13. EVASION OF THE LEGISLATION

(1) Secondary contracts

3.114 Section 10 [s 23] of UCTA ("Evasion by means of secondary contract") reads as if it were designed to ensure that the protection provided by the Act is not lost because of a second contract under which, for example,[231] the party who would otherwise be protected agrees to waive that protection.[232] This problem does not

---

[229] Only in very exceptional cases should the courts consider that the contract is not capable of continuing in existence without the term: M Tenreiro, "The Community Directive on Unfair Terms and National Legal Systems" (1995) 3 ERPL 273. Treitel, p 257, argues that the issue might arise if essential terms were contained in a document that was not binding on the consumer because she did not have a real opportunity to become acquainted with it, as this seems to imply that none of the terms in that document will be binding.

[230] See reg 6(2).

[231] Section 10 was the result of an amendment in Parliament. As Treitel points out (p 239), it does not use the same terminology as the bulk of the Act and this creates some doubts about its precise scope. Interestingly, the language of s 23, while equally elaborate, is different from that of s 10.

[232] There have been difficulties in distinguishing a waiver from a settlement of a claim between the parties. In *Tudor Grange Holdings Ltd v Citibank NA* [1992] Ch 53, the Court of Appeal held that s 10 did not apply to the compromise of a dispute, appeasing previous concerns that it might do so if construed literally: eg L S Sealy, "Unfair Contract Terms Act" [1978] CLJ 15, 19; and F M B Reynolds, "The Unfair Contract Terms Act 1977" [1978] LMCLQ 201, 206. Treitel, pp 240–241, also points out that an agreement to vary an existing contract might be treated as a new contract and therefore within s 10 [s 23]. Hence, Treitel says, the varied term will be totally ineffective even if the original term was only subject to, and satisfied, the test of reasonableness. R Hooley, "A Reasonable Compromise: *Tudor Grange Holdings v Citibank*" [1991] LMCLQ 449, 453–454, suggests that s 10 [s 23] only operates to exclude those terms which would have been totally ineffective in the original contract, and does not affect those terms which would have been subject to the test of reasonableness. See also I Brown, "Secondary Contracts and Section 10 of the Unfair Contract Terms Act" (1992) 108 LQR 223; J Cumberbatch, "The Limits of Compromise: *Tudor Grange Holdings Ltd v Citibank NA*" (1992) 55 MLR 866. In this respect Part II of UCTA is much better in specifically providing that settlements are not affected: s 15(1).

arise in the same way in UTCCR: since these apply to any type of contract, the secondary contract itself could be held to be unfair.[233]

3.115 The legislative history of UCTA in fact suggests that section 10 [s 23] was aimed at a different situation, namely where in an agreement between A and B it is agreed that B will not enforce his rights under a second contract between himself and C.[234] The proposer of the amendment which became section 10 [s 23] gave the example of a consumer who had had central heating installed by one company and then approached another company in the same group to service it. The servicing company should not be permitted to require the consumer to give up any rights he might have against the installer if an exclusion of those rights in the installation contract would not have been valid. Again this problem does not arise in UTCCR as the terms of the secondary contract could be held to be unfair.[235]

(2) Evasion by choice of law

3.116 Each instrument contains provisions designed to ensure that it will apply notwithstanding any attempt to avoid it by a choice of law clause. UCTA will apply, despite a term applying the law of a country outside the UK, when the contract would otherwise be subject to the law of the UK.[236] UTCCR have a parallel provision but referring, not to a term applying the law of a country outside the UK, but to a clause applying the law of a non-Member State in place of that of a Member State.[237] The actual formulation is:

> These Regulations shall apply notwithstanding any contract term which applies or purports to apply the law of a non-Member State, if the contract has a close connection with the territory of the Member States.

---

[233] Unless the waiver were the main subject matter of the secondary contract. This issue is considered in more detail in para 4.189 below.

[234] See Treitel, p 239, referring to *Hansard* (HL) 4 July 1977, vol 385, cols 57–59, 511–514. It is thought that the language of s 23 lends itself better than the language of s 10 to that construction. Section 10 does not apply when the right which the second contract purports to remove is in tort not in contract: *Neptune Orient Lines Ltd v JVC (UK) Ltd (The "Chevalier Roze")* [1983] 2 Lloyd's Rep 438.

[235] In the *Tudor Grange* case (see n 232 above), Browne-Wilkinson VC at [1992] Ch 53, 66–67, suggests that s 10 does not apply where the parties to both the contracts are the same. This interpretation is doubted by E Macdonald, "Mapping The Unfair Contract Terms Act 1977 and the Directive on Unfair Terms in Consumer Contracts" (1994) JBL 441, 453. Chitty describes the scope of the section as "enigmatic": para 14-078. The words of the section seem apt to cover a second contract between the same parties.

[236] UCTA, s 27(2). This applies to all cases of contracts with a consumer resident in the UK if the steps necessary for making the contract were taken there; in other cases, if the term was imposed mainly for the purpose of evading UCTA. The section seems to apply to both express and implicit choices of foreign law: *Benjamin's Sale of Goods* (5th ed 1997) para 25-089. If the law chosen is more favourable to the consumer, he may take advantage of that: Dicey and Morris, para 33-029.

[237] UTCCR, reg 9.

It should be noted that while the parties cannot avoid UTCCR by choosing the law of a non-Member State, they are free to choose the law of another Member State. Thus if a contract which has its closest connection with England is agreed to be subject to the law of some other Member State, UTCCR will not apply. Instead the consumer will receive the protection provided by the Directive as implemented in that other Member State.[238]

3.117　This seems to mean that if the Directive were to be interpreted less (or more) liberally in the law of the Member State chosen than in England, the consumer would receive less (or more) protection.[239] It would also allow the choice of the law of another Member State even though the contract has a closer connection with England and the latter law gives greater protection than is required by the Directive.

3.118　If the term under challenge is affected by both UCTA and UTCCR, it is not clear which anti-avoidance provision should take precedence.[240]

14. PREVENTION

3.119　UCTA renders terms invalid but it does not prevent businesses continuing to use terms which automatically have no effect. The use of terms falling within section 6 [s 20] has been made an offence by orders made under the Fair Trading Act 1973, Part II,[241] but other terms which are of no legal effect,[242] or which if challenged would probably be found not to satisfy the requirement of reasonableness, continued to be used for years after UCTA came into force. This may have been simply because the businesses did not trouble to change them or it may have been a deliberate tactic to deter claims.

3.120　Article 7 of the Directive provides:

> 1. Member States shall ensure that, in the interests of consumers and of competitors, adequate and effective means exist to prevent the continued use of unfair terms in contracts concluded with consumers by sellers or suppliers.
>
> 2. The means referred to in paragraph 1 shall include provisions whereby persons or organizations, having a legitimate interest under national law in protecting consumers, may take action according to the national law concerned before the courts or before competent administrative bodies for a decision as to whether contractual terms

---

[238] Conversely, in an English court UTCCR would be applied not only if the law of a non-Member State had been chosen when the contract had a close connection with England but also if it had no close connection with England but did have one with another Member State: see Dicey and Morris, para 33-042, which also discusses the meaning of "close connection".

[239] Dicey and Morris, para 33-040.

[240] *Ibid.*

[241] Consumer Transactions (Restrictions on Statements) Order 1976, SI 1976 No 1813, as amended by Consumer Transactions (Restrictions on Statements) (Amendment) Order 1978, SI 1978 No 127.

[242] For example, exclusions of liability for death or personal injury.

drawn up for general use are unfair, so that they can apply appropriate and effective means to prevent the continued use of such terms.

3. With due regard for national laws, the legal remedies referred to in paragraph 2 may be directed separately or jointly against a number of sellers or suppliers from the same economic sector or their associations which use or recommend the use of the same general contractual terms or similar terms.

3.121 The 1994 Regulations empowered the DGFT to bring proceedings for an injunction [interdict] against persons appearing to him to be using or recommending the use of unfair terms in contracts concluded with consumers.[243] UTCCR have extended this power to a number of "qualifying bodies", including a variety of industry regulators, all weights and measures departments in Great Britain and the Consumers' Association.[244] Amending Regulations in 2001 added the Financial Services Authority to the list.[245]

3.122 The precise scope of the preventive powers is subject to some debate. For example, it has been questioned whether action can be taken against a firm that purports to "use" an unfair term but does so in a way which means that the term is not effectively incorporated into the contract, or where the term is ineffective for other reasons (for example it is a penalty and therefore void). Consumers will not necessarily know that the term is ineffective and may still be deterred from claiming, or may consider themselves bound by the term.[246] In relation to terms which are ineffective for other reasons, we consider that the term is subject to control: our view is that UTCCR must be interpreted so that such a term is both one of the "terms in contracts concluded between a seller or a supplier and a consumer", and is unfair despite its invalidity, because the indicative list contains examples of terms which, independently of the Directive, would be of no effect under several legal systems.[247] On terms not effectively incorporated, we believe that a court would take a purposive approach to the interpretation of regulation 12 and would hold that a firm is "using ... an unfair term drawn up for general use in contracts concluded with consumers" even if the term is not incorporated.[248]

3.123 Another question is whether the preventive powers can be used where the terms used omit important information. It has been suggested to us that this is a problem. The OFT and other qualifying bodies under UTCCR do not have the

---

[243] 1994 Regulations, reg 8.

[244] Reg 12 and Sched 1. UTCCR contain a number of ancillary powers and obligations: regs 10–13.

[245] Unfair Terms in Consumer Contracts (Amendment) Regulations 2001, SI 2001 No 1186.

[246] E Macdonald, *Exemption Clauses and Unfair Terms* (1999) pp 174 and 193, and "The Emperor's Old Clauses: Unincorporated Clauses, Misleading Terms and the Unfair Terms in Consumer Contracts Regulations" (1999) 58 CLJ 413.

[247] For an example, see the discussion of Sched 2, paras 1(a) (exclusion of liability for death or personal injury) and (1)(c) ("potestative conditions"), para 4.133 below.

[248] Cf E Macdonald, "The Emperor's Old Clauses: Unincorporated Clauses, Misleading Terms and the Unfair Terms in Consumer Contracts Regulations" (1999) 58 CLJ 413, 426–427.

power to specify or suggest the information that should be included, but are limited to drawing attention to the unclear nature of the term and requesting that it be redrafted. However, we are unsure of the extent of this problem. We discuss this further in Part IV.[249]

15. Conclusions

3.124 The problems caused for business in relation to "consumer contracts" by differences between UCTA and UTCCR appear to be caused by a number of factors:

(1) The existence of two instruments is misleading. A term may not be of the type covered by UCTA yet fall foul of UTCCR.

(2) Conversely, a term may have been negotiated with the consumer and so be exempt from UTCCR, but be caught by UCTA.

(3) Terms approved by industry regulators may be exempt from UCTA but may not be exempt from UTCCR.

(4) Several important types of contract are exempt from UCTA but are subject to UTCCR.

(5) While UCTA is fairly precise in what types of exclusion or limitation of liability clause will be invalid in a consumer contract, the scope of application of section 3(2)(b) [s 17(1)(b)] is less than clear, and there are no indicative lists to give further guidance. Conversely, it is difficult to be sure which terms fall outside UTCCR because they are "core terms".

(6) UTCCR seem to have a plain language requirement, but it is hard to be sure to what extent either instrument really requires this or that the term be conspicuous.

(7) The burden of proof of "fairness" seems to be different from that of "reasonableness".

(8) Both UTCCR and UCTA apply to consumer contracts, but the definition of "consumer" for each purpose differs.

(9) Each regime applies only to (broadly speaking) "business liability", but the definitions of business may differ.

(10) UCTA sometimes applies to claims by third party beneficiaries; UTCCR do not.

(11) The very notion of what amounts to a contract may differ under UCTA and UTCCR.

(12) While UTCCR apply to the whole of the UK, UCTA has separate (though very similar) provisions for England and for Scotland.

(13) UTCCR apply only to consumer contracts, while UCTA applies very differently to consumer contracts and non-consumer contracts.

---

[249] See paras 4.195 – 4.198 below.

3.125 It is not clear that all of the differences can be removed without reducing significantly the protection given to consumers. For example, to remove the complete ban on terms excluding a seller's liability for breach of the implied terms under the SGA 1979, sections 12–15, and to rely simply on the "fairness" test under UTCCR, would reduce the protection currently afforded to consumer buyers.[250] Nonetheless, it should be possible to devise a simpler regime with fewer differences and overlaps. How this might be done is considered in Part IV.

---

[250] By UCTA, ss 6(1) and (2).

PART IV
REPLACING UCTA AND UTCCR BY A UNIFIED REGIME

1. INTRODUCTION

4.1 In Part II we identified the problem of overlap and inconsistency between UCTA and UTCCR.[1] The issues were considered in more detail in Part III. Some terms in consumer contracts are subject to both regimes; in relation to other terms, only one of the regimes applies but difficulty is caused by the fact that the concepts, terminology and definitions used in the two regimes, though similar, are subtly different. UCTA can apply to terms in contracts between businesses but UTCCR apply only to consumer contracts.

4.2 Our terms of reference ask us to consider the desirability and feasibility of replacing both instruments by a single regime. We consider that the overlaps and inconsistencies we have identified make it desirable to replace UCTA and UTCCR with a single regime, provided that this can be done in a way which reduces the complexity and makes the legislation easier to understand and apply, while still meeting the requirements of the Directive and certain other policy objectives, principally to maintain the existing level of consumer protection. In this Part of the consultation paper, after considering various general issues, we look in some detail at how the regimes might be combined. At the end we ask consultees whether, overall, the change is desirable.

4.3 This Part concentrates on the regime for unfair terms in consumer contracts. The extension of the kind of controls imposed by UTCCR to business-to-business contracts is considered in Part V.[2] The controls imposed by UCTA on exclusion or restriction of liability by sellers who are not acting in the course of a business (that is, in "private" sales and sales by consumers to businesses) are considered in Part VI.

2. MODELS FOR THE REPLACEMENT REGIME

4.4 A new regime could take one of at least three broad forms:

(1) UCTA could be expanded to apply to all terms (except possibly "core terms") and UTCCR revoked. This could be done, for example, by

---

[1] See para 2.21 above.

[2] We make the provisional proposal that, at least as far as controls over clauses in individual contracts (as opposed to preventive controls) are concerned, it is both desirable and feasible to extend the controls in this way. This would mean that some, or even most, of the current sections of UCTA dealing with exclusion and limitation of liability in business-to-business contracts could be repealed, and the "consumer" regime, with specific modifications, applied to both types of contract. If this extension were not made, the existing controls over exclusion and limitation of liability clauses in business contracts would presumably be retained, either in their existing form or in a form which is closer to that proposed for consumer contracts (for example, in respect of the reasonableness test to be applied and of ancillary matters such as its application to international contracts).

changing the application of section 3(2)(b) [s 17(1)(b)]. At present this section applies to terms used by a business in a consumer contract that would either entitle the business to render a performance substantially different from what was reasonably expected of it, or to render no performance at all. Such terms are valid only if they satisfy the requirement of reasonableness. The section could be amended to apply also to any term (except a "core term", that is the definition of the main subject matter or the price) in a consumer contract which had not been individually negotiated.

(2) UCTA could be repealed, leaving UTCCR. This by itself would result in the protection currently offered to both consumers and non-consumers being significantly reduced unless UTCCR were also amended to make certain types of clause of no effect at all, and to extend the requirement that the terms be fair to certain other types of clause in non-consumer contracts, as under UCTA.[3]

(3) The new regime could follow a new model.

(1) Constraints

4.5 The choice of model is subject to a number of constraints, which are explored in the paragraphs that follow. In outline they are: (a) the requirements of the Directive; (b) the possible desirability of following the wording of the Directive; (c) the need for the new regime to have more uniform concepts, terminology and definitions; and (d) the possible desirability of drafting the whole instrument in a "clear and accessible" way.[4]

(a) Requirements of the Directive

4.6 The UK is obliged to implement the Directive, so that the terms of the new instrument must offer at least as much protection to consumers as the Directive. Thus if it were to be based on UCTA, the expanded Act would have to include quite a number of changes of detail on points at which UCTA seems to offer less protection than UTCCR (this is explored in the next sections of this Part). On the other hand, the Directive allows Member States to provide a greater degree of consumer protection than the Directive requires;[5] so that, from this point of view, provisions of UCTA which are more generous than the Directive could remain.

---

[3] Sections 2(1), 5, 6(1) and (2), 7(2) [ss 16(1)(a), 19, 20(1) and (2), 21(1)(a) and (3)(a)] (clauses of no effect); ss 2(2), 3, 6(3) and 7(3) [ss 16(1)(b), 17, 20(2), 21(1)(a) and (b), 21(3)(a) and (b)] (clauses in non-consumer contracts which are valid if fair and reasonable).

[4] For the sense in which we use this phrase see paras 2.35 – 2.39 above.

[5] Art 8 provides that

> Member States may adopt or retain the most stringent provisions compatible with the Treaty in the area covered by this Directive, to ensure a maximum degree of protection for the consumer.

We do not think that any of the existing or proposed provisions on unfair terms will be incompatible with the Treaty (eg infringe its competition provisions).

(b) The language of the Directive

4.7   UTCCR follow the wording of the Directive very closely. However, there is no obligation on Member States to follow the wording of Directives. Directives are defined by Article 249[6] of the Treaty,[7] which states that

> A directive shall be binding, as to the result to be achieved, upon each Member State to which it is addressed, but shall leave to the national authorities the choice of form and methods.

4.8   It seems that the terminology and concepts of any national legislation implementing a Directive are a matter of "form and methods" and therefore for the discretion of the Member States, provided that the words used achieve the result intended by the Directive.[8]

4.9   Even though the UK is not required to employ the language of the Directive when implementing it, there may be an advantage in doing so. It seems likely that there will be cases in the ECJ on whether Member States have properly implemented the Directive, and whether their courts have applied it correctly.[9] Such cases might give authoritative interpretations of the words of the Directive, for example the meaning of "contract"[10] or of "contrary to the requirement of good faith".[11] If the UK legislation is in similar terms to the Directive, it will be easier to apply the jurisprudence of the ECJ to the interpretation of the UK legislation than if that legislation uses different terminology.

4.10   The price to be paid, however, is the relative unfamiliarity of the terminology of the Directive and the fact that some of the concepts used do not form part of English or Scots legal traditions. The point of European legislation in the form of Directives rather than Regulations is to allow Member States to implement the

---

[6] Formerly Art 189.

[7] Treaty Establishing the European Community (Rome, 1957), as amended by Treaty on European Union (Maastricht, 1992) and Treaty of Amsterdam (1997) (OJ No C 340, 10.11.97, p 173).

[8] This view has been confirmed by the ECJ in *Commission v Germany* (C-131/88) [1991] ECR I-825, para 6. The Court stated:

> ... the transposition of a directive into domestic law does not necessarily require that its provisions be incorporated formally and verbatim in express, specific legislation; a general legal context may, depending on the content of the directive, be adequate for the purpose provided that it does indeed guarantee the full application of the directive in a sufficiently clear and precise manner so that, where the directive is intended to create rights for individuals, the persons concerned can ascertain the full extent of their rights and, where appropriate, rely on them before the national courts.

See also *Commission v Italy* (C-363/85) [1987] ECR 1733; *Commission v Germany* (C-29/84) [1985] ECR 1661.

[9] The first reported case is *Océano Grupo Editorial SA v Roció Murciano Quintero* (C-240/98) [2000] ECR I-4941, on whether the court may raise the question of fairness on its own motion when the consumer fails to defend an action brought by the business.

[10] Cf para 3.106 above.

[11] Cf paras 3.57 – 3.62 above.

legislation in accordance with their own legal traditions. We would go so far as to say that parts of the Directive, in particular the indicative list of terms which may be unfair, are very difficult for even a lawyer from the UK to interpret.[12] It cannot be said that all the examples are "clear and accessible". Keeping to the precise wording of the Directive would mean abandoning the third limb of this project.[13]

(c) Simplicity

4.11 We reported in Part I that respondents to the DTI White Paper complained that having two regimes creates unnecessary complexity.[14] While the elimination of overlaps would help, the gain would be small unless there can also be uniformity of concepts, terminology and definitions, so far as this is compatible with the Directive and policy. Were the new legislation to combine the provisions of UCTA and UTCCR into a single piece of legislation but to preserve all the minor differences between the two existing regimes,[15] there would be no real reduction in complexity.

(d) "Clear and accessible legislation"

4.12 It seems desirable that legislation, particularly legislation which applies to consumers and small businesses, should be as accessible as possible to the lay reader. The third paragraph of our terms of reference asks us to consider

> Making any replacement legislation clearer and more accessible to the reader, so far as is possible without making the law significantly less certain, by using language which is non-technical with simple sentences, by setting out the law in a simple structure following a clear logic and by using presentation which is easy to follow.[16]

4.13 This may mean that the new instrument cannot be modelled closely on either UCTA (which has frequently been said even by lawyers to be very difficult to understand[17]) or UTCCR (which are based closely on the Directive, in itself

---

[12] See further paras 4.118 – 4.122 below.

[13] See para 4.120 below.

[14] Para 2.22 above.

[15] For example, if the UTCCR definition of a consumer contract were used to determine whether the clauses of the contract are caught by a general fairness test, but the UCTA test were used to determine whether the contract is one in which certain terms are automatically of no effect. A practical example of the sort of complexity we have in mind will occur if reg 6 of the draft SSGCR is brought into effect. For the purposes of SGA 1979 ss 13–15 and SOGITA ss 9–11, section 6 of UCTA would be amended to provide a definition of a consumer that is different to the one under UCTA s 12. The section 12 definition would continue to apply to UCTA ss 3 and 4. The principal difference between the two definitions is that for the purposes of s 6 only a natural person may be a consumer.

[16] The broad aim is similar to that of the Tax Law Rewrite project: see Inland Revenue report, The Path to Tax Simplification (December 1995) and The Path to Tax Simplification: A Background Paper.

[17] Professor F M B Reynolds said in 1978:

> The general effect is one of extreme complexity, and it is most unfortunate that such a major consumer-oriented reform ... should be such a dramatic example of

simpler than UCTA but, as we think Part III of this consultation paper shows, far from easy to interpret).

(e) Possible extension to protect businesses

4.14 The second item in our terms of reference, the possible extension of the scope of UTCCR to protect businesses, in particular small businesses, is dealt with in Part V of this consultation paper. Whether or not this is done does not seem to affect the decision on the model to be adopted for the new legislation, as we see nothing to prevent any of the three models being extended in this way. Nor do we see any particular difficulty in incorporating the existing controls over terms in business-to-business contracts into the proposed model.

(f) Scotland

4.15 UCTA has separate provisions for England (Part I) and Scotland (Part II). UTCCR apply to the whole of the UK, with only minor variations for Scotland.[18] It would obviously influence the choice of model were it necessary to maintain separate parts for Scotland under an UCTA model but unnecessary to do so under other models.

4.16 We have considered the differences between Parts I and II of UCTA. Although the language of the two Parts is different, there are few differences in the substantive law between the two regimes. Some of these we provisionally propose should be abolished. Those which we provisionally propose should remain can easily be preserved within a single instrument which could be applied in general throughout the UK. Given that there should be uniformity of such laws throughout the UK and that, for Scotland, consumer law is a reserved matter,[19] we do not see the need for separate parts in any new instrument.

4.17 **It is our provisional proposal that there be a single piece of legislation for the whole of the UK.**

(2) Provisional conclusions on the model to be used

4.18 We think that the most important consideration, after ensuring that the new legislation complies with the Directive, is that the legislation should be reasonably

---

that strange, internally self-referent complexity so often to be found in UK statutes. It will for a considerable period be a bold layman (and perhaps even lawyer) who advises on it with confidence.

"The Unfair Contract Terms Act 1977" [1978] LMCLQ 201, 201–202. See also L S Sealy, "Unfair Contract Terms Act" [1978] CLJ 15, 17, who says: "What a shocking example of 'legislation by reference' – and this in a consumers' measure!"

[18] Reg 3(1) has different definitions of "court", and reg 3(2) substitutes for references to "injunctions" references to "interdicts".

[19] As far as Scotland is concerned, consumer protection is a matter reserved for the Westminster Parliament (Scotland Act 1998, s 30 and Sched 5 (C7)), but for Northern Ireland consumer matters (except consumer safety in relation to goods: see Northern Ireland Act 1998, Sched 3, para 37) fall within the competence of the Northern Ireland Assembly because they are not listed in Sched 3 to the Northern Ireland Act 1998.

clear and simple for businesses and consumers, or at least their advisers, to understand and apply. This means that we should not take the approach of adapting with as few changes as possible either of the existing models, but should use a new model. Inevitably, however, the new model will combine some elements of the existing legislation.

4.19 **We provisionally propose that, so far as possible, the new unified regime should be clearer and more accessible to the reader than the present instruments.**

4.20 As we explained in Part II,[20] in order to give consultees a better idea of what is being proposed, Parliamentary Counsel has produced a draft of the parts of the new instrument which would be required were our provisional proposals in this Part to be accepted.[21] The draft will be found in Appendix B.

3. GENERAL POLICIES

4.21 Before considering in detail the way in which the two regimes may be combined, various issues of general policy need to be canvassed.

(1) No reduction of consumer protection

4.22 We saw in Part III that in some respects UCTA offers consumers significantly greater individual protection than do UTCCR.

4.23 First, certain purported exclusions and restrictions of liability are simply of no effect under UCTA.[22]

4.24 Secondly, terms in consumer contracts which are subject to the requirement of reasonableness under UCTA sections 2(2), 3 and 4 [ss 16(1)(b), 17 and 18] include terms which may have been negotiated, whereas UTCCR apply only to non-negotiated terms.[23]

4.25 Thirdly, the burden of showing that a term is reasonable under UCTA rests on the business, whereas the burden of showing that the term is unfair under UTCCR appears to rest on the consumer.[24]

4.26 Fourthly, we noted in Part III some ways in which the definitions used by UCTA offer slightly more protection to consumers than do UTCCR. Thus section 3

---

[20] Para 2.37 above.

[21] There is not at this stage a full "indicative list" of potentially invalid clauses, and the draft does not deal with the powers of the OFT and others to prevent businesses using unfair terms (see UTCCR regs 10–15 and Sched 1), nor with the extension of the scope of the Regulations to protect businesses (see the second paragraph of the terms of reference at para 1.1 above, and Part V below).

[22] See ss 2(1), 5, 6(1) and (2), 7(2) [ss 16(1)(a), 19, 20(1) and (2), 21(1)(a) and (3)(a)]; para 3.9 above.

[23] Para 3.16 above.

[24] Para 3.79 above.

[s 17] applies to sales by consumers to businesses as well as the more normal reverse case.[25] Terms are not exempt because they reflect the mandatory law of another Member State.[26]

4.27　There is one element of the additional protection that we think may safely be abolished. This is the separate rule that exclusions or restrictions of liability, by means of a term or notice in a "guarantee", of a manufacturer's or distributor's liability in tort [delict] to a person injured by goods proving defective while in consumer use are of no effect.[27] Our reasons are explained more fully below, but are essentially that the changes that were made to the legislation proposed by the Law Commissions before its enactment as UCTA result in this provision giving almost no additional protection. It therefore seems to be unnecessary.[28]

4.28　It is our provisional view that the other elements of additional protection afforded by UCTA should be maintained. Each of them is valuable and desirable. Thus we think that the terms which UCTA renders automatically of no effect should continue to be treated in the same way. Although a court would probably find them "unfair" under UTCCR, it will strengthen the consumer's hand in any negotiations with the supplier if there is absolutely no doubt that they are invalid.[29] In any event, some terms which would exclude or limit a consumer buyer's rights under the SGA 1979, sections 13–15, will have to continue to be of no effect in order to comply with SCGD.[30] In relation to terms that have been negotiated, we argue below that it may be desirable to extend the application of the fairness test to terms in consumer contracts in general, whether or not they were negotiated (as under UCTA), rather than limiting the controls to terms that were not individually negotiated (as under UTCCR).[31] On the other issues we think that the UCTA approach is also the right one; they too are discussed in more detail below.[32] Moreover, we are not aware that the sections of UCTA in question have caused difficulty for businesses, and we have not heard of any call for any of the additional protection given by UCTA to be removed.

4.29　**We provisionally propose that, with the exception of UCTA section 5 [s 19], the additional protection given by UCTA to consumers, beyond that given by UTCCR, should be maintained. If consultees disagree, which other additional protection would they do away with?**

---

[25]　Para 3.41 above.

[26]　Para 3.35 above.

[27]　Section 5 [s 19].

[28]　See para 4.205 below.

[29]　Although mandatory terms may seem to prevent business having the flexibility to offer reduced protection at reduced cost, there are advantages to business in the certainty of knowing that such clauses simply cannot be relied on by either the business or its competitors.

[30]　See para 1.4 above and draft SSGCR, reg 6.

[31]　See paras 4.42 – 4.54 below.

[32]　See paras 4.34 – 4.35, 4.77 – 4.78, 4.146 – 4.150 and 4.152 – 4.167 below.

(2) Incorporation of other statutory and common law rules

4.30 There are a number of other terms sometimes found in consumer contracts which are also of no effect in English or Scots law, either by statute or under common law rules. Statutory examples[33] are terms excluding liability for defective products,[34] for defective premises,[35] or in relation to various forms of carriage, and terms restricting rights of cancellation under consumer legislation.[36] Common law rules would include the rules against penalty clauses and terms excluding liability for fraud.

4.31 We have considered whether there is a case for incorporating these into the new legislation. The advantage of consolidating the rules on "invalid terms" into a single instrument would be that it would make the rules more accessible. The disadvantages are, for statute, that to remove the rules from their existing place to the new instrument would dislocate the existing statutes and, for the common law rules, statement in statutory form might be difficult to achieve and might hinder common law development. We think that to incorporate other statutory and common law rules applying to potentially "unfair" terms in consumer contracts into the proposed legislation would not be appropriate as part of this exercise (though it might well be appropriate to incorporate other statutory provisions or common law rules in the future were there to be a codification of consumer rights). The only exception we would make is to incorporate into the new regime any changes necessitated by SCGD, as these cover a topic which is already central to the existing regimes.

4.32 **Our provisional proposal is that to incorporate other statutory and common law rules applying to potentially "unfair" terms in consumer contracts into the proposed legislation would not be appropriate as part of this exercise, with the exception of any changes necessitated by SCGD.**

4. COMBINING THE REGIMES

4.33 In the sections which follow we consider in detail how the two regimes might best be combined.

(1) Terms of no effect

4.34 We have made the provisional proposal that, with one exception,[37] the protection afforded to consumers by UCTA should not be reduced. It follows that the new instrument should contain a list of terms which will simply be of no effect.

---

[33] A full list can be found in Chitty, paras 14-106 ff.

[34] Consumer Protection Act 1987, s 7.

[35] Defective Premises Act 1972, s 6(3) (England only).

[36] Eg Consumer Credit Act 1974, ss 67 and 173(1); Consumer Protection (Distance Selling) Regulations 2000, SI 2000 No 2334, reg 25.

[37] See para 4.27 above.

4.35　We provisionally propose that the terms set out below, at least in substance, should continue to be of no effect under the new regime:[38]

（1）　exclusions or restrictions of business liability for death or personal injury caused by negligence [breach of duty] (in any type of contract);[39]

（2）　exclusions or restrictions of liability for breach of the implied terms as to title in contracts for sale, hire-purchase or other transfer of property in goods;[40]

（3）　exclusions or restrictions of liability for breach of the implied terms as to description, quality etc in contracts for the supply of goods to a consumer;[41] and

（4）　terms which, in relation to any of the kinds of liability in (1)–(3) above,

（a）　make the liability or its enforcement subject to restrictive or onerous conditions;

（b）　exclude or restrict any right or remedy in respect of the liability, or subject a person to any prejudice in consequence of his pursuing any such right or remedy; or

（c）　exclude or restrict rules of evidence or procedure.[42]

4.36　In relation to consumers there are a number of exemptions contained in UCTA that would exclude certain types of contract from the provisions under which these terms are of no effect.[43] The only such exemption that might be relevant to our proposals here relates to land.[44] We are not clear whether such a term would ever relate "to the creation or transfer of an interest in land, or to the termination

---

[38] We deal later with various ancillary matters, such as the definition of "dealing as consumer", that relate to terms which are no effect: see paras 4.151 – 4.194 below.

[39] Cf UCTA, s 2(1) [s 16(1)(a)]; para 3.9 above. On liability in tort see Part VII below.

[40] Cf UCTA, ss 6(1) and 7(3A) [s 20(1)]; para 3.9 above.

[41] Cf UCTA, ss 6(2) and 7(2) [ss 20(2), 21(1)(a)(i) and (3)(a)]; para 3.9 above. The definitions of "consumer" and "business" are discussed in paras 3.81 – 3.96 above; the question whether the terms listed should be of no effect when the contract is governed by English or Scots law only because the parties have so chosen, in para 3.48 above.

[42] Cf UCTA, s 13: to the extent that Part I prevents the exclusion or restriction of any liability, it also applies to terms of the kind listed, which have the practical effect of excluding or restricting liability without actually doing so. The corresponding provision for Scotland, s 25(3), achieves the same result through an interpretation provision: any reference in Part II to excluding or restricting any liability *includes* terms of this kind. Clause 16 of the draft Bill adopts the latter approach, and cl 17 gives some examples.

[43] UCTA, Sched 1.

[44] UCTA, Sched 1, para 1(b).

of such an interest",[45] but even if it does we think that it should be caught by the new regime.

4.37 **We provisionally propose that, in relation to consumers, the terms listed in paragraph 4.35 should be of no effect even if they relate to the creation, transfer or termination of an interest in land, and would therefore be exempt from control under UCTA.**

4.38 We are not aware of any need for additions to this list. Adding to the list is not strictly within our terms of reference, but if there were a strong case for extending the list it would be possible for us to raise the matter with DTI.

4.39 **If consultees believe that there is a case for any other kind of term found in a consumer contract to be made automatically of no effect, they are invited to submit a reasoned case for its inclusion in the list.**

(2) Terms which must be "fair" or "fair and reasonable"

4.40 **Other terms in consumer contracts will be required to satisfy a test which for the moment we will refer to as a "fairness" test.**

4.41 There remains a question whether the fairness test should apply to *all* other terms or whether at least some terms that have been individually negotiated should continue to be exempted. In Part III we saw that, at present, UTCCR apply to a wide range of terms but only if the term was not individually negotiated, whereas the controls of UCTA section 3 [s 17] apply to consumer contracts whether or not the terms were part of the business's standard terms, but affect only a more limited range of terms.[46] In order to maintain the existing level of consumer protection under UCTA, as we have proposed, on the one hand, and to comply with the Directive on the other, it is necessary to control terms which have been individually negotiated *only* if they are exclusion or limitation of liability clauses. However, in the following section we provisionally propose that the new legislation should apply to *all* terms in consumer contracts (with certain exceptions, such as "core" terms) whether the terms were negotiated or not.[47] This would make it unnecessary to specify exclusion and limitation of liability clauses, and other terms such as indemnity clauses, as UCTA does at present; these will fall under the

---

[45] UCTA, Sched 1, para 1(b). Although we are not aware of any cases specifically on this point, the OFT did mention terms excluding liability for personal injury or negligence in their Guidance on unfair terms in tenancy agreements. However, even if such a term were to be incorporated into a tenancy agreement, we are unsure whether it would relate to "the creation or transfer of an interest in land" in line with the test set out in *Electricity Supply Nominees Ltd v IAF Group Ltd* [1993] 1 WLR 1059, and confirmed in *Unchained Growth III plc v Granby Village (Manchester) Management Co Ltd* [2000] 1 WLR 739 (CA).

[46] Para 3.12 above.

[47] See paras 4.42 – 4.54 below.

general rule.[48] Instead the question will be, what terms should be excluded from the general control. This is taken up after the question of "negotiated terms".[49]

(3) Individually negotiated terms

4.42 UTCCR apply only to terms which were not individually negotiated, though a wider range of terms are covered than by UCTA. Terms that come within UCTA section 3 [s 17] (in effect, those that affect the business's liability or the way it has to perform[50]), and are in a consumer contract, are subject to review whether they were negotiated or not. We have already indicated our provisional view that any greater protection given by UCTA should not be reduced. In the combined instrument, should review of terms which would have been outside the scope of UCTA but within UTCCR (in effect, terms that affect what are the consumer's obligations rather than those of the business[51]) continue to be limited to non-negotiated terms? We believe that, as far as consumer contracts are concerned, the controls should extend even to terms that have been "negotiated", for three reasons.

4.43 First, to limit the extension to terms that have not been individually negotiated while preserving the protection given by UCTA, so that some negotiated terms remain subject to control while others are not, would perpetuate the existing difficulties in determining the scope of the two provisions.[52]

4.44 Secondly, the width of the controls over negotiated terms in consumer contracts under UCTA section 3 [s 17] is such that the extension to all individually negotiated terms (other than "core terms"[53]) would have only a marginal impact on business.

4.45 Thirdly, we believe that there are sound reasons of policy for including negotiated as well as non-negotiated terms.

4.46 We set out in Part II a brief explanation of why terms in standard form contracts are particularly likely to raise issues of unfairness. We accept that they are more likely to be unfair to the consumer than those which have been negotiated. However, the legislative controls imposed by UCTA were not confined to non-negotiated terms, and (we believe) for good reasons. The explanation for this lies in the nature of the problems over unfair terms.

---

[48] A section dealing with business liability for other loss or damage caused by negligence may be needed to cover liability to non-consumers: see paras 5.45 and 8.18 below. It will also be necessary to have provisions dealing with the exclusion of this kind of liability in tort [delict] by means of non-contractual notices: see Part VII below.

[49] See paras 4.55 – 4.76 below.

[50] See para 3.14 above.

[51] *Ibid.*

[52] See paras 3.12 – 3.15 above.

[53] See paras 3.19 – 3.34 above.

4.47 In Part II we suggested that a primary cause of unfavourable terms in contracts is that many customers (in the situation we are now discussing, consumers) are unaware of their existence or their implications. They therefore do not "shop around" for better "small print" terms; instead they concentrate on the matters they can readily understand such as the item offered and the price. The result is that there is no competition over the other terms, and businesses will tend to offer poor terms in order to be able to compete on price. The result may be inefficient if consumers would have been prepared to pay for more favourable terms, and unfair if the consumers were not aware of what they were agreeing and are taken by surprise.

4.48 If the explanation is correct, it certainly suggests that there is less likely to be a problem with terms that were negotiated. First, the consumer will certainly know of their existence, so she is less likely to be taken by surprise. Secondly, if the business is willing to negotiate the terms of the contract and each side understands the issues, there is no reason to suppose that the business will insist on less favourable terms than the consumer wants and is prepared to pay for. However, there are arguments for going further and controlling even terms that have been individually negotiated.

4.49 A first possible argument is that there are some obligations which businesses simply should not be able to evade or restrict, by whatever means.[54] The argument was made in relation to clauses purporting to exclude or restrict the seller's obligations under SGA 1893, sections 12–15. In their First Report the Law Commissions accepted the reasoning of the Molony Committee that such clauses "deny [the consumer] what the law means him to have";[55] "as between the retailer and private consumer the burden of liability under the implied conditions and warranties should fall upon the retailer."[56] However, it is clear that present public policy does not absolutely preclude the exclusion or limitation of some obligations to consumers, provided the particular term is fair and reasonable. Thus in cases not involving death or personal injury, exclusions or limitations of liability for negligence [breach of duty] are permitted if the clause is reasonable. In their Second Report the Law Commissions recommended this on the pragmatic basis that in many cases the victim is likely to be covered by insurance (particularly in relation to property damage) and does not need to pay extra to the business for "double cover". Given present public policy, and the absence of a consensus as to which obligations should be "unalterable", we do not believe that this argument provides support for the imposition of controls upon individually negotiated terms.

---

[54] This argument has often been made in relation to the duty to take reasonable care. In France, for example, it is considered that any attempt to exclude delictual liability is contrary to public policy and ineffective: B Nicholas, *French Law of Contract* (2nd ed 1992) p 232. In English and Scots law this has only been accepted clearly in relation to intentional (or reckless) wrongdoing, for example, fraud: *S Pearson & Son Ltd v Dublin Corpn* [1907] AC 351; see Chitty, para 6-129.

[55] Molony report, para 435, cited in First Report, para 68.

[56] First Report, para 73.

4.50   A second argument is more persuasive. It is that for any negotiations to be meaningful, the customer must genuinely understand the proposed term and must be able to assess its possible impact. Where the customer is a consumer, there are likely to be few cases in which she will have the necessary knowledge (except in relation to the "core" items such as the subject matter of the contract and the price[57]). Therefore it may be better to subject all terms (other than core terms, which the consumer can be expected to understand)[58] to control even when they have been "negotiated".

4.51   The strength of the argument varies with the type of clause. The consumer will find some clauses easier to assess than others. However, many types of clause are difficult for the consumer to assess. A good example is a clause excluding liability for loss or damage caused by negligence [breach of duty]. If the consumer is already fully insured, she may rest easy; but if she is not, to assess the implications of agreeing to such an exclusion will involve having information she is not likely to have. Even a clause which on the face of it seems easy to understand, such as that if a film processor loses the film through negligence it will only be liable for the cost of a new, unexposed film, is actually hard to assess properly without knowing the likelihood of such negligence by the business. Other clauses are even harder for a consumer to assess. For example, the impact of a clause purporting to exclude liability for death or personal injury caused by negligence [breach of duty] is very hard for a consumer to calculate. Though the consumer may be able to envisage the physical effect of death or injury, she is most unlikely to have any real understanding of just how serious the financial consequences of even relatively minor injuries can be, let alone how likely it is that such an injury might occur. The complete ban on businesses excluding or limiting liability for death or personal injury caused by negligence is perhaps most easily justified on this ground.

4.52   Thus it seems appropriate that clauses which exclude or restrict the business's liability to a consumer for negligence [breach of duty] causing death or personal injury should be subject to control whether or not the clause was negotiated: this is, of course, the position under UCTA.[59] The complete ban on businesses excluding their liability for breaches of sections 12–15 of the SGA 1979, whether the exclusion is negotiated or not, can also be supported on this ground as well as

---

[57]   See paras 4.55 – 4.68 below.

[58]   See para 3.32 above.

[59]   The Law Commissions had not recommended a complete ban. The Second Report recommended that such clauses and notices should be completely ineffective only where one party in a comparatively weak position places a high degree of reliance for his personal safety on the care and skill of another, such as in contracts of employment or of carriage, or in relation to car parks (paras 85–94). The report also recommended that the Secretary of State should have order-making powers to extend the protection against such terms to other similar situations (paras 95–97). However, Parliament inserted a complete ban when it became apparent that there were numerous areas where the order-making powers might be required, and after it had been pointed out that such powers had not been very effective in previous application. See *Hansard* (HL) 23 May 1977, vol 383, cols 1102–1103; Second Report, paras 57–58.

on the ground first discussed.[60] With the other types of potentially unfair clause to which UTCCR apply but UCTA does not, the case is less strong but can still be made. A business might "negotiate" other types of clause without the consumer having a clear idea of the risk that the proposed clause represents to her. Suppose it were agreed between a consumer and a builder employed to construct an extension that the builder might make extra charges in some circumstances, or might suspend work or work unusual hours. If this had been negotiated (the latter examples might be the only way the builder could "work in" the customer), should the clauses be subject to threat of review? (We put it in terms of "the threat of review" because it seems unlikely that many genuinely negotiated clauses would actually be held to be unfair.) A lot depends on what is meant by "negotiated". The business may genuinely be prepared to negotiate, but the consumer may not have a full grasp of what she is agreeing or its implications; not realise, for example, how likely the circumstances are to occur, the cost that the builder is genuinely likely to incur, or, in the case of the agreement to allow the builder to work at unusual hours, the risk that neighbours may be able to prevent him from doing so, thereby putting the consumer in breach of contract.

4.53   Therefore we think there is a good case for bringing negotiated terms within the new instrument. An individually negotiated term is very unlikely to be held to be unfair if the business has taken reasonable steps to ensure that the particular consumer understands what has been agreed and its foreseeable implications for her.[61] We note that Denmark, Finland, France and Sweden have not excluded negotiated terms from the scope of their legislation, apparently without problems arising.[62] We also note that the UK Government, in its response to the European Commission Review of the Directive,[63] favoured bringing negotiated clauses into the scope of the controls required by the Directive.[64] The reasons given are similar to those we gave above.

4.54   **Our provisional proposal is that the new regime should apply to both negotiated and non-negotiated terms. We particularly invite comments on the practical and economic impact that this proposal would have.**

---

[60]   Para 4.49 above.

[61]   It does not seem from the consultation papers or reports that the Law Commissions ever considered limiting the controls in consumer contracts to written standard terms.

[62]   Commission Report on the Implementation of Council Directive 93/13/EEC of 5 April 1993 on Unfair Terms in Consumer Contracts (Brussels, 27 April 2000) COM (2000) 248, p 14.

[63]   See para 2.16 above.

[64]   UK Response to the European Commission, DTI, 22 February 2001, response A1(a).

(4) Terms not subject to control

(a) "Core terms"

"DEFINITION OF THE MAIN SUBJECT MATTER" AND WHAT "WAS REASONABLY EXPECTED"

4.55 We suggested earlier that what amounts to a "core term" (or, more properly, the "definition of the main subject matter of the contract") will be exempt from review under UTCCR if it is in plain and intelligible language and is similar to the concept of the performance that the consumer should reasonably expect. However, the two ideas are not interchangeable. We argued[65] that the consumer might "reasonably expect" (because he had been warned of it, for instance) some condition which is not part of the "main subject matter" because it is only to apply in certain situations (for example, a force majeure clause). In order to comply with the Directive, it may therefore be necessary to ensure that terms are subject to review when they do not form part of the main subject matter, even if they were reasonably to be expected. In other words, to ensure that merely "subsidiary"[66] or "incidental"[67] terms are excluded, the definition should continue to refer to the "main subject matter". Conversely, we think that the legislation should make clear what we already believe to be its import, namely that a term will not define the "main subject matter" if it is different from what the consumer reasonably expects.

4.56 Not all Member States have included the exemption for terms which define the main subject matter of the contract.[68] This may solve the problem of defining the scope of the exemption; but we consider that to omit it would have disadvantages.

4.57 First, we believe that, provided the exception is limited to what the consumer should reasonably expect, given what he was told and the other circumstances of the contract, the main subject matter (as opposed to subsidiary or incidental terms) should not be "subject to challenge". If an insurance policy on its face clearly excludes injuries incurred in winter sporting activities, why should that be "subject to challenge"? We would not expect a consumer to be able to challenge a term used by a car dealer stating that it is prepared to supply cars in black only; we do not see that the insurance excluding winter sports injuries is essentially different. Of course, even if these clauses were to be made subject to review, it is very unlikely that either of them would be held to be unfair; but if that is so, there is little point in making them subject to challenge in the first place.

4.58 Secondly, to omit the exception would mean that the legislation would not set out what businesses are expected to do in terms of making it clear to the consumer

---

[65] Para 3.25 above.

[66] The description used by Lord Steyn in *DGFT v First National Bank plc* [2001] UKHL 52, [2002] 1 AC 481 (HL), at [34]; para 3.25 above.

[67] The description used by Lord Bingham: *ibid*, at [12].

[68] The European Commission reports that Denmark, Finland, Greece, Luxembourg, Portugal, Spain and Sweden have not exempted such terms: Commission Report on the Implementation of Council Directive 93/13/EEC of 5 April 1993 on Unfair Terms in Consumer Contracts (Brussels, 27 April 2000) COM (2000) 248, p 15.

what the main subject matter is. We think it would be better to maintain the exception but to try to define its proper scope as clearly as possible.

4.59 We think that it is possible to make the concept of the "core term" rather more concrete than it is at present, and still comply with the Directive,[69] by combining the two tests and qualifying "main subject matter" by what the consumer should reasonably expect. We suggest something along the following lines, excluding from review only those terms which

> set out in plain language the main subject matter of the contract in a way that is not substantially different to what the consumer reasonably expected.

4.60 **We provisionally propose**

(1) **that the new legislation should exclude the main subject matter from the scope of review, but**

(2) **only in so far as**

(a) **it is not substantially different from what the consumer should reasonably expect, and**

(b) **it is stated in plain language.[70]**

ADEQUACY OF THE PRICE

4.61 UCTA does not apply to clauses which set the price payable under the contract. Under UTCCR the adequacy of the price is exempted from review so far as the term in question is "in plain intelligible language".[71] Our provisional view is that a term which fixes the price in a way which is difficult for the consumer to understand should be subject to review, and (insofar as the term was not individually negotiated) this is currently required by the Directive.

4.62 We argued in Part III that the exemption from review of "the adequacy of the price" in regulation 6(2) is already subject to the same kind of limitation as the "definition of the main subject matter of the contract": namely, the "price" means only the amount of the "main price" rather than any price contained in a "subsidiary" or "incidental" term. We think this is a correct approach from the point of view of policy, because only in that case can we be confident that the consumer will not be unfairly surprised and that the amount payable will be

---

[69] It should be recalled that there is no objection to more stringent review than the Directive requires. See para 4.6 above.

[70] On whether this should be changed to a requirement of transparency, see para 4.107 below.

[71] Para 3.19 above. Commission Report on the Implementation of Council Directive 93/13/EEC of 5 April 1993 on Unfair Terms in Consumer Contracts, (Brussels, 27 April 2000) COM (2000) 248, p 15, has raised the question whether the price should be subject to review, noting that several Member States have not transposed this limitation into their law. We are not aware of any demand for price to be reviewable. Most Member States, including the UK, allow for contracts to be avoided where there is a serious disparity coupled with some overreaching behaviour: see O Lando and H Beale (eds), *Principles of European Contract Law, Parts I and II* (Kluwer Law International 1999) pp 263–265.

subject to the discipline of the market. We provisionally propose that the new legislation make this clear. This may require an expansion of the definition of the "adequacy of the price" exemption presently used by UTCCR, in order to ensure that prices set in "subsidiary" or "incidental" terms are not exempted. A suggested draft will be found in Appendix B.[72]

4.63 On the other hand, at least for the purposes of individual review, we see no strong case for bringing a clear term stating the "main price" within the scope of the new legislation. Certainly there are cases in which consumers agree to pay quite exorbitant prices through ignorance of the normal price for such goods or services. Stories of, for example, elderly people being persuaded to pay over the odds for building repairs are only too common.[73] However, an extension of the law in order to deal with this problem is unnecessary and might be undesirable. First, most consumers are relatively alert to the question of price. Secondly, we think that for individual cases there are already adequate remedies. In English law the problem can be dealt with under the doctrine of unconscionable bargains.[74] Although there are not many cases and they relate primarily to land transactions, we consider that the doctrine can apply to the deliberate overcharging of consumers and to exploitation of the consumer's circumstances. While Scots law does not recognise a general doctrine of unconscionable bargains, specific doctrines exist (for example, facility and circumvention) by which grossly unfair contracts can be struck down.[75] Thirdly, given that even in reasonably competitive markets prices do vary significantly (not least because of the different costs faced by traders working in different locations and on different scales, factors which may not be apparent to the average consumer), the authorities might be faced with a large number of challenges to allegedly unfair prices and there would be much scope for argument.[76] Moreover, it would often turn into arguments about the competitiveness of the market, arguments with which neither courts nor many consumer protection organisations are well-equipped to deal.

4.64 A rather different question is whether the bodies listed in Schedule 1 to UTCCR should have power to act against businesses which appear to make a practice of overcharging. This appears to be outside the present powers even of the DGFT. Under the Fair Trading Act 1973, Part III, the DGFT may take proceedings

---

[72] See clause 6.

[73] See the DTI consultation paper, "Proposals to amend the Consumer Protection (Cancellation of Contracts Concluded Away from Business Premises) Regulations 1987", published on 10 June 1998; also G Holgate, "Curbing Doorstep Selling" (1999) 18 Tr Law 33.

[74] See Chitty, paras 7-075 to 7-088.

[75] See H MacQueen and J Thomson, *Contract Law in Scotland* (2000) pp 147 ff.

[76] If the price were to be subjected to review, we think that the test for fairness of the price would have to be much stricter than that for other terms. It could either be set in terms of a factor above the market price (eg at least twice the normal market price) or, preferably, in terms of the deliberate overreaching of ill-informed consumers (eg the elderly persons who are overcharged for building work) or exploitation of their urgent needs (eg the mini-cab driver who is asked to take an injured person to hospital when no ambulance is available and who charges what both parties know to be several times the normal fare).

against businesses persisting in a course of conduct which is detrimental and unfair to consumers,[77] but for this purpose "unfair" is defined to mean in breach of the criminal law[78] or

> in breach of contract or in breach of a duty (other than a contractual duty) owed to any person by virtue of any enactment or rule of law and enforceable by civil proceedings ...[79]

Overcharging, even if it leads to the contract being voidable for unconscionability, is not a breach of duty any more than is use of unfair terms (even terms automatically void under UCTA).[80]

4.65 Previous Directors-General have proposed an extension of their powers to enable them to deal with "unconscionable practices", which would include

> that the terms and conditions on, or subject to, which the consumer transaction was entered by the consumer are so harsh or adverse to the consumer as to be inequitable.[81]

4.66 Moreover, the Government's response to the European Commission's Review of the Directive[82] states that the Government accepts that there is a need to protect vulnerable consumers against deliberate overcharging in certain circumstances. It therefore favours retaining the exemption for the price/quality ratio *except* where the price is exorbitant or grossly contravenes the ordinary principles of fair dealing.[83]

4.67 In our view it may well be desirable for the DGFT to have a power to act against those who charge exorbitant prices, but it is strictly outside the terms of reference of this project. We consider it more appropriate for this to be considered under any review of the Fair Trading Act 1973, rather than as part of the present exercise.

4.68 **Our provisional conclusion is that the adequacy of the price should not be reviewable under the legislation, where**

> (1) **having to make the payment, or the way in which it is calculated, is not substantially different from what the consumer, in the light of what he was told when or before the contract was made and all the other circumstances, should reasonably expect, and**

---

[77] Fair Trading Act 1973, s 34.

[78] Section 34(2).

[79] Section 34(3).

[80] There seems to be no right to compensation, as distinct from avoidance of the contract. That is so in the analogous case of non-disclosure: *Bank Keyser Ullman SA v Skandia (UK) Insurance Co Ltd* [1990] 1 QB 665, CA (aff'd on other grounds [1991] 2 AC 249); see Chitty 6-135.

[81] Trading Malpractices (OFT, July 1990) para 5.27.

[82] See para 2.16 above.

[83] UK Response to the European Commission, DTI, 22 February 2001, response A1(c)(ii).

**(2) the price is not one contained in a subsidiary term,
provided that the price is stated in plain language.**[84]

(b) Mandatory and permitted terms

4.69 We noted in Part III various differences between the existing regimes on this issue.[85] Given that this is a question of exemption from the Directive, there is no legal objection to UK law allowing narrower exceptions than does the Directive.[86]

4.70 We have already expressed disquiet that the Directive exempts terms which reflect the principles, as opposed to the requirements, of international conventions.[87] **We provisionally propose that terms required or authorised by an international convention to which the UK is party should be exempt from the new "reasonableness" regime, but not terms which merely reflect the principles of such a convention.**

4.71 We think that both regimes exempt a term which merely reflects what would be the law even in the absence of the term, and we think that it is proper to exempt terms that in substance are not significantly different[88] to the "default rule" that would otherwise apply under the general law, subject to one qualification. As we noted in Part III, the current exemption under UTCCR has the consequence that such terms cannot be challenged even if they are not in "plain intelligible language". This appears to give rise to real difficulties: the OFT has found

> clauses which reflect the general contractual position concerning damages for breach of contract, but in a misleading way. Contracts sometimes give the impression that, if they are cancelled by the consumer, the company can recover all the profit it would have made. In law the supplier actually has a duty to "mitigate his losses" ...[89]

4.72 We think that the DGFT and the other authorised bodies should have power to prevent the use of standardised terms that reflect the "default rules" but do so in such a way that the consumer may be misled. The invalidation of such terms in a particular contract will make no difference to the legal position of the parties to that contract, because the misleading term will be replaced by the general law that it reflects; but, for the sake of simplicity, we think it best to follow UTCCR in using the same test for both prevention and invalidation.

---

[84] On the requirements we would impose in this respect see para 4.104 below.

[85] See paras 3.35 – 3.40 above.

[86] See para 4.6 above.

[87] See para 3.38 above.

[88] To the detriment of the consumer.

[89] Unfair Contract Terms Bulletin 3 (OFT 188, March 1997) p 12.

4.73 **We provisionally propose that the exemption for terms which reflect what would be the law in the absence of contrary agreement should not apply unless the terms are in plain language.**[90]

4.74 We see no reason to follow UTCCR in exempting terms which do not reflect the law of the relevant part of the UK but the law of some other Member State.[91] **We provisionally propose that a term should not be exempt merely because it represents the law of another Member State.**

4.75 It is our understanding that the Directive may not exempt from the fairness test terms approved by industry regulators unless the terms are *required* by that regulator.[92] We think that in principle terms which are required by a regulator should be exempt, but those that have merely been approved by a regulator should not be exempt. A term might be approved by a regulator in one context but be applied in another in which it operates unfairly.

4.76 **It is our provisional proposal that terms required by regulators should be exempt, but not those merely approved by a regulator.**[93]

(5) Excluded contracts

(a) Consumers as suppliers

4.77 There are some contracts under which the consumer supplies goods or services to the business (for example when a private motorist sells a car to a dealer). If such a contract contains terms that operate to the detriment of the consumer, they are subject to the controls of UCTA.[94] The position under UTCCR is not wholly clear.[95]

4.78 **It is our provisional proposal that the new legislation should make it clear that it applies where the consumer is the seller or supplier.**

(b) Insurance contracts and contracts for the transfer of land or securities

4.79 The terms of these are exempt from UCTA but will be subject to the new regime as they are subject to UTCCR.[96]

---

[90] On the requirements we would impose in this respect see para 4.104 above.

[91] Para 3.36 above.

[92] Para 3.40 above.

[93] Even the fact that a term has been required by a regulator will not protect it if it is one of those which are of no effect under UCTA: see para 3.40 above. We propose that this position should continue.

[94] Note that UCTA prevents the consumer from excluding or restricting certain liabilities to the business: see para 3.9 above. This is considered in Part VI below.

[95] See para 3.39 above.

[96] See para 3.43 above. As to whether the exemptions should continue to apply as far as, under the new regime, terms would continue to be simply of no effect, see para 4.36 above.

(c) Employment contracts

4.80   In Part III we noted that, whereas employment contracts appear to be outside the scope of UTCCR, they are to some extent within UCTA, and that some courts have treated the employer as acting in the course of its business and the employee as a consumer.[97] Such contracts would therefore fall within the definition of a consumer contract unless specifically exempted. We think that the employee should in any event be able to limit her liability for negligence towards the employer, as currently in England under UCTA Schedule 1, paragraph 1(4).[98] Subject to that, we see no reason to exempt employment contracts from the regime we propose. But they could be included in the regime without necessarily being treated as consumer contracts or subjected to the same controls as consumer contracts. It is arguable that the employee is in the "business" of hiring out her labour, and that the contract should therefore be subject to the controls which in Part V below we propose should apply to business-to-business contracts. This might have implications for the level of protection provided. Under our proposals, the controls applicable to business-to-business contracts would in some respects be less stringent than those applicable to consumer contracts, and, if contracts of employment were regarded as business-to-business contracts, employees would to that extent be less well protected. Terms of employment which have been individually negotiated, for example, would not be subject to control.[99] Again, there is at present no provision for policing the use of unfair terms in business-to-business contracts, and it is debatable whether any such provision should now be made;[100] categorising employment contracts as consumer contracts might therefore bring them within the scope of preventive controls which would not otherwise apply.

4.81   Our provisional view is that the features of business-to-business contracts which justify treating them differently from consumer contracts are not necessarily shared by employment contracts, even if employment contracts are not really consumer contracts either; and that it might be best to subject employment contracts to much the same *regime* as consumer contracts, while acknowledging that in some respects they constitute a separate category of their own. This might even involve dealing with them in a separate part of the legislation, though we have not attempted to do this in the draft Bill. **We invite views on**

---

[97]   See para 3.45 above.

[98]   This exemption does not apply in Scots law.

[99]   See paras 5.41 – 5.59 below.

[100]   See paras 5.98 – 5.111 below. There may be other differences too. It is arguably inappropriate, for example, to allow terms in business-to-business contracts to be found unfair simply because they are not "transparent" (paras 5.80 – 5.81 below); if this view prevails, *and* employment contracts are treated as business-to-business contracts, non-transparent terms of employment would be binding where they are not otherwise unfair. Again, we suggest at paras 5.84 – 5.88 below that the new indicative list of terms which may be found unfair should be narrower for business-to-business contracts than for consumer contracts; and this would have implications for the burden of proof in the case of terms which fall within the wider list but not the narrower.

   (1) **whether contracts of employment should be covered by the new regime at all; and**

   (2) **if so, whether they should count as consumer contracts, or as business-to-business contracts, or as a separate category subject to some (but not necessarily all) of the controls that apply to consumer contracts.**

(d) International contracts

4.82 Although both consumer and non-consumer "cross-border" contracts for the supply of goods are exempt from UCTA, there is no exemption for cross-border contracts of sale in SCGD. Thus the absolute ban on sellers to consumers restricting their liability for breaches of sections 13–15 of the SGA 1979 will in future have to apply to cross-border sale contracts. Other cross-border contracts for the supply of goods are not uncommon: for example, some UK car hire companies will provide cars at overseas locations.[101] Such contracts are covered by UTCCR, which equally have no exemption for international contracts. It would be possible to distinguish these other contracts from sales, merely subjecting them to the "reasonableness" regime of the new legislation, but it is our provisional view that there is no reason to reduce the consumer's protection from the level he would enjoy were the goods to be supplied in the UK.[102] We also consider that the prohibition on sellers contracting out of their obligations as to title (which applies whether or not the other party deals as a consumer) should apply to cross-border contracts. **We provisionally propose that the controls should apply to terms in cross-border contracts for the supply of goods to consumers in the same way as they would apply to the same terms in a domestic contract.**

(e) Choice of UK law

4.83 We saw in Part III that UCTA also exempts from the operation of the Act contracts in which English or Scots law applies only because the parties have chosen that law to govern their contract; but that there is no such exemption in UTCCR. Thus under the new regime, in the rather unlikely event of a consumer contract being made subject to English or Scots law when that law would not otherwise apply, the "reasonableness" requirement would still be relevant.

4.84 Nor is there an exception for any such contracts in SCGD. It follows that the absolute ban on sellers contracting out of their obligations to consumers as to conformity will have to be maintained even if the parties have chosen English or Scots law when it would not otherwise apply.

---

[101] Car hire companies' websites reveal that in some cases the contract will be with a subsidiary in the location overseas, but in others it is stated that the consumer's contract will be with the UK company.

[102] The DTI has proposed that changes required by SCGD in the case of contracts of sale should also be made in relation to other contracts for the supply of goods. See para 4.160 below.

4.85   It does not necessarily follow that the list of terms which, under the new legislation, will continue to be of no effect at all[103] should apply to other types of contract under which the ownership or possession of goods passes just because the parties have chosen that it should be governed by English or Scottish law.[104] However, we see no strong reason why, in a consumer contract, this exemption should continue, and at least one reason why it should not. The consumer, faced with the prospect of making a contract under the law of the supplier's country because the supplier will not agree to the law of the consumer's country, might be willing to accept English or Scots law as a compromise just because she believes that under Scots or English law the consumer has strong rights. It would be misleading were those rights not to apply in full to her contract.

4.86   **We provisionally conclude that there should be no special treatment of consumer contracts to which English or Scots law applies only through the choice of the parties.**

(6) The test to be applied

4.87   We suggested earlier that there appears to be very little difference, if any, between the "requirement of reasonableness" ["fair and reasonable" test] under UCTA and the test of "fairness" used by the Directive and UTCCR; and we explained that there is no necessity for the legislation implementing the Directive to follow its wording, provided that the test employed affords no less protection to consumers. We also explained the advantages and disadvantages of adopting each model.

4.88   Our provisional view is that the legislation should attempt to give the greatest possible guidance to both business and consumer.[105] This means departing from the wording of the Directive and also expanding somewhat on the "fair and reasonable" criterion of UCTA.

(a) The basic test

4.89   The basic criterion used in the Directive is whether or not the term is unfair; that in UCTA, whether or not the clause is fair and reasonable. If there is any difference between them, we consider that the new legislation should use the latter since the double requirement must make it more favourable to the consumer. It is possible that "fair" by itself might be read as meaning that, so long as the business was not acting unfairly in any subjective sense (for example, it had no intention of harming the consumer's interest), the term is not unfair.[106] The "fair and reasonable" criterion may give more guidance and we think it would be preferable to adopt it. To avoid all doubt it could be stated that everything required by good

---

[103]   See paras 4.34 – 4.35 above.

[104]   Nor, in contracts of sale, to obligations as to title; para 3.9 above.

[105]   So far as possible, it should also be the same as the test to be used in judging terms in contracts with non-consumers: see para 5.74 below.

[106]   Although we do not believe that this would be a correct interpretation of the Directive or UTCCR.

faith should also be required by this test, but our provisional view is that this is unnecessary.

4.90   UTCCR uses the phrase "significant imbalance in the parties' rights and obligations arising under the contract, to the detriment of the consumer." We do not find the concept of imbalance, stated as baldly as it is in the Directive, helpful. It tends to suggest that a harsh clause may be justified if it can be shown that the contract is a reasonable balance in terms of value for money. This is often not the point. As we showed earlier,[107] frequently the harsh terms are "balanced" by a low price, but the consumer did not appreciate the harshness of the terms or did not want such a deal, and therefore it is unfair. But we think that the more general question of fair balance between the interests of the parties is central to the question of fairness.[108] We think it might be referred to in the guidelines we propose below.[109]

4.91   As we saw in Part III,[110] the phrase "significant imbalance" in UTCCR[111] is capable of a variety of interpretations. It at least seems to mean that minor, "insignificant" imbalances are not subject to review; in other words that a term is not subject to review unless a certain threshold is crossed. Given that under the new legislation almost any term might fall within the scope of the review, should a threshold requirement of this type be included? In our view, this depends on the question of burden of proof. If the business will have the burden of showing the fairness of any term which departs from the general law in a way that the consumer claims to be against his interests, there seems to be some merit in a threshold requirement to avoid the business having to justify even trivial departures from the general rule. If, however, the burden of proving that the term is not fair and reasonable is to be on the consumer (where the term is not one on the so-called "grey list" of terms likely to be unfair), there seems to be no need for a threshold. The burden of proof issue is discussed below,[112] but for the moment we will assume that a threshold requirement is not necessary.

4.92   UTCCR state that only terms which are detrimental to the consumer can be challenged. (This problem did not arise under UCTA because the terms subject to its control were all clauses in which the business tried to limit its liability or, in the case of an indemnity clause, put an additional burden on the consumer.) The new legislation will have to include a similar provision.

4.93   Both UTCCR and UCTA apply the test of fairness as of the time the contract was made.[113] We consider that the new legislation should do the same.

---

[107]   Paras 2.5 – 2.7 above.

[108]   Paras 3.57 – 3.71 above.

[109]   See paras 4.95 – 4.103 below.

[110]   See paras 3.57 – 3.62 above.

[111]   Reg 5(1).

[112]   See para 4.146 below.

[113]   Para 3.54 above.

4.94   **We provisionally propose that the basic test in the new legislation should be whether, judged by reference to the time the contract was made, the term is a fair and reasonable one; and that it is not necessary to include an explicit reference to good faith. We ask consultees whether they agree with this and, if not, what test they think should be used.**

(b) Factors to be taken into account

4.95   A question which we have found difficult is whether the "fair and reasonable" test should be supplemented by guidelines or lists of factors to be taken into account in assessing fairness and reasonableness, or should be left to stand alone. UCTA has some guidelines both in section 11 [s 24] and in Schedule 2. The recitals to the Directive[114] refer to various factors (the strength of the bargaining position of the parties, whether the consumer had an inducement to agree to the term, and whether the goods or services were sold or supplied to the special order of the customer) which appear to be taken from Schedule 2 to UCTA, and these were included in the 1994 Regulations. However, there is no such list in the Directive itself and the factors have been omitted from UTCCR.

FAIRNESS IN SUBSTANCE

4.96   We think that it would be useful to include at least a list of factors for assessing the fairness of the substance of the term, in order to provide consumers, businesses and the courts with the clearest possible guidance on how this test should be applied. We suggest that the new legislation should spell out a series of factors which should be taken into account, building in some or all of the guidelines in Schedule 2 to UCTA.[115] We suggest that in the guidelines as to substance there should be a reference to the balance of the interests of the parties, and the risks to the consumer. We should also include references to

(a)   the extent to which the term (on its own or in conjunction with other terms) differs from what would apply in the absence of express provision on the point, or from terms required by any relevant authority;[116]

(b)   the possibility and likelihood of insurance (as in UCTA section 11(4) [s 24(3)] but in broader terms); and

(c)   other ways in which the consumer might protect his position (for example, getting advice on the transaction from an expert).[117]

---

[114] See Recital 16. The Directive is set out at Appendix E below.

[115] We do not include item (d) because we think it would go better in the "grey" list.

[116] Cf mandatory and permitted terms: paras 4.69 – 4.76 above.

[117] We considered adding (in line with Recital 17) whether the transaction was an unusual one for the business, so that it was fair for it to use terms placing less risk on it than for more usual transactions. This we understand to be the thrust of UCTA, Sched 2(e). We suspect that it is of very limited relevance to consumer transactions as opposed to business-to-business contracts.

4.97 We are less certain whether guidelines as to procedural fairness will be useful. One view is that these would also give useful guidance to businesses that wish to try to ensure that their terms will be fair and reasonable to consumers; and they may help consumers or their advisers when confronted by a business which argues, for instance, that the clause is reasonable in its own interests and if the consumer didn't like it she should not have entered the contract. Another view is that a list of procedural factors may weaken the hand of the consumer or of the agency trying to prevent use of the term, as it gives greater scope for the business to argue that because the procedure used to make the contract was fair (for example that the document was in clear terms and the consumer had time to read it in advance) the terms in it should not be regarded as unfair. The Unfair Contract Terms Unit of the OFT has told us that on occasion businesses have attempted to justify the use of harsh terms in this way. To list the procedural ways in which harsh terms may be made palatable might therefore weaken the efforts to get rid of harsh terms.

4.98 We do not think that terms fall into only two groups, those which are fair and those which are unfair in any circumstances. Certainly some clauses are unfair to consumers in almost all circumstances; but there are clauses which might be fair were the consumer warned of them in clear enough language, so that he can readily understand the implications, but which are unfair without such a warning. No doubt preventive action will concentrate on those terms which are so much against the consumer interest that they could never be made fair by procedural steps, but it is important that it be possible for both individual consumers and the bodies empowered to take preventive action to be able to challenge terms on the ground that, for example, they were not properly explained or the consumer had effectively no choice. For these cases we believe that a list of factors of procedural fairness will also be helpful to both businesses and consumers.

4.99 Our suggestion is that there should be a reference to the fairness of the term in the light of the circumstances existing when the contract was made. This would include

(a) the consumer's knowledge and understanding, and

(b) the strength of the bargaining positions of the parties,

as well as the other matters referred to by Article 4(1) of the Directive (the nature of the goods and services and the other terms of the contract or of any other contract on which it is dependent).

4.100 The consumer's knowledge and understanding should be considered in the light of

(a) previous dealings, if any;

(b) whether the consumer knew of the term;

(c) whether she understood the meaning and implications of the term;

(d) what consumers in her position would normally expect of a contract of the general type which appeared to her to be on offer; and

(e)   the complexity of the matter.

The following would also be relevant in all cases, but particularly when the matter is complex:

(f)   the information given to the consumer about the terms, at or before the time the contract was made;

(g)   whether the contract was "transparent";[118]

(h)   the way the contract was explained to the consumer;[119]

(i)   whether she had a reasonable opportunity to absorb the information before making the contract;

(j)   whether she took, or could reasonably be expected to take, professional advice; and

(k)   whether she had a realistic subsequent opportunity to cancel the contract without charge.

4.101   Factors relevant to the relative bargaining strength of the parties would include

(a)   whether the transaction was an unusual one for either of the parties;

(b)   whether the consumer was offered a choice over the term;

(c)   whether she had an opportunity to seek a more favourable term;

(d)   whether she had an opportunity to enter into a similar contract with other persons, but without that term;

(e)   whether there were alternative means by which her requirements could have been met; and

(f)   whether it was reasonable, given her abilities, for her to take up any such opportunities.

4.102   This list is rather fuller than that in UCTA but tries to set out what we understand to be the major issues in relation to unfair terms. In particular we have indicated the factors that we think are relevant to inequality of bargaining power, which we think is an ambiguous and much misunderstood phrase.[120]

4.103   **We ask for consultees' views on our provisional proposal that the new legislation should contain detailed guidelines on the application of the**

---

[118]   See paras 4.104 – 4.109 below.

[119]   It would be possible to include references to plain and intelligible/simple language, ease of reading the document, prominence, etc – but we consider that this might be too much detail for legislation rather than guidance notes to businesses.

[120]   Case law suggests that the phrase is used in two senses: (a) lack of sophistication and (b) lack of market power. See for example Lord Denning's reference to "his bargaining power which is grievously impaired by reason of his needs or desires, or by ignorance or infirmity": *Lloyds Bank Ltd v Bundy* [1975] QB 326, 339 (CA). Compare with *Dawnay, Day & Co Ltd v De Braconier D'Alphen* [1997] IRLR 285, 292 (HC); and *St Albans City and District Council v International Computers Ltd* [1995] FSR 686 (QBD), where bargaining power is viewed as a matter of position and strength within the market place.

"fair and reasonable" test, and on the contents of those guidelines proposed at paragraphs 4.96 and 4.99 – 4.101 above.

(c) Plain and intelligible language

4.104 In Part III we noted that UTCCR require all terms to be in plain and intelligible language, and that a "core term" which is not in plain and intelligible language will lose the exemption it would normally enjoy; but that otherwise the only explicit sanction is that the clause will be interpreted in the way most favourable to the consumer. We consider that the use of plain and intelligible language is a vital aspect of fairness and we think that it should be listed specifically among the factors that should be taken into account in assessing fairness. The language should also be unambiguous, if that is not already covered by the phrase "plain and intelligible".[121]

4.105 Like the OFT,[122] however, we think that it is not sufficient that the term is in plain and intelligible language if it is in print that is hard to read, if the terms are not readily accessible to the consumer, or if the layout of the contract document is hard to follow. We think that all these factors (which collectively we refer to as "transparency") should be made relevant to the decision on fairness.

4.106 **We provisionally propose**

  (1) **that the factors to be taken into account in assessing fairness should include whether the contract is "transparent", in the sense of being expressed in plain language, presented in a clear manner and accessible to the consumer; and**

  (2) **that transparency should also be a condition of exemption for "core" and default terms.[123]**

4.107 There is a further question: should it be possible for the court to hold that a term is unfair *simply* because it is not "transparent"? In other words should the court have power, if it considers it appropriate, to hold the term to be unfair even though, had it been transparent, it would have been fair? Earlier we argued that a term may be "unfair" under UTCCR because of the process by which it was "agreed"; for example, if it was contained in a separate document that was only incorporated into the contract by reference and the consumer had no chance to examine it. We see no difference in principle between such a term and one that is not transparent because of the language, the size of print or the layout of the contract.

4.108 Incorporating the transparency factor in the list, as we have proposed, would mean that (like any of the other factors we suggest) it might be the principal or even the sole ground on which a term was held to be unfair. However, we do not think that a finding of lack of transparency should lead *automatically* to a finding

---

[121] See Treitel, p 256.

[122] Cf para 3.75, n 156 above.

[123] See paras 4.60, 4.68 and 4.73 above.

of unfairness. That might lead to difficulties, for example, if a core term was not transparent. It might invalidate the contract, which might not be in the consumer's interest.

4.109 **We provisionally propose that, whilst lack of transparency should not automatically render a term unfair, it should be made clear that a term may be found unfair principally or solely on that ground.**

4.110 Whether it is necessary to state the rule of interpretation in favour of the consumer in the new instrument is a matter on which we are uncertain. It will apply as a matter of common law and it may be unnecessary to state it. However, doing so is unlikely to do any harm and we think that it should therefore be stated in the new instrument.

4.111 **We provisionally propose that the rule of interpretation in favour of the consumer should be stated in the new instrument. We would welcome consultees' views on what form this statement should take.**[124]

(d) Indicative lists

4.112 UTCCR contain an indicative list, or "grey" list, copied from the Annex to the Directive. It appears that legislation needs to contain such a list in order to comply with the Directive.[125] In any event the indicative list appears to have been found useful, at least by the OFT in its work in seeking to eliminate unfair terms, and we are not aware of any call to remove it. Two questions may be asked. First, should the indicative list be expanded to include other clauses which have been found to be unfair? Secondly, not all the examples on the indicative list are easy to understand. The language is complex and the examples sometimes refer to concepts from other legal systems which seem to have no exact equivalent in the laws of England and Scotland. Should the list be reformulated, "translating" the examples into terms which are recognisable to readers from the UK and, if it is permissible to do so, omitting altogether any that are not?[126]

AN EXPANDED LIST

4.113 On the first question, it seems sensible to consider whether there are any terms which the OFT has required firms to stop using, or organisations to cease

---

[124] The draft Bill in Appendix B does not include such a provision.

[125] Chitty, para 15-051, says the Annex must be included because of Art 3(3). That is perhaps not obvious on the wording but the European Commission has brought infringement proceedings against Denmark, Finland and Sweden, whose legislation did not originally contain an indicative list. See Report from the Commission on the Implementation of Council Directive 93/13/EEC of 5 April 1993 on Unfair Terms in Consumer Contracts, COM(2000) 248 final of 27 April 2000, para III(2) p 16. However, on 31 January 2002 Advocate General Geelhoed issued an opinion on the Swedish case above stating that the indicative list did not have to be transposed into domestic legislation because it was illustrative and not prescriptive and binding. The Court has yet to give its judgment in this case.

[126] Whether this is permissible is discussed in paras 4.6 – 4.10 above.

recommending, although the terms are not listed. This suggests that at least the following types of clause should be added to the list: [127]

(1) terms allowing a supplier to impose an unfair financial burden, such as giving it the power to demand an advance or stage payment or (in the case of a utility supplier) a payment based on an estimate at its discretion; [128]

(2) terms transferring unfair risks to consumers, for example through indemnity clauses or clauses which permit the supplier to impose additional charges; [129]

(3) onerous enforcement clauses, such as clauses allowing a supplier to repossess goods from the consumer or to sell goods left in the supplier's hands when the consumer is in breach of contract without first giving the consumer the chance to cure the breach, or despite the breach being slight; [130]

(4) exclusions of the consumer's right to assign guarantees or agreements; [131]

(5) consumer declarations about contractual circumstances, such as that the consumer has read the terms of the agreement or has examined goods prior to purchase; [132]

(6) exclusions or limitations of the consumer's non-contractual rights under data protection or other legislation; [133]

(7) terms allowing the supplier to deliver or perform in a manner or at a time left to its discretion; [134] and

(8) terms giving the supplier the right to determine unilaterally whether the consumer is in breach of contract or has acted improperly. [135]

4.114 There are potentially unfair terms in financial services agreements which are not included in either the existing list or the list of additions suggested above. However, the Financial Services Authority has power to issue separate guidance dealing with these. [136] We understand that it intends to do so and therefore such terms need not be included in the general legislation on unfair terms.

---

[127] This list is taken from Unfair Contract Terms Bulletin 13 (OFT 330, April 2001) p 69 with some additions from Unfair Contract Terms Guidance (OFT 311, February 2001) Annex A.

[128] See OFT Guidance, Annex A, Group 18(a). This refers also to deposits though these will usually fall within Sched 2, para 1(d).

[129] *Ibid*, Group 18(b). Some additional charges will fall within Sched 2, para 1(l).

[130] *Ibid*, Group 18(c). We omit clauses permitting landlords to repossess premises, for the reasons given in para 4.115.

[131] *Ibid*, Group 18(d).

[132] *Ibid*, Group 18(e).

[133] *Ibid*, Group 18(f).

[134] *Ibid*, Group 18(g).

[135] *Ibid*.

[136] Financial Services and Markets Act 2000, ss 157 and 158.

4.115 The OFT has recently issued a Guidance on Unfair Terms in Tenancy Agreements.[137] We do not include examples from this area in the consultation paper because the issue is currently being examined by the Law Commission in the context of its work on housing tenure.[138]

4.116 It would seem sensible to add contractual terms which purport to exclude or restrict the business's liability in tort [delict] for loss or damage other than death or personal injury. These terms are subject to the reasonableness test under UCTA,[139] and it is up to the business to show that the term is fair and reasonable.[140] When we come to discuss the burden of proof, it will be seen that one possibility is that businesses will bear the burden of showing that any term on the list is fair, but that with other terms the burden of showing that the term is unfair will be on the consumer. If this is the solution finally adopted, it will be important to add these terms to the list in order to preserve the current position. Further, although if terms are unfair the bodies listed in Schedule 1 to UTCCR can act to prevent their use even if they are not listed, it would be clearer for all concerned if they appeared on the list.[141] We also think that it should be possible to add to the list by Ministerial Order.

4.117 **It is our provisional proposal that the legislation should include a new version of the indicative list, containing not only what is required by the Directive but the additional terms set out in paragraphs 4.113 and 4.116 above. We ask consultees if they agree with these additions and if there are any other terms which should be listed.**

REFORMULATING THE LIST IN UK TERMS

4.118 The second question, whether the list should be reformulated in terms which would be more directly applicable to UK law, and which would be more readily understandable to UK readers, is not easy to answer. To "translate" the list into UK terms, while ensuring that it complies with the Directive, is not easy. Moreover, as we shall see below,[142] some of the existing paragraphs have no real relevance to UK law, or seem to cover terms that, in the context of UK law, do not seem unfair. We do not believe that correct implementation of the Directive requires the legislation to include a direct equivalent to every paragraph of the Annex to the Directive, any more than it requires legislation in identical language,[143] though there is no clear authority on this point.

---

[137] OFT 356 (November 2001).

[138] See Renting Homes – 1: Status and Security (2002) Consultation Paper No 162.

[139] Section 2(2); see para 3.10, n 25 above. They are not covered by UTCCR Sched 2, para 1(b), which refers only to "contractual obligations". Notices which are not themselves terms of a contract and which exclude liability in tort [delict] are discussed in Part VII below.

[140] Section 11(5).

[141] Terms which would limit the supplier's liability for death or personal injury fall within Sched 2, para 1(a), but the indicative list does not refer to liability for other losses.

[142] Para 4.133 below.

[143] See paras 4.7 – 4.10 above.

4.119 A second point is that the OFT, particularly in its Unfair Contract Terms Guidance ("OFT Guidance"),[144] has done a great deal to explain how in its view the indicative list applies to various types of contract term. A possible drawback of reformulating the indicative list would be that the experience in using it, particularly in the OFT, might be lost. If the indicative list were to be reformulated, officials and others used to applying the indicative list would have to adjust to the new list.

4.120 On the other hand, to keep the indicative list in its present form would mean abandoning, as least as far as the list is concerned, any attempt to make the new legislation clear and accessible to the reader.[145] We therefore think that we should attempt to "translate" the indicative list. It is our view that in reformulating the list it should be possible to draw on the experience of the OFT and the guidance that it has so usefully issued. If the reformulation can be made successfully, the result would be a list which is no harder to apply than the OFT Guidance but which is more authoritative and avoids the need for a preliminary "translation" process. We also think that the reformulation can be sufficiently close to the terms of the Annex to the Directive that it is most unlikely that infringement proceedings would be threatened.

4.121 **We provisionally propose that the indicative list should be reformulated in terms which are more directly applicable to UK law and more readily comprehensible to UK readers.**

4.122 However, it seems to us that whether the list can be reformulated successfully can only be tested by experiment. To enable consultees to assess whether reformulation is likely to be successful and therefore worth pursuing, this consultation paper considers the reformulation of a number of paragraphs. The draft Bill in Appendix B contains the relevant provisions for consultees to evaluate. The consultation paper discusses, and the draft Bill provides replacements for,[146] paragraphs 1(a)–(e) of Schedule 2 to UTCCR. We think this is a sufficient sample to reveal the main issues that would be involved in preparing a complete new list along the lines suggested above. Once again we should stress that the inclusion of these drafts in the consultation paper does not create any presumption that this will be the approach the Law Commissions will finally recommend.[147]

TERMS WHICH ARE ALWAYS OF NO EFFECT

4.123 A preliminary point is that the indicative list serves two purposes. One is to give information to businesses and consumers as to what, in an individual case, is likely to be regarded as an unfair clause. The second is to make it easier for the OFT (and the other bodies listed in Schedule 1) to ensure that unfair terms are not

---

[144] OFT 311 (February 2001).

[145] See paras 2.35 – 2.39 above.

[146] Sched 2.

[147] See para 2.38 above.

used by businesses, and for businesses to know what terms are likely to be unacceptable. The second purpose may make it desirable to have a wider list than is needed for the first purpose. Under UCTA certain clauses are automatically ineffective, and we have provisionally proposed that this should remain the case under the new legislation.[148] Some of these terms appear in the indicative list. For the first purpose it is not necessary to include them in the new list, but it has been suggested to us that they should be included for the second purpose. However, to make it clear that there can be no doubt that these clauses are null, we propose that they be placed in a separate list. We think that this can be done by a clause simply referring to the sections of the new legislation which render the terms of no effect.[149]

4.124　**We invite views as to whether the list, and therefore the preventive powers under UTCCR regulations 10-15, should be extended so as explicitly to include contract terms which are automatically of no effect under other parts of the new legislation.[150]**

THE NEW EXAMPLES

4.125　Even if the list is reformulated using more familiar language and concepts, it may be hard for the lay reader to appreciate, from a general description of the type of clause, what is actually involved. We think it would be useful to include specific examples of clauses in the list. There would be a provision that the examples are not to be interpreted as limiting the way in which the general words of each item in the list are to be construed. We think it might also be helpful if the new legislation included examples of the kinds of term which are brought within the scope of UCTA by section 13 [s 25(3)].[151] So that consultees may see what we intend, the next paragraph gives some draft examples, and more are contained in Schedule 2 to the draft Bill in Appendix B. Alternatively, it may be thought better to leave examples to publications such as the OFT Guidance.

4.126　The examples of the kinds of term which are brought within the scope of UCTA by section 13 [s 25(3)] might be as follows:

(1)　making the consumer's rights or remedies subject to restrictive conditions (for example, that claims must be notified within a short period, or that defective repairs will only be put right if the goods are returned to a particular place at the consumer's expense);

(2)　excluding or restricting any right or remedy that would otherwise be available to the consumer (for example, preventing the consumer from terminating the contract, or limiting the damages that may be claimed, or

---

[148]　Paras 4.34 – 4.35 above.

[149]　Sched 2 to the draft Bill contains no such clause because the Bill does not yet replicate the preventive powers under UTCCR regs 10–15 to which such a clause would be relevant.

[150]　The issue of non-contractual notices that purport to exclude business liability in tort [delict] for death or personal injury caused by negligence is discussed in Part VII below.

[151]　See para 4.35(4) and n 42 above.

preventing the consumer from deducting any compensation due to her from any payments still due by the consumer);

(3) providing that a consumer who exercises her rights or remedies will be subject to some prejudice (for example, providing that the consumer will invalidate any rights which she has against the business if she exercises a right to have defective work put right by a third party); and

(4) excluding or restricting rules of evidence or procedure (for example, providing that a decision of the business, or a third party, that work done is not defective is to be conclusive).

Such terms would probably fall within at least one category in the indicative list,[152] so, if the new indicative list is to include examples, arguably there should be examples of these terms too. However, whereas the indicative list is relevant only to the provisions that prevent reliance on terms which are unfair, UCTA section 13 [s 25(3)] applies equally for the purpose of the provisions that render certain terms automatically invalid. Its counterpart in the new legislation therefore cannot appear solely in the new indicative list. In the draft Bill, clause 16 provides that certain kinds of term or notice count as an "exclusion or restriction of liability" and clause 17 gives one or more examples of each kind. Paragraph 1 of the new indicative list in Schedule 2 includes terms in a consumer contract which attempt to exclude or restrict liability to the consumer for breach of contract, and cross-refers to the examples of this in clause 17.

Liability for death or personal injury

4.127 UTCCR Schedule 2, paragraph 1(a) refers to terms which have the object or effect of

> excluding or limiting the legal liability of a seller or supplier in the event of the death of a consumer or personal injury to the latter resulting from an act or omission of that seller or supplier.

Many of the terms which fall under this sub-paragraph are automatically of no effect, because the liability in question is either for negligence [breach of duty][153] or for a failure of the goods supplied to comply with the implied terms as to quality or correspondence with description or sample under the SGA 1979 or parallel legislation or common law rules for other contracts.[154] Thus they would be covered by the provision proposed in the previous paragraphs. However it is conceivable that liability for death or personal injury might arise from failure to comply with some other express or implied term of the contract. This would fall under the "fair and reasonable test" provisionally proposed for terms in general, and such clauses should arguably be referred to in the reformulated list. But very few cases will fall into this category, and we therefore doubt that it would be

---

[152] UTCCR Sched 2, para 1(b): see para 4.128 below.

[153] This cannot be excluded or restricted under UCTA s 2(1) [s 16(1)(a)]; and see clause 1 of the draft Bill.

[154] This cannot be excluded or restricted under UCTA ss 6(2) and 7(2) [ss 20(1), 21(1)(a) and (3)(a)]; and see clauses 4 and 5 of the draft Bill.

helpful to refer to it in the Schedule. **We invite views on whether the reformulated list should refer to any clause which purports to exclude or restrict a business's liability for the death of or personal injury to a consumer and is not covered by the part of the list dealing with clauses that are automatically of no effect.**

Exclusion and limitation of liability clauses

4.128 Paragraph 1(b) of UTCCR Schedule 2 refers to terms

> inappropriately excluding or limiting the legal rights of the consumer vis-à-vis the seller or supplier or another party in the event of total or partial non-performance or inadequate performance by the seller or supplier of any of the contractual obligations, including the option of offsetting a debt owed to the seller or supplier against any claim which the consumer may have against him.

Again, many of the clauses that fall within this will automatically be of no effect, but there will be many others which will be subject to the proposed "fair and reasonable" test, so the substance of this paragraph must be retained. We think it is unnecessary and confusing to refer to the various ways in which the contract may have been broken by the business,[155] and suggest referring simply to "breach of contract". On the other hand, when it comes to types of exclusion or restriction, we think that it would be useful to give more than the single example of set-off. For reasons we have explained,[156] other examples are contained in the draft Bill in clause 16, which is supplemented by examples in clause 17. Paragraph 1 of Schedule 2 to the draft Bill therefore refers simply to "Terms which attempt to exclude or restrict liability to the consumer for breach of contract", and refers to clause 17 for examples of such terms.

4.129 The final words of UCTA section 13(1) [s 25(5)[157]] provide:

> ... and (to that extent) sections 2 and 5 to 7 also prevent excluding or restricting liability by reference to terms and notices which exclude or restrict the relevant obligation or duty.

---

[155] This wording probably reflects the tradition of some continental systems which treat total and partial non-performance, and different forms of non-performance such as non-performance and defective performance, under separate legal provisions and lack a unitary concept of breach of contract. A prime example is the German BGB. Recent reform proposals would introduce the unitary notion: see H-W Micklitz, "The New German Sales Law: Changing Patterns on the Regulation of Product Quality" in (2002) Journal of Consumer Policy (forthcoming).

[156] See para 4.126 above.

[157] Section 25(5) provides:

> In sections 15 and 16 and 19 to 21 of this Act, any reference to excluding or restricting liability for breach of an obligation or duty shall include a reference to excluding or restricting the obligation or duty itself.

4.130 These words have been judicially criticised as "obscure".[158] They were aimed at clauses which attempt to exclude altogether some obligation or duty that otherwise would exist, for example a clause which purports to exclude "all conditions or warranties, express or implied", or to deny that there is any obligation to take reasonable care.[159] The idea seems to be that a clause which attempts to prevent the business having an obligation or duty which it would have in the absence of the clause, should be treated as an exclusion of liability for breach of the duty. As Slade LJ said, delivering the judgment of the Court of Appeal in *Phillips Products Ltd v Hyland*:

> ... in considering whether there has been a breach of any obligation ... or of any duty ..., the court has to leave out of account, at this stage, the contract term which is relied on by the defence as defeating the plaintiffs' claim for breach of such obligation or such duty ...[160]

This has been described as a "but for" test.[161]

4.131 To ensure that this rule is preserved, clause 16(1)(e) of the draft Bill provides that a term which excludes or restricts an obligation or duty should be treated as an exclusion or restriction of the liability to which that obligation or duty would give rise; and clause 17(5) gives as an example a term which excludes "all conditions and warranties".

Consumer bound when the business is not

4.132 UTCCR Schedule 2, paragraph 1(c) lists terms which have the object or effect of

---

[158] By Lord Donaldson MR in *Stewart Gill Ltd v Horatio Myer & Co Ltd* [1992] QB 600, 605–606.

[159] In the case of a notice excluding liability in tort [delict], the target was a notice that purports to exclude the duty of care. See the draft clause 12(2) in the Second Report, p 147.

[160] [1987] 1 WLR 659, 664.

[161] Both the "but for" test and the last part of s 13(1) [s 25(5)] have been criticised for failing to draw a "distinction between the purely verbal displacement of a primary duty and the circumstantial displacement of the primary duty": D Yates, *Exclusion Clauses in Contracts* (2nd ed 1982) p 78; E Macdonald, *Exemption Clauses and Unfair Terms* (1999) pp 92–95. What seems to be meant is that the court should not pretend that the term does not exist at all; rather it should decide whether in all the circumstances including the existence of the clause (which might have been drawn to the consumer's attention), the duty would arise. Thus if a car is sold "with all faults", and in all the circumstances of the case it is clear that the consumer intends to buy the car "as it is", the clause should not be treated as "excluding a duty" and therefore of no effect. On the other hand if the only reason that there might be no obligation to deliver a car of satisfactory quality is that there is a clause to that effect in the terms of the written contract signed by the consumer, but (for instance) there is no reason to think that the consumer was aware of the clause, the clause should be treated as excluding the duty. Thus, as in *Smith v Eric S Bush* [1990] 1 AC 831 (HL), the court will not treat such a clause as preventing the duty arising but as an exclusion/limitation clause that is subject to the controls. See also *McCullagh v Lane Fox & Partners Ltd* [1996] 1 EGLR 35. We do not think that the proposed formulation would prevent a court from reaching a just result in the first sort of case where, for instance, neither party intended that the seller should be under any obligation as to quality; it would simply conclude that, even if the clause were invalid, the circumstances of the case did not give rise to any obligation or duty.

making an agreement binding on the consumer whereas provision of services by the seller or supplier is subject to a condition whose realisation depends on his own will alone.

4.133 This appears to refer to two situations neither of which, so far as we are aware, is common in the UK. The first is where the consumer is said to be bound by an offer which has not been accepted by the business.[162] The second is the so-called "potestative condition", where the business's obligation to perform is dependent on the occurrence of some condition and the occurrence or non-occurrence of that condition is entirely within the control of the business.[163] An example might be a loan agreement which purports to bind the consumer/borrower but which states that the business/lender is under no obligation to advance any money unless the loan is approved by its managers.

4.134 We doubt whether either type of clause is commonly found in consumer contracts in the UK. Quite apart from UTCCR, we consider it very unlikely that the consumer would be bound by the contract in either case. In the first case the consumer would normally be free to withdraw the offer and in the second the court would probably hold that the contract was no more than a declaration of intent by the business. However, were such terms to be used in the UK they would be very misleading to consumers, who would be unlikely to know their rights; and it seems sensible to retain them in the list so that it is clear that action may be taken to prevent their use.[164]

4.135 There is another situation which may fall within the paragraph. A contract may be concluded but one party may not be obliged to perform its main obligations until a condition is fulfilled [in Scots law, "purified"]. For example, a sale of land might be subject to planning permission. If the non-consumer is expected to take steps which are a necessary preliminary for fulfilment of the condition, such as making a proper application for permission, but excludes liability for failing to do so, the term could be unfair. However, we doubt whether this situation is sufficiently common in consumer contracts to make it worth including in the new list.

Deposits and retention of money paid

4.136 Paragraph 1(d) of UTCCR Schedule 2 refers to terms

---

[162] In a number of legal systems an offer, at least when it is stated as having a time limit, is irrevocable within that time: see H Kötz, *European Contract law: Formation, Validity and Content of Contract: Contract and Third Parties*, vol 1 (1997) p 23. In English law the offer may be revoked at any time before acceptance unless the offeror has promised to keep it open and either the promise was made by deed or the offeree provided consideration for it. In Scots law, the offer can also be revoked at any time before acceptance unless the offeror has promised to keep it open. As the promise is made in the course of business, there is no need for it to be constituted in writing. There is no need for the offeree/promisee to have provided consideration: Requirements of Writing (Scotland) Act 1995, s 1(2)(a)(ii).

[163] B Nicholas, *French Law of Contract* (2nd ed 1992) pp 159 ff.

[164] See para 2 of Sched 2 to the draft Bill. For a discussion of preventing the use of unfair terms which are in any event of no legal effect, see para 3.119 above.

permitting the seller or supplier to retain sums paid by the consumer where the latter decides not to conclude or perform the contract, without providing for the consumer to receive compensation of an equivalent amount from the seller or supplier where the latter is the party cancelling the contract.[165]

4.137 This paragraph appears to cover a number of different situations:

(1) where the consumer is entitled to withdraw from the contract, but will lose a sum paid (probably a deposit);[166] the business is equally entitled to withdraw, but without having to pay an equivalent amount to the consumer;[167]

(2) where, if the consumer wrongfully refuses to perform the contract, he will lose a sum paid; but there is no provision for an equivalent amount to be paid by the business if it wrongfully refuses to perform;[168] and

(3) (possibly) where the consumer will lose a sum paid if he decides justifiably not to perform because the business has committed a serious breach of the contract.[169]

4.138 Our difficulty is that we are not convinced that in any of the three situations the paragraph produces results that are sensible for UK law. In the first, we think that a term providing that, if the consumer cancels, he will lose a deposit paid, may be fair even if the agreement also gives the business the right to cancel but in that event merely requires the business to return the consumer's deposit (rather than twice the deposit as paragraph (d) appears to require). In the second case, the paragraph seems to propose inappropriate solutions: we do not see why there needs to be a corresponding penalty clause.

---

[165] As a matter of construction the paragraph does not seem to require that the "loss of deposit" be matched by compensation where the business is not given a right to cancel. Nor does it govern the case where the deposit is simply unreasonably large: but see para 1(e).

[166] The paragraph refers to the consumer deciding not to "conclude or perform"; but in English and Scots law if the contract is not concluded the business will have no right to retain any sums paid but equally cannot be liable to pay compensation. (The consumer would not have the right to recover a payment if the arrangement were an "option" contract, but this cannot be what is contemplated since under an option the business would not have the right to withdraw.)

[167] Thus a holiday-maker may have the right to cancel her booking until a number of days before the holiday, losing her deposit, but without further liability; the holiday company may have the right to cancel the holiday if, for example, insufficient bookings are received for it to be viable. It seems that under UTCCR the "loss of deposit clause" would be "potentially unfair" unless the holiday company, were it to cancel, would be liable not only to refund the deposit, but also to pay the same amount again to the holiday-maker.

[168] It is not clear whether this means that the "loss of deposit" clause must be matched by a clause providing for agreed compensation of an equivalent amount, or whether it would suffice that the business should be liable for at least an equivalent amount of unliquidated damages.

[169] This is referred to in the OFT Guidance, para 4.2, though to treat the paragraph as referring to this situation seems to give little weight to the second part of it.

4.139   We note that the OFT has attempted to make sense of paragraph 1(d) by interpreting it as striking at all clauses which provide that the consumer, whether he has the right to withdraw or has broken the contract, will lose prepayments of amounts that go beyond the business's loss.[170] We think that it would be better to replace the sub-paragraph by a provision covering a term which would entitle the business, when the consumer exercises a right to withdraw from the contract or when the contract is terminated for the consumer's breach, to retain a payment (made by way of deposit or otherwise) which is not reasonable in amount.[171] We consider that this would be sufficiently close to the paragraph in the Annex to the Directive from which UTCCR Schedule 2, paragraph 1(d) is copied to avoid any real risk of challenge for non-implementation. **We provisionally propose that paragraph 1(d) of the indicative list be replaced by a reference to a term entitling the business, on withdrawal by the consumer or termination of the contract because of the consumer's breach, to retain a pre-payment which is not reasonable in amount.**

Penalty clauses

4.140   Paragraph 1(e) of UTCCR Schedule 2 refers to terms

> requiring any consumer who fails to fulfil his obligation to pay a disproportionately high sum in compensation.

4.141   This would apply to clauses by which a party agrees that, if she breaks the contract, she will pay a fixed or determinable sum as compensation, and the sum exceeds a genuine pre-estimate of the likely loss. In UK law such clauses are regarded as "penalty" clauses and are unenforceable.[172] Thus there is no need to include them on the list for the purposes of protecting individual consumers; but to do so makes it easier for the OFT and others to prevent their use.[173] We consider that this paragraph should be reformulated in terms which make clear what test is to be applied (that is, explain the penalty rule).[174]

4.142   The OFT Guidance points out that the sub-paragraph also covers clauses which require the consumer to reimburse the business for its costs, without limiting

---

[170]   OFT Guidance, para 4.5.

[171]   This effectively applies the "penalty clause rule" to deposits and forfeiture of payment clauses, whether the consumer is in breach of contract or is exercising a contractual right to withdraw.

[172]   See *Dunlop Pneumatic Tyre Co Ltd v New Garage & Motor Co Ltd* [1915] AC 79 (HL).

[173]   In fact the paragraph may go slightly wider than "penalty clauses". Whether a clause is penal is, in English and Scots law, determined by asking whether it was a genuine pre-estimate of the loss judged at the time the contract was made. If it was, the clause is valid even if the amount agreed turns out to be much greater than the actual loss. The paragraph seems to reflect the continental tradition, which is to ask whether the sum is disproportionate to the loss actually suffered. However, as the fairness of the term is to be judged as of the time the contract is made, we think that the paragraph can only be read as referring to the anticipated loss, as the actual loss cannot be known at that time.

[174]   Our draft reflects current law in the UK, but the Scottish Law Commission has proposed significant amendments: see the Report on Penalty Clauses (1999) Scot Law Com No 171.

them to what was reasonable, or to reimburse its expenses without taking into account what could reasonably have been avoided. We consider that the reformulation should cover these points,[175] and paragraph 4 of Schedule 2 to the draft Bill accordingly gives examples of terms which it would cover.

4.143 **It is our provisional view that the list should contain examples. We invite comments on this general question as well as on the individual examples that we have discussed, and on the relevant parts of the draft Bill,[176] in terms of both substance and style.**

Existing exemptions

4.144 Like the Annex to the Directive, paragraph 2 of UTCCR Schedule 2 exempts certain types of term from the indicative list. The exceptions relate to terms in financial services contracts allowing termination by the supplier, or allowing it to alter interest rates and other charges, where there is a valid reason;[177] allowing suppliers to alter unilaterally the conditions of contracts of an indefinite duration, provided adequate notice is given and the consumer has the right to terminate the contract; various terms in transactions in transferable securities, financial instruments and other products or services;[178] and price indexation clauses.[179] We are not aware that these exemptions have caused any difficulty. In any event they do not prevent the clause being held to be unfair.

4.145 **We invite views as to whether the types of terms listed in paragraph 2 of UTCCR Schedule 2 should continue to be set out as exceptions to the indicative list.**

(e) Burden of showing that term is reasonable

4.146 Under UCTA the burden of showing that a term is reasonable is on the party claiming that the term satisfies the requirement of reasonableness, but of course this affects only a limited range of terms. The new legislation, like UTCCR, will affect a wider range of terms. Would it be appropriate to place the burden on the business to show that any of its terms (other than exempt "core" terms) is fair? Or would it be better (as in UTCCR) to leave the burden on the consumer in all cases; or something in between? We have not found these questions to be easy.

---

[175] The OFT Guidance also refers to "disguised penalties", in the sense of payments that must be made when the consumer exercises a so-called right to withdraw from the contract. These will be within the proposed reformulation of sub-para (d): see above.

[176] Sched 2.

[177] Para 2(a) and (b).

[178] Para 2(c).

[179] Para 2(d).

4.147 We do not think it would be right to apply the UTCCR approach of leaving it to the consumer to show that the term is unfair in all cases.[180] This would weaken the consumer's position in comparison to the position under UCTA.[181]

4.148 One alternative approach is to say that, even though the new legislation would affect a greater range of terms, it would still be justifiable to place the burden on the business. This is because the reasonableness of the term will not come into question unless it alters the consumer's rights or obligations from what they would otherwise be under the normal rules of contract law for the kind of transaction in question.[182] It does not seem inappropriate to require the business to justify this departure from the normal rule, whether it be, for example, a clause allowing the retailer to charge the manufacturer's list price at the date of delivery or a limitation of liability clause.[183]

4.149 A second alternative is to say that a business which follows the proposed guidance by avoiding the listed terms should get some benefit from doing so. Therefore a business which includes in its contract a term which is in the list of terms that are potentially unfair should bear the burden of proving that the term is fair and reasonable. Other terms should also be subject to review but only if the consumer shows, or the court is satisfied,[184] that the term is not fair.

4.150 **We invite views on the question whether (a) the burden of proving that a term is fair should always rest on the business, or (b) the consumer should have to show that the term is unfair unless the term in question is on the indicative list. (The draft in Appendix B contains alternative formulations on this point.)**

(7) Ancillary questions

4.151 In this section we deal with a number of ancillary questions, concerning the definitions of "consumer", "business" and "contract"; the position of third party beneficiaries; the effect of invalid exclusions or restrictions of liability; and attempts to evade the statutory controls.

---

[180] Subject to the point that the court may raise unfairness of its own motion: see para 3.80 above.

[181] On the general policy of not reducing existing consumer protection, see paras 4.22 – 4.29 above.

[182] If this approach were to be followed, it would probably be necessary to introduce a "threshold" test along the lines that the term should not be subject to challenge unless it caused a significant imbalance to the detriment of the consumer: see para 4.91 above.

[183] The burden of proof in collective proceedings is a separate issue: see paras 4.201 – 4.202 below.

[184] This is to deal with the problem identified in *Océano Grupo Editorial SA v Roció Murciano Quintero (C-240/98)* [2000] ECR I-4941 of the consumer who does not defend an action against her. See para 3.80 above.

(a) Definitions

"CONSUMER"

4.152 We noted in Part III that the definition of "consumer" under UTCCR differs from that of a person who "deals as consumer" under UCTA.[185]

Should companies ever count as consumers?

4.153 In the *R & B Customs* case[186] it was held that a company may deal as a consumer under UCTA, so that a clause excluding the supplier's liability to the company was of no effect. We return to this question in Part V where we discuss the protection needed for businesses. (Our provisional conclusion is that the definition of consumer can be limited to natural persons as under UTCCR. Companies will still be protected, but by a "reasonableness" test.)[187]

"In the course of business"

4.154 We also take up in Part V the question whether a natural person who makes a contract to obtain goods or services "related to" her business but not "in the course of" it should be treated as a consumer. (Our provisional conclusion is that this is not necessary.)

Mixed transactions

4.155 Some transactions, particularly purchases, may be made partly for business and partly for private purposes. Furthermore, the degree of intended business and private use can vary significantly. For example, a sole trader might purchase a vehicle for use in the business during the week, using it privately at weekends; whereas an individual might purchase a car for personal use, occasionally using it in the course of employment.[188] We therefore think that the most appropriate method of classifying these transactions as either consumer or business would be to assess each on its facts, according to the purpose for which it was predominantly intended.

4.156 Neither UCTA nor UTCCR seem to deal with the issue whether or not such a transaction should count as a consumer contract.[189] This does not seem to have

---

[185] Para 3.81 above.

[186] [1988] 1 WLR 321; see para 3.85 above.

[187] See Part V below. Draft SSGCR reg 6(1) would amend UCTA s 6 so that, for the purposes of SGA 1979 ss13–15 and SOGITA ss 9–11, a person would deal as consumer only if he is a natural person.

[188] Companies usually provide a procedure for claiming expenses in such situations.

[189] UCTA s 5 [s 19] does deal with "mixed" transactions; it applies when goods are being used or are in a person's possession "otherwise than exclusively for the purposes of a business". It seems that this formula was used because under s 5 it is the liability of the manufacturer or other person offering the guarantee which is in question, not that of the supplier, and it was thought that, as by definition there is no contract between manufacturer or other person and the claimant, the question of whether the contract of sale with the supplier was or was not made by the claimant "dealing as consumer" was not relevant. See the Second Report, para 102.

given rise to difficulties and we think that the decision as to whether a transaction is a business or a consumer transaction should continue to be determined by the judiciary.

4.157 **We provisionally propose that there should be no provision for "mixed" transactions in the new legislation, and that it should be left to the determination of the judge according to the predominant purpose of each transaction.**

"Goods of a type ordinarily supplied for private use and consumption"

4.158 We have seen that under UCTA, where the contract is one for the sale or supply of goods, a party will be "dealing as consumer" only if the goods supplied are of a type ordinarily supplied for private use or consumption.[190] There is no equivalent limitation in UTCCR. The aim of the restriction in UCTA (which was taken from the earlier SOGITA) was to make it easier for the seller or supplier to know whether the customer was to be treated as a consumer.[191] The Law Commissions considered a parallel requirement for consumer services contracts but concluded that it is not possible to identify a service as being of a kind normally provided for private (as opposed to business) use.[192] Should this aspect of UCTA be preserved?

4.159 For sales, the question is answered by SCGD, which prevents sellers of goods to consumers from contracting out of their obligations as to conformity whether or not the goods supplied are of a type ordinarily supplied for private use or consumption.

4.160 There remains the issue whether this requirement should continue to apply to contracts for the supply of goods other than sale in which terms excluding the supplier's liability are of no effect if the other party is "dealing as consumer". The advantage to suppliers of knowing more clearly where they stand has to be set against (a) the added complexity of continuing to have two definitions within the same piece of legislation and (b) the slightly reduced protection that consumers would have if this exception were retained. We note that the draft regulations proposed by the DTI for the implementation of SCGD would effect the same change in the case of non-sale contracts as SCGD requires in the case of contracts of sale.[193]

4.161 **Our provisional view is that the present requirement that, for a contract for the supply of goods to qualify as a consumer contract, the goods supplied under the contract should be of a type ordinarily supplied for private use or consumption should not be retained – whether or not the**

---

[190] Section 12(1)(c) [s 25]. The restriction seems to derive from the Molony report (see para 400).

[191] First Report, para 86.

[192] Second Report, para 150.

[193] Draft SSGCR, reg 6(3).

contract is one of sale (in which case this requirement must in any event be abandoned so as to comply with SCGD).

Sales by auction or competitive tender

4.162 The terms used at auction sales are subject to UTCCR but a buyer at auction or by competitive tender does not deal as a consumer within UCTA.[194] In practical terms the impact of this is that the seller may exclude or restrict its liability under SGA 1979 sections 13–15, provided the term satisfies the requirement of reasonableness. The question of auction sales had divided the members of the Law Commissions, some taking the view that the terms at auction should not be subject to any control at all, others being in favour of the solution ultimately adopted, but all were agreed that there should be no absolute ban on contracting out at auction. The principal reason appears to have been that it will often be difficult for the auctioneer to know whether the buyer is or is not a trader.[195]

4.163 The exemption cannot continue in its present form because SCGD provides only a limited exemption for sales at auction:

> Member States may provide that the expression "consumer goods" does not cover second-hand goods sold at public auction where consumers have the opportunity of attending the sale in person.[196]

Member States may allow sellers of second-hand goods generally to limit their liability but only by fixing a shorter time period, of no less than one year, during which the seller will be liable for non-conformity.[197]

4.164 **We provisionally propose that sales by auction of second-hand goods, where the consumer can be present at the sale, should continue to be exempted from the absolute ban on contracting out which applies to other consumer sales.** (Auction sales would not be distinguished from other consumer contracts for any other purpose; and exclusions of liability for conformity would still be subject to the reasonableness test.)

4.165 SCGD contains no explicit mention of sales by competitive tender.[198] Therefore **we provisionally propose that sales by competitive tender no longer be exempted from counting as "consumer" contracts.**

---

[194] UCTA, s 12(2) [s 25]; see para 3.87 above.

[195] See the Second Report, paras 115–119, especially 115(b). Of the various arguments in favour of treating auction sales differently, this is the one which seems still to apply after the decision that all sales made in the course of business should be subjected to the reasonableness test.

[196] Art 1(3). Draft SSGCR reg 6(2) would amend UCTA s 6 to provide that, for the purposes of SGA 1979 ss 13–15 or SOGITA ss 9–11, a person will not "be regarded as dealing as consumer if (a) the goods in question are second-hand goods, and (b) the contract is made at public auction where persons dealing as consumers have the opportunity of attending in person."

[197] Art 7(1), second para.

Holding oneself out as making the contract in the course of a business

4.166 UCTA excludes from the definition of "consumer" a person who holds himself out as making the contract in the course of a business.[199] Although it seems rather unfair that a person who has held himself out as buying in the course of a business should nonetheless be able to claim the protection due to a consumer, there is no equivalent rule in SCGD; therefore this limitation can no longer apply even to the absolute ban on contracting out in contracts of sale. It would be possible to preserve the exception in relation to other contracts for the supply of goods, but we see less advantage in doing so than in having a uniform regime for all contracts for the supply of goods to consumers. This is also what is proposed by the DTI.[200] Similarly it would be possible to preserve the exception in relation to contracts other than those for the supply of goods, but again we think it is more important to ensure consistency than to withhold the statutory protection in a few cases where it is arguably not deserved.

4.167 **We provisionally propose**

    (1)   that the absolute ban on contracting out in consumer contracts should apply in favour of a person who is in fact a consumer even if he has held himself out as making the contract in the course of a business – whether or not the contract is one of sale (in which case this is required by SCGD) – and

    (2)   that, for the purpose of determining whether a contract other than one for the sale or supply of goods is a consumer contract, and is therefore subject to the fair and reasonable test, the definition of a consumer should include such a person.

"BUSINESS"

"Occasional sales"

4.168 We suggested in Part III that there is probably no difference between the definitions of business in UCTA and UTCCR over the question of "occasional sales",[201] but this depends on which of two possible interpretations will be taken by the courts.

4.169 **We think that it should be made clear in the new legislation that a contract will be made in the course of a business if it "relates" to the business, even if it is a contract for the sale of an item not normally sold.**

---

[198] It is perhaps arguable that the word "auction" in consumer Directives should be interpreted to include sales by competitive tender. This is because Council Directive 1997/7/EC on the protection of consumers in respect of distance contracts (the "Distance Selling Directive") OJ L114, 4/6/1997, p 19, which gives cancellation rights to consumers who "shop" on the internet, does not apply to on-line auctions (Art 3(1)); see Consumer Protection (Distance Selling) Regulations 2000, SI 2000 No 2334, reg 5(1)(f). This is presumably because it is not feasible to sell by auction if the buyer has a right to cancel. The same is true, however, of sale by competitive tender; and it may therefore be that sale by competitive tender is to be considered as a form of sale by auction for the purpose of both that Directive and (by analogy) SCGD.

[199] Section 12(1)(a) [s 25(1)].

[200] Draft SSGCR, reg 6(3).

[201] See para 3.94 above.

Contracts with government departments or local or public authorities

4.170 We also suggested that there may possibly be a difference in that the definition of "business" in UCTA explicitly includes "the activities of any government department or local or public authority".[202] It is likely that UTCCR apply to contracts under which public authorities sell or supply to consumers, but this is not completely clear. Contracts in the normal sense between government departments or local or public authorities and consumers are common and we see no good reason for excluding their terms from the controls which will apply to other consumer contracts.

4.171 **We provisionally propose that the new legislation should make it clear that contracts with government departments or local or public authorities may count as consumer contracts.**

"CONTRACT"

4.172 In Part III we said that it is uncertain whether, or to what extent, UTCCR apply to arrangements under which goods or services are supplied and which do not amount to contracts under UK law. It has been argued that the ECJ may develop an autonomous interpretation of the word "contract" in the Directive so that the Directive will apply to some such arrangements.[203]

4.173 Unless it is required by the Directive, we do not think that there is a particular need to ensure that the UK legislation does include such arrangements. Supply under non-contractual arrangements is principally relevant to privatised industries which are subject to regulation, and we understand that the firms involved are normally required by the terms of their licence to use terms which are fair to consumers. We have not heard of significant problems and assume that this provides adequate control. Nor do we think that other non-contractual arrangements for the supply of services (for example, health or education) are appropriate to bring within the scheme of the legislation.

4.174 Were the ECJ to take an autonomous view of contract so as to include any such arrangements, it would be necessary to ensure that the UK legislation implemented this. In our view that can be achieved simply by referring in the new legislation to consumer "contracts". This can then be interpreted by UK courts in line with any ruling from the European Court in Luxembourg.

4.175 **We provisionally propose that the new legislation should refer simply to "contracts", so that it may be interpreted in line with any ECJ interpretation of what constitutes a contract for the purposes of the Directive.**

(b) Third party beneficiaries

4.176 We explained in Part III that third party beneficiaries of a contract who have the right to enforce a term of the contract under the Contracts (Rights of Third

---

[202] Section 14 [s 25(1)].

[203] Para 3.106 above.

Parties) Act 1999 cannot rely on any provisions of UCTA except section 2(1).[204] In Scots law a third party with a *ius quaesitum tertio* is unlikely to be able to rely on many of the provisions of UCTA as he is unlikely to be regarded as a party to the contract. However, he may apparently rely on any part of section 16, so that he may challenge clauses excluding business liability not only for death or personal injury but also for other loss or damage caused by breach of duty. UTCCR do not seem to apply to third party beneficiaries at all and, while the language of SCGD is not incompatible with its application to third party beneficiaries, we do not believe that it will be held to apply in favour of them.

4.177   Because this matter has been covered by very recent legislation in England, and we have received no complaint as to its operation, we propose that the new legislation should take the same approach as the existing law. Thus (in England) the promisor would be prevented from limiting its liability[205] to the third party for death or personal injury caused by negligence; in other cases the third party would not be able to challenge the fairness of the terms. In cases in which the promisee takes action to enforce the terms of the contract for the third party's benefit the terms would be subject to the usual controls. In Scotland there has been no call for change, and we provisionally propose that the status quo be preserved there also, so that such terms should be of no effect in the first case and be subject to challenge in both the other situations.

4.178   **We provisionally propose no change in any of the UK jurisdictions as to the rules governing the right of third party beneficiaries to challenge unfair terms in the contracts from which they derive their rights.**

(c) Effect of invalid exclusion or restriction

4.179   If an exclusion or restriction of liability or other term is invalid under UCTA it is simply of no effect, but the remainder of the contract stands.[206] This causes no problem with exclusion and limitation of liability clauses; the parties revert to the general rules on liability. UTCCR cover a greater range of terms and, while in many cases the contract will be workable without the offending term, this may not always be the case.[207] Regulation 8 therefore provides that the offending term shall not be binding on the consumer and the contract shall continue to bind the parties "if it is capable of continuing in existence without the unfair term". Given that the new legislation will cover the same wide range of terms, there must be the possibility that, when the unreasonable terms have been removed, the remainder of the contract will be insufficient to be enforceable (or to be enforced without hardship to one party or the other).

4.180   **Our provisional conclusion is that an equivalent is needed to UTCCR regulation 8 (effect of unfair term).**

---

[204]   Which prevents the exclusion or restriction of business liability for death or personal injury caused by negligence.

[205]   If this were business liability: see para 3.9 above.

[206]   See paras 3.108 – 3.113 above.

[207]   Only in very exceptional cases should the courts consider that the contract is not capable of continuing in existence without the term: M Tenreiro, "The Community Directive on Unfair Terms and National Legal Systems" (1995) 3 ERPL 273.

4.181 There is a difficult point as to exactly how this should be implemented. Under UCTA the question is whether the term (normally an exclusion or limitation of liability clause) is "a fair and reasonable one to be included"[208] or, for Scotland, whether it was "fair and reasonable to incorporate" the term in a contract.[209] In Part III we concluded that, in Scotland, a term which partly offends Part II of UCTA is wholly ineffective.[210] We also noted that, in *Stewart Gill Ltd v Horatio Myer & Co Ltd*,[211] the Court of Appeal held that the words of Part I mean that (in England) an unreasonable part of a term cannot be severed so that the rest can then be relied upon. Stuart Smith LJ said:

> Nor does it appear to me to be consistent with the policy and purpose of the Act to permit a contractor to impose a contractual term, which taken as a whole is completely unreasonable, to put a blue pencil through the most offensive parts and say that what is left is reasonable and sufficient to exclude or restrict his liability in a manner relied upon.[212]

4.182 This approach has a significant function in consumer protection: it prevents the business from using over-wide clauses and then, when challenged, seeking to rely on only the parts of the clause that may be reasonable.

4.183 UTCCR provide that "an unfair term ... shall not be binding".[213] It is not clear whether the court can put a blue pencil through the offending parts of a clause and leave the rest, but it seems likely that it can. Suppose a single clause were to provide that the consumer might be required to pay a higher price in two different circumstances, and the extra charge in one situation would be entirely fair but not that in the other; could the court strike out the unfair charge leaving the fair one? It seems likely that the court is entitled, under UTCCR, to treat a clause as divisible into separate "terms" and to strike down only those which are unfair, leaving the rest.[214] However, it would be possible for the new legislation to require

---

[208] Section 11(1).

[209] Section 24(1).

[210] See para 3.110 above.

[211] [1992] QB 600 (CA).

[212] [1992] QB 600, 609. Lord Donaldson MR put it graphically, at p 607:

> The issue is whether "the term [the whole term and nothing but the term] shall have been a fair and reasonable one to be included."

A previous, unreported Court of Appeal case, *Trolex Products Ltd v Merrol Fire Protection Engineers Ltd*, 20 November 1991, seems to disagree to some extent. The court held that where a term purports to exclude liability which under UCTA cannot be excluded in any circumstances and also liability which can be excluded subject to the test of reasonableness, the term is ineffective to exclude the former liability but could be upheld as reasonable in respect of the latter exclusion. The court expressly left open the question of whether one can sever when only reasonableness is in issue (ie when no part is automatically unfair).

[213] Reg 8(1).

[214] This gets some support from *DGFT v First National Bank plc* [2001] UKHL 52, [2002] 1 AC 481 (HL), where Counsel for the DGFT seems to have accepted that the first part of the clause in question, stating that interest was payable on the amount outstanding, was fair but not the subsequent parts of the clause, providing that interest should be payable even after

that the court strike down the clause as a whole, in order to deter businesses from including over-wide clauses in the hope of deterring claims and then, if the claimant persists nonetheless, seeking to rely on the parts of the clause that are reasonable.

4.184 We are conscious of this advantage of the "no blue pencil" approach. However, the approach works better with exclusion clauses, which are always to some extent to the consumer's disadvantage, than it would with other potentially unfair terms, which might be combined with terms that actually benefit the consumer. Once controls go wider than exclusion clauses, it is our provisional view that to strike down the whole of a clause because a part of it is unfair may result in the consumer losing parts of the clause which are beneficial to him.

4.185 We think, however, that the new legislation could reach a satisfactory compromise between the two approaches by treating the whole clause as invalidated except to the extent that it is beneficial to the consumer. Accordingly, clause 6(2) of the draft Bill provides that clause 6 will apply only to the part of the term that is detrimental.

4.186 **We provisionally propose that the new legislation should state that, where part of a term is detrimental to the consumer and the rest is not, it is only the detrimental part that is of no effect if it is unfair.**

(d) Evasion of the controls

SECONDARY CONTRACTS

4.187 It is obviously important to ensure that the controls over unreasonable terms are not circumvented by businesses providing fair terms in one contract and then securing the consumer's agreement to a separate contract which limits the consumer's rights under the first one, except where the second contract is part of a genuine settlement of an existing dispute. Section 10 of UCTA [s 23[215]], which may in part be aimed at this problem, has given rise to difficulties of interpretation as it is not easy to distinguish the unacceptable evasion from the (acceptable) settlement.

4.188 Under the unified regime it may not be necessary to have a specific provision for "evasions", as the regime will apply to any kind of term, so that the terms of the secondary contract itself might simply be declared unenforceable. Instead a specific exception could be made for settlements, though even this may not be strictly necessary as the agreement to drop the claim and the promise to pay a sum in settlement would presumably be "core terms".

4.189 However, the "core terms" exemption gives some pause for doubt on the question of "evasions". If the secondary contract were no more than an agreement, in advance of any dispute having arisen (that is, not a settlement) that the consumer would not enforce her rights under the main contract, that would seem to be a core term of the secondary contract and therefore exempt from control. Of course

---

judgment and that the obligation to pay it should not merge with the judgment. See the speech of Lord Hope, at [41].

[215] This is in rather different (and clearer) terms.

this is unlikely, if only because it would be so blatant; it is much more likely that the "evasive" clause would be hidden in a larger contract (for example, to service the goods bought). We think that this problem can be overcome by subjecting any term in the secondary contract to the same controls to which it would have been subject had it been in the main contract (where of course it would not have been a core term). There should be an exception for genuine settlements.

4.190 The other problem at which section 10 [s 23] of UCTA was aimed was the case of an agreement between A and B in which it is agreed that B will not enforce his rights under a second contract between himself and C. This will equally not need specific provision under the new regime unless the point made in the previous paragraph is a real risk.

4.191 However, if, as we provisionally propose, the new legislation preserves those sections of UCTA which render certain clauses of no effect, a provision will be needed to prevent evasion of *these* by secondary contract (the relevant term of a secondary contract should also be of no effect, rather than being subject to a reasonableness test). We think the formula we suggested at paragraph 4.189 above would achieve the right result in this case also. Again there should be an exception for genuine settlements.

4.192 **Our provisional conclusion is that there should be a provision subjecting terms in "secondary contracts" to the same controls as if they appeared in the main contract. Genuine agreements to settle an existing dispute should be exempted.**

EVASION BY CHOICE OF LAW

4.193 Consumers should not be deprived of their rights by a clause stating that the contract shall be subject to a foreign law when the contract would otherwise be governed by the law of England or of Scotland. UTCCR seem to allow the choice of the law of another Member State although the contract has a close connection, or even its closest connection, with a UK jurisdiction.[216] This seems wrong in principle, since UK legislation may give greater protection than that of the Member State chosen and to subject the contract to the latter law might well be unfair.

4.194 **It should be made clear that the rules on unfair clauses in consumer contracts are mandatory so that, if the contract has a close connection to the UK, they will be applied under the Rome Convention despite a choice of another system of law.[217]**

(8) Prevention

4.195 UTCCR have extended the power to bring proceedings for an injunction [interdict] against persons appearing to be using or recommending the use of unfair terms in contracts concluded with consumers to a number of "qualifying bodies", including not only the DGFT but a variety of industry regulators, all

---

[216] See para 3.116 above.

[217] As yet the draft Bill includes no provision to this effect.

weights and measures departments in Great Britain, the Consumers' Association and, most recently, the Financial Services Authority.[218] Whether or not this was required by the Directive, there seems no reason to change the provisions if they are working well.

4.196 It is possible that the scope and terms of review of unreasonable clauses under the new instrument will be slightly wider than under UTCCR.[219] It would not be sensible to confine the preventive powers just to those required by the Directive.

4.197 In Part III we noted doubts about the position where a term has not effectively been incorporated into the contract – is the business "using" the term?[220] – and as to whether a term may be unfair simply because it is not "in plain, intelligible language". Earlier we suggested that lack of "transparency"[221] of a term should be a ground for saying that the term is unfair.[222]

4.198 **We provisionally propose that, to avoid any doubt, the legislation should provide that the authorised bodies may take steps to prevent a business purporting to use a term which in practice the business does not effectively incorporate into the contract, and also any term which is unfair because it is not transparent even if in substance the term is fair.**

4.199 We also noted in Part III that it has been suggested that terms which omit important information might not be regulated effectively under the current regime.[223] However, we are unsure to what extent this is a problem and whether it is necessary to increase the qualifying bodies' powers in this area.

4.200 **We invite views on whether and to what extent the omission of important information from terms should be subject to preventive control in the new legislation.**

4.201 The burden of proof was discussed in relation to the reasonableness test above.[224] It is suggested that a similar burden of proof could apply to preventive proceedings.

4.202 **We invite views on the question of who should bear the burden of proof in preventive proceedings.**

4.203 It is only possible for an authorised body to act against a term which is used or recommended for use regularly. This does not necessarily mean, however, that the authorised body should never be able to act against a term which was negotiated.

---

[218] Reg 12 and Sched 1. The Regulations contain a number of ancillary powers and obligations: regs 10–13. The FSA was added by the Unfair Terms in Consumer Contracts (Amendment) Regulations 2001.

[219] See, eg, para 4.194 above.

[220] Para 3.122 above.

[221] For the sense in which we use the word "transparent" see para 4.105 above.

[222] See para 4.106 above.

[223] See para 3.123 above.

[224] Paras 4.146 – 4.150 above.

We have been told that some firms are making a practice of "negotiating" the deposit to be paid by the consumer when she signs a contract for work and materials, but that the "negotiations" almost inevitably result in the consumer paying an unfairly large deposit. This is because the limits within which the salespersons can negotiate are tightly defined and if they make an agreement outside the limits they stand to lose their commission. This raises the question whether the authorised bodies should be empowered under the new legislation to act against particular "practices of negotiating unfair terms".[225]

4.204 **We provisionally propose that the listed bodies should have power to act against the use or proposal of any non-negotiated term which either would be of no effect or would be unreasonable under the proposed new regime. We invite views as to whether they should also have powers to act against practices of *negotiating* terms which are nonetheless unfair.**

(9) Provisions no longer required

4.205 There are three provisions in UCTA which may not need to be reproduced in the new legislation. The first is section 5 [s 19], which prevents exclusion or restriction of liability, by means of a term or notice in a "guarantee", of a manufacturer's or distributor's liability in tort [delict] to a person injured by goods proving defective while in consumer use. The question here is whether there is any need for a separate provision on guarantees. When it was first drafted, as part of the original Law Commission Bill,[226] the clause that became section 5 [s 19] would have had a substantial effect because what is now UCTA section 2 [s 16] was much narrower in its effect. The ban on excluding or restricting liability for death or personal injury caused by negligence would have been limited initially to the liability of employers to their employees, of carriers to passengers, of the occupiers or managers of car parks to users and to liability for accidents involving devices for the movement of persons.[227] There would have been power to extend the ban to other kinds of business liability by Ministerial Order.[228] In the event, Parliament passed section 2(1) [s 16(1)(a)] in very broad terms so that, quite apart from UCTA section 5 [s 19], a manufacturer can never exclude its liability for death or injury caused by negligence.

4.206 What the section does achieve is to prevent a manufacturer or distributor excluding its liability for other loss or damage caused to a consumer, whereas under section 2(2) [s 16(1)(b)] such a clause may be valid if it is fair and reasonable. In practice the only liability in question will be liability for damage to other property of the consumer.[229] This was seen by the Law Commissions to be

---

[225] An alternative would be to leave this question for more general legislation on unfair trading: cf para 4.67 above.

[226] Second Report, draft Bill, cl 10.

[227] Second Report, para 94; see para 2.12 above.

[228] Second Report, para 97.

[229] The manufacturer will not be liable in tort to the consumer for defects in the goods themselves after the decision of the House of Lords in *Murphy v Brentwood District Council* [1991] 1 AC 398. It is in theory possible for the manufacturer to be liable for defects in the goods under the principle of *Junior Books Ltd v Veitchi Co Ltd* [1983] 1 AC 520, which was

of importance.[230] However, its importance has been very much diminished by the Consumer Protection Act 1987. The 1987 Act makes the manufacturer or distributor liable for a defect in the goods without fault having to be proved by the consumer,[231] and it applies not only to death or personal injury but also to property damage above the value of £275.[232] That liability cannot be excluded.[233] Thus section 5 [s 19] seems to bite only in those cases where there is property damage of less than £275, and all it does is to make the clause automatically invalid rather than subject to a fair and reasonable test. Meanwhile, the overlaps in coverage between this section and section 2 of UCTA [s 16] and the Consumer Protection Act 1987 add significantly to the complexity of the law and make the position confusing to non-lawyers and lawyers alike. It is our provisional view that the additional protection provided by section 5 [s 19] is of such slight value to consumers that its value is outweighed by the complexity it causes.

4.207 **We provisionally propose that section 5 [s 19] of UCTA should not be reproduced in the new legislation.**

4.208 The second provision that may no longer be needed is UCTA section 9 [s 22]. Section 9(1) [s 22(a)] was inserted to ensure that the so-called doctrine of fundamental breach, under which a party might escape the effect of a clause which would otherwise limit his rights by terminating the contract for fundamental breach, would not prevent a valid clause applying. The doctrine has been overruled by the House of Lords.[234] Section 9(2) [s 22(b)] appears to have been aimed at the associated understanding that if the contract had been affirmed, the clause would be binding.

4.209 **Our provisional view is that neither part of section 9 [s 22(a), (b)] of UCTA is still required.**

4.210 The last is section 28, which was a temporary measure pending implementation of the Athens Convention. The Convention has now been implemented by the Merchant Shipping Act 1995, Schedule 6.

4.211 **Our provisional view is that section 28 of UCTA can now be repealed without replacement.[235]**

---

not overruled by the Murphy case. However, that depends on the consumer being able to show a special relationship with the manufacturer, and, as Lord Roskill pointed out in the *Junior Books* case (at p 547), that is very unlikely to occur in a consumer transaction.

[230] See the Second Report, paras 98–105.

[231] Section 2.

[232] Section 5(4).

[233] Section 7.

[234] *Photo Production Ltd v Securicor Transport Ltd* [1980] AC 827.

[235] And with it Merchant Shipping Act 1995, s 184(2). Discussions are currently under way to amend the Convention. We are told that, in the unlikely event that the Government is unhappy with the amendments, it would consider denouncing the Convention. If this were to occur, the proposed legislation would have to include a section comparable to s 28.

PART V
EXTENDING THE PROTECTION AGAINST UNFAIR TERMS TO BUSINESSES

1. INTRODUCTION

5.1　In Part III we examined the differences between UCTA and UTCCR, and we noted that UTCCR affect a wider range of potentially unfair clauses than UCTA, but that UTCCR apply only to consumer contracts. We also noted that UTCCR provide mechanisms designed to prevent the use of unfair terms, which UCTA does not. In this Part we consider whether (or to what extent) the protection given by UTCCR to consumers should be extended beyond consumer contracts to contracts between businesses, especially small businesses. We also consider whether, if this extension were made, some of the existing controls over exclusion and restrictions of liability under UCTA – which apply whether or not the clause was negotiated – could be removed; and how the rest of the existing controls of UCTA should be brought within the proposed new legislation.

2. EXISTING PROTECTION IN BUSINESS-TO-BUSINESS CONTRACTS

5.2　In Part III we pointed out that many of the controls against unfair terms contained in UCTA apply to contracts between one business and another ("business-to-business" contracts). Thus section 2 [s 16] applies to any exclusion or restriction of "business liability"[1] for negligence[2] whether the victim was acting in the course of business or not. Sections 6 and 7 [ss 20, 21] apply to the exclusion or restriction of various implied terms in contracts of sale, hire-purchase, barter, hire and work and materials.[3] While any exception or restriction on the obligation to give good title is automatically void, where the buyer or person to whom the goods were supplied is not dealing as a consumer, the exclusion or restriction of liabilities for breach of the other implied terms may be valid if it satisfies the requirement of reasonableness. These provisions apply to business-to-business contracts even if they were negotiated between the parties. Section 3 [s 17] applies in favour of a party who is dealing on the other's "written standard terms of business".[4]

---

[1]　See s 1(3). Part II (Scotland) does not use this phrase but the effect of s 16 is similar.

[2]　In Scotland, breach of duty as defined in s 25(1). Similarly, for England s 8 (which amends the Misrepresentation Act 1967, s 3) applies to any kind of contract but only to clauses excluding or restricting liability, or the remedies available, for misrepresentation.

[3]　Section 6 [s 20] applies to sale and hire-purchase, covering clauses which exclude or restrict liability for breach of the implied terms as to title, etc, and conformity with description or sample, quality or fitness for a particular purpose; s 7 does the equivalent for other types of contract "under or in pursuance" of which possession or ownership of goods passes. Section 21 (Scotland), while in slightly different terms, has the same effect. Section 6(1) [s 29(1)] prevents any business seller from excluding or restricting its liability under SGA 1979, s 12, whether or not the buyer is a consumer.

[4]　On s 17 see para 3.13, n 36 above.

5.3   We also saw that the controls of UCTA are largely restricted to exclusions or limitations of liability. Even section 3 [s 17] applies only to terms which purport to allow the party whose terms they are to perform in a way which is substantially different from what was reasonably expected, or not to perform at all.

5.4   Thus under the existing legislation a party who is acting in the course of a business is not protected against unfair terms which, for example, relate to his own performance rather than that of the other party. Some protection is provided by the common law, for example in relation to penalty clauses, but this is narrow and to some degree uncertain in its scope of application.[5]

5.5   The terms in consumer contracts which are regulated by UTCCR are significantly wider in scope than exclusion of liability clauses. UTCCR subject all the terms of the contract other than the "core terms" to a fairness test. Examples of potentially unfair clauses against which businesses, unlike consumers, are not protected include:

(1)   deposits and forfeiture of money paid clauses;

(2)   default rates of interest (unless these can be shown to be penalties);

(3)   automatic extension of contract clauses;

(4)   price variation clauses;

(5)   entire agreement clauses;

(6)   arbitration clauses;

(7)   jurisdiction clauses; and

(8)   termination clauses.

5.6   Consumer contracts are also subject to another layer of control under UTCCR which has no equivalent under UCTA. UTCCR give the DGFT and other authorised bodies the power to prevent the use or recommendation of unfair terms. The OFT has made wide and very effective use of these powers and, though it states that the use of unfair terms is still widespread, the impact of these controls on the market is far greater than would ever be achieved by individual consumers challenging the terms in their particular contracts. This is clearly demonstrated by the large numbers of terms which have been removed after intervention by the OFT when the term in question was either of no effect under UCTA, or almost certainly would be ineffective because it could not satisfy the statutory reasonableness test.

3. THE CASE FOR "INDIVIDUAL" CONTROLS OVER BUSINESS-TO-BUSINESS CONTRACTS

5.7   In passing UCTA, Parliament accepted that there is a case for "individual" control over some types of term in business-to-business contracts. (We use the word "individual" to distinguish these controls from the "preventive" controls referred to in the previous paragraph. "Preventive" controls will be discussed in Section 11

---

[5]   See paras 2.1 and 4.141 above.

of this Part.) As we explained in Part II,[6] unfairness may occur simply because one party may "agree" to terms without being aware of what they contain or of their impact (obviously this is a particular risk when the first party "agrees" to the other's standard terms); or one party may find it has no choice but to agree because all suppliers offer similar terms and it lacks sufficient bargaining power to get the terms altered. This may then leave it exposed. For example, a retailer might be advised that in its contracts with consumers it cannot use a clause allowing it to increase the price of goods, at least without giving the consumer the opportunity to cancel the contract, but find that the manufacturer or distributor which supplies him insists on his placing an order which is at a price to be fixed at the date of delivery and which cannot be cancelled. The plight of retailers was the main example given by the Law Commissions in discussing whether business sellers should be able to exclude or limit their liability under the SGA 1979 only if the clause was fair and reasonable.[7] However, in cases decided under UCTA and its predecessor, SOGITA, the courts have also found exemption clauses in individual business-to-business contracts to be unreasonable in a wide range of other circumstances.[8]

---

[6] See paras 2.4 – 2.8 above.

[7] First Report, paras 96–113. See also Tenreiro, who argues that some businesses find themselves "coincés entre deux réalités" as a result of terms which they cannot impose upon consumers, but which are imposed upon them by businesses further up the commercial chain: M Tenreiro and E Ferioli, "Examen comparatif des législations nationales transposant la directive 93/13/CEE" at the 1999 Brussels Conference "The 'Unfair Terms' Directive, Five Years On: Evaluation and Future Perspectives". Similarly H E Brandner and P Ulmer, "The Community Directive on Unfair Terms in Consumer Contracts: Some Critical Remarks on the Proposal Submitted by the EC Commission" (1991) 28 CMLR 647, 650, who conclude:

> Consideration should ... be given to the possibility of controlling the terms of unilaterally preformulated (standard) contracts either at all commercial levels, or at least at all commercial levels in those chains of sale which extend unbroken to the ultimate consumer.

The European Commission has also stated that

> extending control of unfair terms to the general terms and conditions used in relations between firms would make it easier for firms to shift their obligations vis-à-vis consumers to a higher level in the marketing chain.

Report on the Implementation of Council Directive 93/13/EEC of 5 April 1993 on Unfair Terms in Consumer Contracts (Brussels, 27.4.2000) COM (2000) 248, p 32.

[8] See *Gray v Chartered Trust Plc*, unreported 18 April 1984; *Rees Hough Ltd v Redland Reinforced Plastics Ltd* (1984) 27 BLR 136; *Stag Line Ltd v Tyne Shiprepair Group Ltd (The "Zinnia")* [1984] 2 Lloyd's Rep 211; *Phillips Products Ltd v Hyland* [1987] 1 WLR 659; *Charlotte Thirty Ltd v Croker Ltd* (1990) 24 Con LR 46; *Building Services (London) Ltd v Kerryredd Engineering Ltd*, unreported 12 April 1991; *Stewart Gill Ltd v Horatio Myer & Co Ltd* [1992] QB 600; *Edmund Murray Ltd v BSP International Foundations Ltd* (1993) 33 Con LR 1; *Fastframe Franchises Ltd v Lohinski*, unreported 3 March 1993; *Lease Management Services Ltd v Purnell Secretarial Services Ltd* (1994) 13 Tr LR 337; *Fillite Ltd v APV Pasilac Ltd*, unreported 26 January 1995; *Knight Machinery (Holdings) Ltd v Rennie* 1995 SLT 166; *The Salvage Association v CAP Financial Services Ltd* [1995] FSR 654; *AEG (UK) Ltd v Logic Resource Ltd*, unreported 20 October 1995; *St Albans City and District Council v International Computers Ltd* [1996] 4 All ER 481 (CA); *Sovereign Finance Ltd v Silver Crest Furniture Ltd* (1997) 16 Tr LR 370 (QB); *Esso Petroleum Co Ltd v Milton* [1997] 1 WLR 938; *Overseas*

4. Terms which are of no effect in business-to-business contracts

5.8 Under the existing law, certain terms are simply of no effect in business-to-business contracts. Clauses which purport to exclude business liability for death or personal injury caused by negligence or breach of duty fall into this group, and this should continue under the new legislation.[9] There are two further situations in which clauses in business contracts may be of no effect under UCTA. Before we consider extending the "fairness" test to other terms, this section considers whether terms should continue to be of no effect in these two situations.

(1) Business purchasers as consumers

5.9 We saw in Part III that in the *R & B Customs* case the Court of Appeal held that a company may "deal as consumer" within UCTA if it enters a transaction which is only incidental to its business activity and which is not of a kind it makes with any degree of regularity.[10] The effect is that any clause excluding or restricting the other party's liability for breach of sections 13–15 of the SGA 1979, or for breach of other equivalent legislation, is of no effect. There is a question whether a company or even a natural person making a contract to obtain goods or services "related to" but not "in the course of" business should continue to be treated as a consumer.[11]

5.10 We note that a number of Commonwealth jurisdictions do treat some business purchases as if they were consumer transactions so that any exclusion or restriction of liability under sale of goods and similar legislation will be ineffective.[12] Usually this applies only to buyers that are not corporations and if

---

Medical Supplies Ltd v Orient Transport Services Ltd [1999] 1 All ER (Comm) 981; *Pegler Ltd v Wang (UK) Ltd (No 1)* [2000] BLR 218; *Messer UK Ltd v Britvic Soft Drinks Ltd* [2002] EWCA Civ 548.

[9] It will be seen that the draft Bill treats all attempts to exclude business liability for negligence, including death or personal injury, in a single clause, cl 1. For the reasons for this see para 8.18 below.

[10] *R & B Customs Brokers Co Ltd v United Dominions Trust Ltd* [1988] 1 WLR 321 (purchase of car for personal and business use of directors): see para 3.85 above, where it is noted that in *Stevenson v Rogers* [1999] QB 1028 (sale by fisherman of his old working boat held to be made in course of business within SGA 1979, s 14(2)) Potter LJ, delivering the leading judgment, seems to cast some doubt on the *R & B* case. Only a natural person may count as a consumer under UTCCR. The ECJ has held in relation to another Directive that a trader cannot claim that because the transaction (a contract to advertise the sale of the business) was not a normal part of his business, he is entitled to the protection granted by the Directive to "consumers": see para 3.85, n 174 above. It has been held that a transaction will be made in the course of business if it is "integral to the business" even if it was not one made regularly: *Chester Grosvenor Hotel Co v Alfred McAlpine Management* (1991) 56 BLR 115 (QBD) (contract for refurbishment of hotel). See also *Chapman v Aberdeen Construction Group plc* 1993 SLT 1205.

[11] Draft SSGCR reg 6(1) would amend UCTA s 6 so that, for the purposes of SGA 1979 ss 13–15 and SOGITA 1973 ss 9–11, a person would deal as a consumer only if he is a natural person. However, a natural person would continue to be regarded as a consumer unless the contract were not made "in the course of a business." SCGD requires that contracts be treated as consumer contracts only if they are made "for purposes which are not related to" business: Art 1(1).

[12] See Appendix A, esp paras A.4 – A.7, A.12 – A.15 and A.19.

the goods were bought by the business for use, rather than for re-sale or manufacture into other goods.[13] The result is probably somewhat similar to the result in the *R & B Customs* case, in that purchases of goods bought regularly as materials or stock-in-trade will fall outside the controls.

5.11 We are not convinced, however, that clauses in business-to-business contracts should ever be treated as automatically ineffective, even if the contract was not a regular one for the business. We think it would be sufficient that they be subject to a fair and reasonable test. Although in the *R & B Customs* case the goods supplied may not have been either an item bought regularly by the company or integral to its business, the form of the transaction[14] may have been perfectly familiar to it and there seems little reason to hold the clause absolutely ineffective rather than subject to a reasonableness test. A second point is that the supplier will find it difficult to know whether the buying company is "dealing as consumer" without quite detailed enquiry as to the nature of its business. The same arguments apply, we believe, when the buyer is a natural person making the contract for purposes related to his business.

5.12 **It is our provisional view that a person who makes a contract to obtain goods or services "related to", even if not "in the course of", his business should be treated as dealing as a business and not as a consumer.[15]**

(2) Obligations as to title in the sale of goods

5.13 Section 6(1) [s 20(1)] of UCTA prevents any seller from excluding or restricting his obligations under the SGA 1979 section 12 (seller's implied undertakings as to title), irrespective of whether he is a business or a purely private seller and irrespective of whether the buyer is buying for business or private purposes. Section 7(3A) [s 21(3A)] does the equivalent in relation to implied terms as to title in other contracts for the transfer of goods under the Supply of Goods and Services Act 1982, section 2. It seems to us that the implied obligations in the respective sections reflect a fundamental principle of the law of moveable property, namely, that a seller or supplier of goods should have a good title to pass to the purchaser. At least in the business-to-business contracts with which this

---

[13] Eg Australia's federal Trade Practices Act 1974, s 4B; see para A.4 below.

[14] Essentially the transaction in *R & B Customs Brokers Co Ltd v United Dominions Trust Ltd* [1988] 1 WLR 321 was one in which a finance company provided a loan for the purchase of a car from a dealer and took quasi-security over the goods by buying the title from the dealer. The form is potentially confusing because the buyer may assume that it will have rights against the dealer, whereas its rights will normally be against the finance company, which, as it will not have seen the car, will not wish to take responsibility for its condition. This problem is well known in commercial circles and its ill effects are easily avoided by the buyer obtaining a full warranty from the dealer.

[15] In principle there might be an issue over the converse case, when it is the party supplying the goods or service who is making the contract for purposes related to his business but the transaction is not made regularly. In *Stevenson v Rogers* [1999] QB 1028 a transaction of this kind (the sale by a fisherman of his old working boat) was held to be made in the course of his business within SGA 1979, s 14(2). We think that the same approach would and should be applied to the question whether a supplier using a potentially unfair term is acting in the course of his business.

Part is concerned, no seller or supplier should be able to exclude this obligation.[16] Moreover, we are not aware of any difficulties over these provisions.

5.14 **We provisionally propose that the substance of UCTA sections 6(1) and 7(3A) [ss 20(1), 21(3A)] should be incorporated into the new legislation.**

5. THE CASE FOR EXTENDING THE RANGE OF TERMS SUBJECT TO A "FAIRNESS" TEST IN INDIVIDUAL BUSINESS-TO-BUSINESS CONTRACTS

5.15 There are two issues that arise in relation to extending the range of terms subject to a "fairness" test: the extent to which the arguments, discussed earlier,[17] relating to unfair terms in standard form contracts apply to business-to-business contracts; and the extent to which terms that do not exclude or restrict liability should be subject to a fairness test in business-to-business contracts.

(1) Unfair terms in standard form contracts

5.16 We have argued earlier that standard form contracts present particular problems of unfair surprise and lack of choice,[18] especially in the consumer context. We identified the main reason as a market failure caused by the cost of acquiring information. However, unfair terms, and particularly unfair terms in standard form contracts, are regularly to be found in business-to-business contracts. Standard forms are used in transactions between all types of business because the cost of customising each transaction can be prohibitive for both sides.[19] The use of standard terms is not in itself a sign that one of the parties is in a weak bargaining position. Indeed, the terms of many standard forms are entirely fair and reasonable. Unfortunately, this is not always the case.

5.17 We believe that in the business-to-business context standard form contracts cause problems which are similar to, if not so severe as, those affecting consumer contracts. First, while in an ideal world a contracting party should read and ascertain the impact of the terms on offer, in the real world this involves costs to a business. Simply to have someone read through the terms is time-consuming. This is particularly the case if the terms are hard to understand. But even when the clause is in clear terms it may be difficult to know how it will affect the customer, especially if to evaluate its impact requires information (such as the other party's reliability) which the customer will not have readily available.[20] Secondly, a

---

[16] The position in "private sales" and sales by consumers to businesses is considered in Part VI below.

[17] See paras 4.42 – 4.54 above.

[18] See paras 2.4 – 2.7 above.

[19] See para 2.2 above.

[20] See C Joerges, "The Europeanisation of Private Law as a Rationalisation Process and as a Contest of Disciplines – an Analysis of the Directive on Unfair Terms in Consumer Contracts" (1995) 3 ERPL 175. Joerges argues that the negotiation of contractual terms is associated with transactional costs and that such costs are minimised by standardised terms, except where individual negotiation makes economic sense, such as in determining the adequacy of price and main subject matter of the contract. This is, he says, why the Directive in Art 4(2) prohibits control over the adequacy of price and main subject matter. If this

business customer may have very little more bargaining power as against a supplier than would a consumer.[21] For example, a business supplier that sells all its output to a single purchaser (as in the case of a manufacturer of components for a major car maker) will not be in a strong negotiating position. However the problem is not confined to this case. It may exist whenever the proposed purchase is of relatively low volume or value.

5.18   It is probable that the problems for business customers in general are less severe than they are for consumers. The business customer is more likely to have the expertise to understand the terms or the resources to seek legal advice; it is more likely to have some influence over a supplier if it intends to make similar purchases in future; and it may be able to call on a trade association to negotiate better terms on its behalf. Even if it is obliged to accept unfavourable terms, it may be able to insure against the risk. But the cases that come before the courts suggest that unfair terms are still a real problem in business-to-business contracts.

(2) Terms that do not exclude or restrict liability

5.19   In business-to-business contracts UCTA affects only various forms of exemption clauses, though this is defined broadly by UCTA, especially section 3 [s 17]. As we have said, the effect of that section is that a term which purports to allow the business whose standard terms are used to perform in a way which is "substantially different from that which was reasonably expected", or not to perform at all, is subject to control. In contrast, a term which affects the other party's obligations, such as a term requiring the other to pay an increased price, is not. This made sense when the focus was on exclusion and limitation of liability; but, looked at from the perspective of potentially unfair terms in general, the justification for this restriction is far from evident. The terms listed earlier as not being caught by UCTA[22] have an equal potential for unfairness as do many of the clauses which UCTA requires to be fair and reasonable. It does not seem to us that, for instance, the clause purporting to allow the seller to charge an increased price (which, as we have said, is not caught by UCTA) is any less likely to be unfair than a clause allowing the seller to vary the specification of the goods or services to be provided (which is within UCTA). Our provisional view is that both should be subject to control.

5.20   Further arguments might be made. First, on a purely practical level, it is sometimes difficult to draw a clear dividing line between the consumer and the businessman. Under the current law it is not always obvious whether a person is acting "in the course of a business" (UCTA, s 12 [s 25(1)]) or "for purposes relating to ... trade" (UTCCR, reg 3(1)).[23] One commentator, when considering the International Air Transport Association's (IATA) general conditions of

_____

rationalisation of the Directive is accepted, he says, it would suggest that the regulation of standardised terms be extended to business relations and not restricted to consumer contracts.

[21]   See para 2.6 above.

[22]   Para 5.5 above. Examples drawn from case law are given at para 2.30, n 39 above.

[23]   See for example, the discussions over the _R & B Customs_ case at para 3.85 above.

carriage, has wondered which regime applies to a traveller whose primary purpose is to go on holiday but who takes the opportunity of having a business meeting abroad.[24] Or if a solicitor buys a vehicle for use both in his business and for domestic use, how is the transaction to be categorised? Though in many cases it may be clear whether the transaction in question is a consumer transaction or a commercial transaction, there are clearly a number of cases which could with equal accuracy be characterised either way. It would be simpler to have a single regime for most cases, all terms being subject to the fairness test.[25] The court can apply the test in a flexible way to take account of the facts of the particular situation.

5.21 Secondly, the "overlap" makes the continuing existence of two different, exclusive, regulatory regimes questionable. As we will explain in this Part, we do not accept that terms in consumer and in business-to-business contracts should be treated in the same way in all respects, because we believe that the needs of the parties differ in the two situations; but we think that in general terms it is not desirable for the two sets of rules to differ without good reason.

5.22 A third argument is that an extension of the existing controls would bring our law into line with that of several of our competitors. As can be seen from the more detailed account in Appendix A to this consultation paper, a number of countries have controls over unfair terms in business-to-business contracts that go beyond what is provided in the UK. These further controls take three basic forms (a single country often having more than one form of control):

(1) Some countries treat small businesses, or some small businesses such as artisans and farmers, simply as if they were consumers. This may apply only for certain types of contract such as sales, as in some Canadian provinces,[26] and render exclusion clauses of no effect. More usually it means that a very wide range of unfair terms are subject to a test of fairness. The Netherlands is an example. The French courts at one time held that a business buying goods or services outside its field of professional expertise is to be treated like a consumer ("*non-professionel*"). More recent cases have held that this does not apply to purchases directly related to the business (for example if a printing company purchases electricity) but the possibility remains that it will apply in other cases.[27]

(2) Some countries have wide-ranging controls over unfair terms of all types in individual business-to-business contracts. This may be a general power to strike down harsh contracts or clauses, as under the American doctrine of

<hr>

[24] D Grant, "The Unfair Terms in Consumer Contracts Regulations and the IATA General Conditions of Carriage – a United Kingdom Consumer's Perspective" [1998] JBL 123, 125.

[25] Other than those exclusions and restrictions of liability that are to remain of no effect in consumer cases: see paras 4.34 – 4.35 above. In this situation it will continue to be necessary to decide on which side of the line the particular case falls.

[26] Eg Saskatchewan: see para A.19 below.

[27] See paras A.30 – A.32 below.

unconscionability[28] and section 36 of Sweden's Contracts Act,[29] or it may be that legislation aimed primarily at consumers can be applied by analogy, or at the court's discretion, to business-to-business contracts also. Thus the German BGB[30] has lists of clauses which are always of no effect and which are presumed to be unfair unless shown otherwise;[31] and while these lists are stated to apply to consumer contracts,[32] the German courts apply them to business-to-business contracts relying on the "general clause" of BGB article 307.[33] This provides that clauses which are contrary to good faith are not valid. The position in the Netherlands is similar.[34]

(3) A number of countries, including the Netherlands and Sweden, have preventive controls over the use of clauses in business-to-business contracts. This is discussed further later in this Part.[35]

5.23 Lastly, in the European context it has been argued that the Directive should be extended to business contracts in order to promote the objectives of the Treaty of Rome[36] – the harmonisation of consumer protection law across Europe, thus increasing the movement of trade and competition and thereby raising the standard of living.[37] An extension of our law would go some way to achieving the

---

[28] This is a doctrine of equitable origins which was incorporated in modern form into the Uniform Commercial Code, Art 302, and has subsequently been adopted in this form as a principle of common law. In business-to-business contracts it has chiefly been used against unfair exemption clauses ("disclaimers").

[29] See para A.50 below.

[30] See para A.33 below. The provisions of the BGB are new, replacing the earlier Act on Standard Terms (AGBG) of 1976.

[31] Arts 10 and 11.

[32] Art 24.

[33] Art 9.

[34] See Butterworths, paras 6.236 and 6.237.

[35] See paras 5.97 – 5.110 below.

[36] Treaty Establishing the European Community (Rome, 1957).

[37] Collins has argued that the Directive is not essentially concerned with the fairness of contracts between two parties. Rather, it seeks to establish the necessary conditions under which citizens have access through markets to high quality goods and services at competitive prices, and that, as such, the logic of harmonisation and of enhancing competition and consumer choice should equally well apply to standard form contracts between businesses. Collins argues that even if the sole purpose behind the Directive was to improve the standard of living of its citizens by establishing a market which supplies high quality goods and services at competitive services, then, since most consumer products pass through a chain of supply between businesses, to allow businesses to challenge the fairness of standard form contracts would achieve this aim most effectively, as businesses have more resources to insist upon conformity to contracts than consumers: H Collins, "Good Faith in European Contract Law" (1994) 14 OJLS 229. It is possible that EC legislation will move in this direction. The European Commission's preliminary views are set out in its Report from the Commission on the Implementation of Directive 93/13/EEC of 5 April 1993 on Unfair Terms in Consumer Contracts, COM (2000) 248, 27 April 2000, pp 31–32. The Report specifically mentions that some firms are in a weak position when confronted with general contractual terms imposed upon them, that extending the control of terms would make it easier for firms to shift their obligations vis-à-vis the consumer to a higher level in the

same result. It is difficult to gauge the strength of this argument but it is not inconceivable that overseas firms would be readier to do business in the UK if they knew that under UK law they would have protection from any unfair terms used by their UK counterparts, particularly if they are used to having such protection under their own domestic law.

5.24 We should emphasise a point made in Part II. So many terms in business-to-business contracts are already subject to control under UCTA section 3 [s 17][38] that to subject *all* terms to control as under UTCCR, as we will provisionally propose, would not be such a great change as it might at first sight appear to be. (It may also be noted that we do not intend to extend the controls over terms in business-to-business contracts to clauses that were negotiated.[39]) Nonetheless our proposal would deal with a number of types of clause that have caused justified complaints, such as clauses locking businesses into long-term contracts for photocopiers and similar equipment at escalating prices.

5.25 **Our provisional view is that a good case can be made for extending the power to challenge unfair terms in at least some individual business-to-business contracts from the types of term subject to the reasonableness test of UCTA to the wider range covered (for consumer contracts) by UTCCR.**

6. THE RANGE OF BUSINESSES TO BE PROTECTED

5.26 We now go on to consider whether this extension should apply to all, or only to a limited type of, business-to-business contracts. We consider first whether any extension should be limited to protecting *small* businesses. Secondly we consider an alternative, which would be to limit the extension to transactions which are not of a kind the business disadvantaged by the term makes on a regular basis (so that it is an "occasional business customer"); and thirdly we consider whether the controls should apply to all business contracts.

(1) Small businesses

5.27 Our terms of reference ask us to consider whether extended protection is particularly necessary for small businesses. It must be the case that problems are more likely where the party affected by a term is a sole trader or small business. A sole trader or small business is less likely than a larger business to have staff with the knowledge and skills to understand the impact of the other party's clauses, especially if they are not in readily understandable language;[40] and is unlikely to

---

marketing chain, and that in many contracts of adherence it is difficult to find any difference between the "adherent" regardless of whether the person is labelled a consumer or not. The Report also notes that this situation could also be covered by European competition law.

[38] Para 3.13 above.

[39] See para 5.44 below.

[40] Collins suspects that businesses "frequently overlook or fail to comprehend the small print proffered in standard form contracts": H Collins, "Good Faith in European Contract Law" (1994) 14 OJLS 229, 235.

have the bargaining power to persuade the other party to modify its terms. In many ways the position of a small business is closely analogous to that of a consumer. We have seen that several countries simply treat small businesses, or certain types of small business, as if they were consumers.[41] Thus the small business is given protection identical to that of consumers, including in some cases rules which render certain types of clause of no effect at all.

5.28 However, though the problems posed by unfair terms may be worse for small businesses, they are not confined to them. This may be demonstrated simply by the number of cases in which the courts have found clauses in business-to-business contracts to be unreasonable under UCTA even though the party affected was not a small business. There have been some cases in which a clause was held to be unreasonable and the business in whose favour the decision was reached was said to be a small business.[42] But there have been more in which it was said that the parties were of unequal bargaining power without mentioning the size of the "weaker" business.[43] This suggests that the courts do not necessarily consider bargaining power to be a function of size.

5.29 A factor that seems to be more critical than whether the complaining party is a small business is whether or not it has dealt on the other party's standard form of contract. There seems to have been only one reported case in England in which a clause which had been negotiated was held to be unreasonable.[44]

5.30 It seems likely that the factors listed in paragraph 5.18, as mitigating the problems caused by standard form contracts for businesses, are much less relevant for a small business than for a medium-sized or large one. As we suggested earlier,[45] in many ways small businesses seem to be in a similar position to consumers. Thus there appears to be a case for extending the controls so that they at least protect small businesses. However, the justification for extending the protection given to businesses may be wider than this.

---

[41] We outline our findings as to what controls over business-to-business contracts exist in other jurisdictions in Appendix A below.

[42] See for example *AEG (UK) Ltd v Logic Resource Ltd,* unreported 20 October 1995 (CA); *Gray v Chartered Trust Plc,* unreported 18 April 1984 (QBD); *Lease Management Services Ltd v Purnell Secretarial Services Ltd* (1994) 13 Tr LR 337 (CA).

[43] See *Fillite (Runcorn) Ltd v APV Pasilac Ltd,* unreported 22 April 1993 (CA); *Overseas Medical Supplies Ltd v Orient Transport Services Ltd* [1999] 1 All ER (Comm) 981 (CA); *St Albans City and District Council v International Computers Ltd* [1996] 4 All ER 481 (CA); *Stag Line Ltd v Tyne Shiprepair Group Ltd (The "Zinnia")* [1984] 2 Lloyd's Rep 211 (QBD). We have found 34 cases involving the use of standard terms in business-to-business contracts. The courts found the terms to be unreasonable in 19 of these, but only 5 of these 19 specifically make reference to one party being a small business.

[44] *The Salvage Association v CAP Financial Services Ltd* [1995] FSR 654. It appears that the defendant failed to adduce any evidence to show that the limitation figure was reasonable.

[45] Para 5.27 above.

(2) Occasional business customers

5.31 An alternative argument is that what matters is not so much the size of the customer's business but the balance of bargaining expertise and bargaining power. This is borne out by the reported cases under UCTA, insofar as one can rely on these as a guide. As we have said, in cases in which a clause was held to be unreasonable there has been more emphasis on the unequal bargaining power of the parties than on their relative size.

5.32 A major determinant of bargaining power is whether the transaction a business is entering is of a kind it makes regularly or, conversely, is an unusual one for it to enter. When the transaction is of a kind which the business enters regularly, it is less likely to be at a disadvantage vis-à-vis the other party. It is more likely to have relevant expertise; the cost of finding out the meaning of the terms on offer can be spread over a larger number of transactions; and, as it can hold out to the other party the prospect of regular repeat orders, it may have some bargaining power. Conversely, if the transaction is not one it enters regularly, for example if a business buys equipment for use or contracts for occasional services rather than inventory or routine services, it is likely to be in a weaker position. This is true whatever the size of the business: a large business making the occasional purchase of goods or services which are outside its field of expertise may not be in a much better position than a small business in the same situation.[46]

5.33 Therefore it can be argued that, while business customers do not need protection in their routine transactions, since for these they can be expected to develop or buy in the necessary expertise and are likely to have more bargaining power, protection may still be justified in transactions which are not part of the routine business of the customer – when, in other words, the business is an "occasional business customer".

5.34 However, we do not believe that the fact that a particular transaction is routine for the business is alone sufficient to ensure fairness. For example, the supplier whose entire output is usually bought by a car manufacturer or a supermarket chain lacks any real bargaining power, and a farmer buying seed[47] may face unfair terms, though all these are "routine" transactions for the weaker party. Thus we believe that it would not be sufficient to give protection to "occasional business customers"; it would be necessary to protect at least small businesses also.

(3) General protection for business

5.35 A third argument is that the new legislation should follow the pattern of UCTA. The protection provided by the requirement of reasonableness under UCTA is

---

[46] Kidner gives the example of a business buying light-bulbs, saying that most business buyers of consumer goods would have no greater expertise than a private buyer: R Kidner, "The Unfair Contract Terms Act 1977 – Who Deals as Consumer?" (1987) 38 NILQ 46, 49. The same argument may be made in respect of much more important transactions, involving large sums and high risk to the purchaser, for example the purchase of a computer system.

[47] As in *George Mitchell (Chesterhall) Ltd v Finney Lock Seeds Ltd* [1983] QB 284; see para 5.109 below.

not formally limited to small or occasional business customers.[48] In cases involving small businesses, and cases where the transaction is of a kind the business does not make regularly, these are factors (and probably important factors) which can be taken into account in assessing reasonableness, but in principle any business can claim the protection of UCTA.[49]

5.36 There would be advantages in this approach. To provide a separate regime for small businesses, or for small businesses and occasional transactions, would create even more complexity; it has not proved necessary in relation to the broad range of terms already controlled by UCTA; and it would cause difficulties for business. It seems likely that businesses wish to have a fairly good idea of which regime governs their terms. Were controls to be applied only to protect small businesses and "occasional business customers", the other business might not be able to tell which regime would apply.

5.37 First, how is a business to know whether it is dealing with a small or a large business? It is true that there is legislation which distinguishes between "small" and other businesses. The Late Payment of Commercial Debts (Interest) Act 1998 provides for a term to be implied into contracts that interest shall be payable on debts paid late. This has been brought into force progressively. At first it applied only where the supplier was a small business (under 50 employees) and the purchaser a large business (over 50 employees) or a public authority.[50] It was then extended to the case where a small business was purchasing from a public authority,[51] and most recently it has been applied as between small businesses.[52] The burden of proving that a business is small rests on the business but there is no requirement that the small business warn its contracting partner in advance. It would be useful to know whether this has caused practical problems. It will be possible for the supplier to discover from industry sources the approximate size of a potential customer.

5.38 Equally, particularly where there has been no previous dealing between them, how is a business to know whether a transaction is or is not a regular one for its customer? The very difficulty for a supplier of distinguishing between its various customers could be a factor which the court can take into account in assessing the

---

[48] We noted earlier that in *R & B Customs Brokers Co Ltd v United Dominions Trust Ltd* [1988] 1 WLR 321 it was held that a business which buys goods which are not integral to its business, and for which the transaction is not regular, is not buying "in the course of a business" and is therefore "dealing as consumer". As a result the exclusion clause in the contract was of no effect at all. We argue that this decision gives the business buyer an unnecessary degree of protection: para 4.153 above.

[49] A brief survey we have made did not suggest that cases in which the terms were found to be unreasonable were likely to fall into one of these two categories, but it is doubtful if this shows anything about the extent of the use of unfair terms.

[50] Late Payment of Commercial Debts (Interest) Act 1998 (Commencement No 1) Order 1998, SI 1998 No 2479.

[51] Late Payment of Commercial Debts (Interest) Act 1998 (Commencement No 2) Order 1999, SI 1999 No 1816.

[52] Late Payment of Commercial Debts (Interest) Act 1998 (Commencement No 4) Order 2000, SI 2000 No 2740.

reasonableness of the term in question. Moreover, apart from the isolated decision in the *R & B Customs* case,[53] this distinction is not one normally used in contract law and, even if it can be justified in theory, it is not clear that it is workable in practice: detailed factual investigations are likely to be involved in order to determine which regime applies.

5.39 Thus in relation to the question of extending the range of clauses which must satisfy the fairness test to protect business customers, we are not convinced that the extension should be made only to small businesses or only to "occasional business customers".

5.40 **Our provisional view is that it would be better to treat all businesses alike in being able to benefit from the protection, allowing the courts to take into account the size of the business, and whether it makes transactions of the kind in question regularly or only occasionally, in assessing the fairness of the terms complained of. We ask consultees whether they agree. If not, how would they prefer to see the protection limited?**

7. "STANDARD" OR "NON-NEGOTIATED" TERMS, OR ALL TERMS?

(1) Should any controls apply to negotiated contracts?

5.41 In 1975, when considering what the scope of control should be in relation to business contracts, the Law Commissions concluded that control was most necessary where, even though both parties are acting in the course of a business,

> one party requires the other to accept terms which the former has decided upon in advance as being generally advantageous to him, and the customer must either accept those terms or not enter into the contract: that is, where there is a standard form contract.[54]

The Second Report rejected more general controls on the ground that this would constitute too great an interference with freedom of contract, noting that "injustice is unlikely where the parties have been able to negotiate the provisions of the contract on equal terms".[55]

5.42 On the other hand, we have seen that the "reasonableness" requirement imposed by UCTA sections 2(2) [s 16(1)(b)], 6(3) [s 20(2)(ii)] and 7(3) [s 21(1), (3)] in business-to-business contracts applies to terms in contracts which have been fully

---

[53] Para 3.85 above.

[54] Second Report, para 147.

[55] *Ibid.* Respect for the principle of freedom of contract can also be seen in UTCCR, which only apply controls to those contract terms which have not been "individually negotiated". The original European Commission Proposal provided for an unfairness control in relation to "a contractual term" without distinguishing between negotiated and non-negotiated terms. In a number of countries the law on collective regulation of contract terms has not been restricted to standard form contracts. See T Wilhelmsson, "The Implementation of the EC Directive on Unfair Contract Terms in Finland" [1997] ERPL 151. Similarly, in France, Arts L 132-1 to L 135-1 of the *Code de la Consommation* apply to all contracts between professionals and consumers, regardless of the form of the contract.

negotiated. We have also made the provisional proposal that, in consumer contracts, controls over unfair terms should not be limited to "non-negotiated" terms.[56] If the new legislation is to extend the controls to cover a wider range of clauses in business-to-business contracts, what approach should it take to this question? Should the controls apply to all "unfair" terms, whether negotiated or not? Or should the existing controls over negotiated terms in UCTA be retained, but the wider controls apply only to terms that are standard terms of business (the test under UCTA) or have not been individually negotiated (the test under UTCCR)?[57] Or should all the existing controls be replaced by a "fairness test" applicable only to standard or non-negotiated terms?

(a) Extended controls

5.43   Our provisional view is that it is not necessary to extend the general controls to terms which have been negotiated between businesses. We accept that there may be cases where, even though a business negotiated over a clause and thus was aware of the nature of the terms being offered to it and their possible consequences, it was obliged to accept those terms and the consequent risk, which could not be passed on to a third party. For example, a farmer who supplies a supermarket chain will in practice have very little influence over the terms on which his product is purchased. The fact that a negotiating process has taken place may not change the position that the contract contains terms which are unfair to one of the parties.[58] It may be argued that unless the negotiation has resulted in an amendment of the clause in question in favour of the weaker party, the clause should remain subject to the control of the court.[59] However, where the business concerned has been given the opportunity to negotiate a particular term in its contract, it will at least be aware of the term, and so have had the chance to consider the possible consequences of entering into a contract on that basis. Even if it does not have the bargaining power to ensure that the term is not included in the contract, it may be able to safeguard its position by ensuring that other terms of the contract are more favourable, or, alternatively, by accepting the risk and insuring against it. It can be argued to be an unreasonable interference with freedom of contract to allow the business to object to the term when, with hindsight, it appears that it is not advantageous. In particular, it is important that a business should not be encouraged to embark on litigation, or to threaten to embark on litigation, to challenge the fairness of a term, when its primary reason for doing so is to delay having to implement the contractual obligations which it has undertaken.

---

[56]   Para 4.54 above. The difference between "standard terms" and "non-negotiated terms" is explored in paras 5.48 – 5.59 below.

[57]   We consider which of these tests would be the more appropriate at paras 5.57 – 5.59 below.

[58]   The view taken by the European Parliament and the European Commission in relation to the original proposal for the Directive for contracts between consumers and businesses. See E Alexandriou, "Implementation of the EC Directive on Unfair Contract Terms in Greece" (1997) 5 ERPL 173, 178.

[59]   This suggestion was made in relation to consumer contracts by T Wilhelmsson at the 1999 Brussels Conference, "The 'Unfair Terms' Directive, Five Years On", in Workshop 1, "The Scope of the Directive: Non-Negotiated Terms in Consumer Contracts", p 94, 101.

5.44 **We provisionally propose that, for business-to-business contracts, the "fairness test" be extended to cover the same range of terms as would be subject to the fairness test under our proposals for consumer contracts, but only where the term in question "has not been negotiated" or is "standard".[60]**

(b) Existing controls

5.45 Should the provisions in UCTA that in business-to-business contracts[61] require even negotiated exclusion clauses to be reasonable be retained? It would not be illogical to say that the kinds of exclusion clauses covered by UCTA sections 2(2) [s 16(1)(b)], 6(3) [s 20(2)] and 7(3) [s 21(1), (3)] are so risky, or so anti-social, that they should be the subject of control even when they were negotiated, but that other terms should only be challenged if they were "standard" or "non-negotiated". We think that the substance of UCTA section 2(2) [s 16(1)(b)], which of course applies to non-contractual notices as well as contract terms, should be retained, but we are not convinced that those in sections 6(3) and 7(3) [ss 20(2)(ii), 21(1)(ii)] are still needed. To maintain them would add to the complexity of the legislation; and we suspect that it would in practice affect the outcome in very few cases. We have already said that there seems to have been only one reported case in England and Wales in which a clause which had been negotiated was held to be unreasonable.[62]

5.46 Limiting the exclusion in this way to "individually negotiated terms" or "standard terms of business" (and thus following the approach of the current section 3 [s 17] of UCTA) would ensure that businesses are not deprived of protection from unfair terms in an area where it is needed, while preserving freedom of contract as far as possible.[63] At the same time it would simplify the law, as with only a few exceptions all terms in business contracts would be subject to a single regime.[64]

---

[60] If however it were decided that negotiated terms should be caught by the legislation only if they fall within the scope of the present UCTA s 3(2) [s 17(1)] (in other words, they are terms which purport to exclude or restrict the business's liability for breach of contract, or allow it to perform in a way substantially different from what was reasonably expected or not to perform at all: see para 3.14 above) and the other controls should apply only to terms which were not negotiated, it would be desirable to harmonise the two tests: under UTCCR whether the term was "individually negotiated", and under UCTA whether it was part of the written standard terms of business. The decision on which to adopt might depend on our final recommendation as to whether to apply the controls to all terms in consumer contracts, whether or not negotiated. If this were not done, so that in consumer contracts also only non-individually negotiated clauses were subject to control, it would seem better to adopt the same approach for business-to-business contracts, or businesses would face different tests for what was "negotiated" for consumer contracts and business-to-business contracts.

[61] Private sales and sales by consumers to businesses are considered in Part VI below.

[62] *The Salvage Association v CAP Financial Services Ltd* [1995] FSR 654. It appears that the defendant failed to adduce any evidence to show that the limitation figure was reasonable.

[63] We consider which in the next section.

[64] Where the terms would continue to be of no effect, see paras 5.8 – 5.14 above; and where contracts or particular terms are exempt from control, see paras 5.64 – 5.65 below.

5.47 **We would welcome evidence from consultees on whether in practice there are significant numbers of terms which were not standard, or which were negotiated, and which are seen as unfair. Our provisional conclusion is that the controls over negotiated exclusion clauses in UCTA sections 6 and 7 [ss 20(2)(ii), 21(1)(ii)] are not needed and that it would suffice to have the general fairness test over "standard" or "non-negotiated" terms.**

(2) "Standard terms" or "not individually negotiated terms"?

5.48 There remains the question of whether the controls should be over "standard terms" as under UCTA section 3 [s 17] or "not individually negotiated terms" as under UTCCR. We need to define what is meant by each of these phrases.

5.49 UCTA refers to "written standard terms of business" (or, in the case of Scotland, "standard form contract", but section 17(2) limits this to written standard terms of business). When considering whether or not to define "standard terms of business", the Law Commissions rejected the lack of negotiation as a defining feature, noting that there are cases in which some, but not all, terms of the contract may be negotiated.[65] In the event it was decided to leave the phrase undefined. It has been interpreted flexibly by the courts.

5.50 First, it has been held that a term may be a "written standard term of business" even though other parts of the contract, including other standard terms, have been negotiated by the parties, provided the terms remain "standard". In *St Albans City and District Council v International Computers Ltd*[66] Nourse LJ (with whom the other members of the court agreed) said that to "deal" on the other's standard terms means simply to make the final contract on those terms. The question was one of fact: had any negotiations left the standard terms "effectively untouched"?[67]

5.51 Secondly, it is possible that one term may be treated as a "written standard term" within section 3 [s 17] even though some of the other standard terms have been altered as the result of negotiation: in other words, that the question whether a term is standard will be treated "term by term". However, such authority as exists seems divided. In *Pegler Ltd v Wang (UK) Ltd (No 1)*[68] the evidence showed that Wang was prepared to negotiate on clauses defining the moments of delivery, performance, passing of risk and other matters but not on its standard exclusion clauses. Peter Bowsher QC, sitting as a High Court judge, found that the exclusion clause in question was still a standard term, even though Wang was prepared to accept a small variation of the term limiting its liability to losses of a certain amount: "A standard term is nonetheless a standard term even though the party putting forward that term is willing to negotiate some small variations of

---

[65] See Second Report, para 156.

[66] [1996] 4 All ER 481 (CA). This is the only Court of Appeal case. The real issue here was over the meaning of the word "dealing", but the court quoted a passage from the judgment in *The Salvage Association v CAP Financial Services Ltd* [1995] FSR 654 without criticism.

[67] [1996] 4 All ER 481, 491g.

[68] [2000] BLR 218.

that term."[69] In *The Salvage Association v CAP Financial Services Ltd*,[70] however, Thayne Forbes J held that the second contract in that case was not on CAP written standard terms as they had been the subject of negotiation, although they were "closely based on and followed" those terms.[71]

5.52 It is necessary that the term in question is one that is used with some regularity. Lord Dunpark in *McCrone v Boots Farm Sales Ltd*[72] said that the phrase "standard form contract" (the Scottish counterpart of "written standard terms"[73])

> is, in my opinion, wide enough to include any contract, whether wholly written or partly oral, which includes a set of fixed terms or conditions which the proponer applies, without material variation, to contracts of the kind in question.

5.53 Other judges have been less demanding. Thus in *British Fermentation Products v Compair Reavell*,[74] it was said that it might be enough that the term was "at least usually used".[75] Nonetheless, it is probable that the terms in question must be used for a large proportion of contracts of the relevant type before the criterion of being "standard" written terms is met.

5.54 In this respect UTCCR are different. A term is not individually negotiated "where it has been drafted in advance and the consumer has therefore not been able to influence the substance of the term".[76] Thus it appears not to matter whether the term has been used before or was drafted in advance for use in the particular contract. It seems that the question must be taken "term by term".

5.55 If controls over unfair terms in business-to-business contracts are to be extended, but the controls are to be restricted to "standard" or "non-negotiated" terms, should the legislation follow the UCTA or the UTCCR approach? We suggest that a "term by term" approach is better, simply because a party will often

---

[69] At para 73.

[70] [1995] FSR 654.

[71] The terms were not imposed upon the claimant, but

> were fully negotiable between parties of equal bargaining power and ... [the defendant] was prepared to engage in a meaningful process of negotiation ... as to those terms.

[1995] FSR 654, 672.

[72] 1981 SC 68, 74. Cited in *Pegler Ltd v Wang (UK) Ltd (No 1)* [2000] BLR 218; *British Fermentation Products v Compair Reavell* [1999] BLR 352; and *Fillite (Runcorn) Ltd v APV Pasilac Ltd,* unreported 22 April 1993 (QBD).

[73] UCTA s 17.

[74] [1999] BLR 352.

[75] At p 361. In *Oval (717) Ltd v Aegon Insurance Co (UK) Ltd* (1997) 54 Con LR 74 it was enough that the contract had been used on at least one other previous occasion, as evidenced by the fact that a copy of the previous contract was sent to the claimant as a draft contract; but that does not show that it would have been treated as "standard" if there had been evidence of the use of other terms on a regular basis.

[76] Reg 5(2).

concentrate its attention on some terms but not others.[77] For instance, the "standard terms" may well include provisions dealing with the amounts payable under the contract; for example, standard scale fees. A party might well consider these in some detail and attempt to negotiate them while having no understanding of other terms in the standard form.

5.56 **We provisionally propose that, if controls are to be limited to standard terms, the question should be whether the particular term is standard rather than whether any of the standard terms have been subject to negotiation.**

5.57 We have not found it easy to decide whether the controls should be extended to a clause merely because it has been drafted in advance by one party and not subsequently negotiated. On the one hand we suspect that most clauses are drafted by one party or the other "in advance" of the contract being agreed – save in very high value transactions, it must be unusual for the parties to sit down together to draft the clauses. If the clause was drawn up for the particular contract, rather than being standard, the party who drafted it is less likely to refuse to alter it. On the other hand it is quite difficult to distinguish "standard terms" from those merely drafted in advance, particularly when the "standard form" may in fact be an electronic document and the clauses are printed out for each transaction.

5.58 In the end we have reached the provisional conclusion that the controls should apply to clauses that have been drafted in advance by one party and not subsequently negotiated, because this is the test which we think will be the easier one to apply when, as we think will be more and more often the case, the "standard form" will not be a printed document but an electronic one.[78]

5.59 **We provisionally propose that, if controls are to be limited to terms that are in some way standard, they should apply to any term which has been drafted in advance and has not been negotiated, whether or not the term is one regularly used by the proponent.**

8. EXEMPTIONS FROM THE NEW REGIME

(1) "Core" terms

5.60 In Part III we considered the exemption from UTCCR's fairness test of the "core terms" (more accurately, the definition of the main subject matter and the

---

[77] An example of this can be seen in *South West Water Services Ltd v International Computers Ltd* [1999] BLR 420. Here SWW, a water company, sought a software package to handle its billing. The chosen supplier was one of several firms. SWW was described as a very aggressive negotiator. (It is apparent that when the contract was being negotiated, the balance of power lay with SWW, who were described by ICL as making a number of demands on a "take it or leave it" basis.) The contract was won against fierce competition. Nevertheless, the contract was concluded on ICL's terms and conditions which contained a clause restricting ICL's liability. This clause was held to be unreasonable.

[78] See S Wilson and S Bone, "Businesses, Standard Terms and the Unfair Contract Terms Act 1977" [2002] Journal of Obligations and Remedies 29.

adequacy of the price), and proposed a reformulated version which should make these exemptions rather clearer.[79]

5.61   **We provisionally propose that the same formulation of the "core terms" should apply to business-to-business contracts as to consumer contracts.**

(2) Mandatory and permitted terms

5.62   In Part III we considered the question of terms which either are required by law or which are in substance the same as those which would apply in the absence of an express term (the "default" rules). We considered that both are exempt under the existing law and should remain so under the new legislation, provided however that they are "transparent". As to terms required or approved by industry regulators, only terms *required* by regulators should be exempt from the new "reasonableness" regime.[80]

5.63   **We provisionally propose that the same rules on mandatory and permitted terms should apply to business-to-business contracts as to consumer contracts.**

(3) Excluded contracts

(a) Terms not subject to UCTA in business-to-business contracts

5.64   In Part II we noted that certain contracts are excluded from the operation of UCTA, even when they are consumer contracts. They are:

(1)   contracts of insurance;[81]

(2)   any contract so far as it relates to the creation or transfer of any interest in land, or the termination of such an interest;[82]

(3)   any contract so far as it relates to the creation or transfer of securities or of any right or interest in securities; and[83]

(4)   (for Scotland) contracts of guarantee.[84]

5.65   There are other exclusions which in practice affect only business-to-business contracts:

(1)   any contract so far as it relates to the creation or transfer of a right or interest in any patent, trade mark, copyright or design right, registered

---

[79]   Paras 4.60 and 4.68 above.

[80]   See para 4.76 above.

[81]   Sched 1, para 1(a) (England); for Scotland, s 15(3)(a)(i).

[82]   Sched 1, para (b) (England); for Scotland, these are not listed in s 15(2) and are therefore excluded. The Act however does apply "to a grant of any right or permission to enter upon or use land not amounting to an estate or interest in land": s 15(2)(e).

[83]   Sched 1, para (e) (England); for Scotland, these are not listed in s 15(2) and are therefore excluded.

[84]   These are not listed in s 15(2) and are therefore excluded.

design, technical or commercial information or other intellectual property, or relates to the termination of any such right or interest;[85]

    (2)   any contract so far as it relates

        (i)   to the formation or dissolution of a company (which means any body corporate or unincorporated association, and includes a partnership), or

        (ii)   to its constitution or the rights or obligations of its corporators or members;[86] and

    (3)   (except in so far as the contract purports to exclude or restrict liability for negligence or breach of duty in respect of death or personal injury)

        (a)   any contract of marine salvage or towage;

        (b)   any charterparty of a ship or hovercraft; and

        (c)   any contract for the carriage of goods by ship or hovercraft.[87]

5.66   **We are not aware of calls for business-to-business contracts of the types excluded from UCTA to be brought within the scope of the unfair terms legislation. We would be interested to hear any evidence suggesting that any of them should be covered, but provisionally we propose to maintain the existing exemptions.**

(b) International contracts

5.67   As we noted in Part III, UCTA section 26[88] exempts from the operation of certain sections of the Act any contract for the supply of goods which is made by parties in different States and which involves carriage of the goods between States, offer and acceptance across State borders or delivery in a different State to that where the contract was made. We have proposed that all the provisions to protect consumers should apply to "cross-border" contracts.[89] Should international business-to-business contracts continue to be exempt?

5.68   In their First Report, the Law Commissions gave three reasons for exempting international supply contracts: (a) that, where goods were exported from the UK to another country, it was for the legal system of that country rather than that of our own to specify how far contractual freedom should be limited or controlled in the interests of consumers or other purchasers; (b) that contracts of an international character ordinarily involved transactions of some size between parties who were engaged in commerce and who wished to be free to negotiate their own terms; and (c) that it would be undesirable to make proposals which

---

[85]   Sched 1, para 1(c) (England); for Scotland, these are not listed in s 15(2) and are therefore excluded.

[86]   Sched 1, para 1(d) (England); for Scotland, s 15(3)(a)(ii).

[87]   Sched 1, paras 2 and 3 (England); for Scotland, s 15(3)(b) and (4).

[88]   As amended by Contracts (Applicable Law) Act 1990, s 5 and Sched 4.

[89]   Para 4.82 above.

would place UK exporters under restrictions which would not apply to some of their foreign competitors.[90]

5.69 It seems likely that conditions have changed to some extent since 1977. For instance, we suspect that there are now many small "cross-border" contracts within the EU, and many of them may be between parties who are not regularly involved in that kind of commerce. Moreover, one of the aims of recent EU legislation on contracts has been to increase the confidence of consumers in making contracts under other legal systems than their own (many of which will be cross-border contracts) and so to enhance the operation of the single market.[91] It would be odd to pursue this aim for consumers but to ignore it for business-to-business transactions, which must have the potential to play an equal role in the development of the single market. However, we are not aware of any calls for changes to the law on this point affecting business-to-business contracts.

5.70 **We invite views on the question whether international business-to-business contracts should be exempt from the controls proposed for domestic contracts.**

(c) Choice of English or Scots law

5.71 UCTA also exempts from its operation contracts in which English or Scots law applies only because the parties have chosen the law of a part of the UK to govern their contract.[92] The aim of this exemption was to avoid discouraging "foreign businessmen from agreeing to arbitrate their disputes in England or Scotland".[93]

5.72 **We invite views on whether the exemption for contracts subject to the law of a part of the UK only by choice of the parties should continue to apply to the new regime for business-to-business contracts.**

(d) Utilities and the definition of contract

5.73 Agreements for the supply of gas, electricity or telecommunications to businesses would be within the new regime because they are now regarded as contracts in the strict sense.[94] Where a utility agreement is not a contract (as appears to be so in the case of agreements for the supply of water[95]) it is at present outside the scope of UCTA, but is subject to a regulatory framework which Parliament presumably

---

[90] First Report, para 120. The Second Report noted that there had been some criticism of the definition of an international sale (which was derived from Art 1 of the annex to the Convention relating to a Uniform Law of International Sale of Goods (The Hague, 1964), reproduced in Sched 1 to the Uniform Laws on International Sales Act 1967), but recommended that the same approach be maintained: para 235.

[91] See SCGD, Recitals 2 and 5; the Directive, Recital 6.

[92] Section 27(1). The choice of law may be either express or implicit: see *Benjamin's Sale of Goods* (5th ed 1997) para 25-086.

[93] Second Report, para 232.

[94] See para 3.106, n 211 above.

[95] *Ibid.*

regards as adequate. We therefore see no reason to include such agreements within the new legislation except to the extent that this is required by the Directive. Since the Directive applies only to consumer contracts, non-contractual utility agreements with businesses can safely be excluded. Even if the ECJ were to develop the concept of a "contract" in such a way as to include non-contractual utility agreements, this would not affect business-to-business agreements because they are outside the scope of the Directive in any event. **Our provisional view is that the new regime need not extend to non-contractual agreements between utility suppliers and businesses.**

9. THE TEST TO BE APPLIED

(1) The basic test

5.74 In Part III, we provisionally proposed that the basic test in the new legislation for consumer contracts should be whether, judged by reference to the time the contract was made, the term was a fair and reasonable one.[96] We see no reason to make the basic "fair and reasonable" test any different for business-to-business contracts from the test we propose for consumer contracts.

5.75 **We provisionally propose that the same "fair and reasonable" test should apply to business-to-business contracts as we propose for consumer contracts.**

(2) Plain and intelligible language

5.76 We have provisionally proposed that, for consumer contracts, lack of transparency (by which we mean not only that the language is plain and intelligible but that the terms are readily accessible to the consumer, and that the layout of the contract document is easy to follow) should be listed among the factors that should be taken into account in assessing fairness.[97]

5.77 The extent to which an exclusion clause is transparent is already a factor to be taken into account under UCTA. Schedule 2, guideline (c) directs the court to consider

> whether the customer knew or ought reasonably to have known of the existence and extent of the term (having regard, among other things, to any custom of the trade and any previous course of dealing between the parties).

5.78 The transparency of the term must be directly relevant to this question. Some cases have referred to the difficulty of understanding a clause as one ground for holding it to be unreasonable.[98] Where a term is clear, that is often a factor in the

---

[96] Para 4.94 above.

[97] Para 4.106 above.

[98] *Stag Line Ltd v Tyne Shiprepair Group Ltd (The "Zinnia")* [1984] 2 Lloyd's Rep 211, 222, *per* Staughton J; *George Mitchell (Chesterhall) Ltd v Finney Lock Seeds Ltd* [1983] QB 284, 314, *per* Kerr LJ; *Knight Machinery (Holdings) Ltd v Rennie* 1995 SLT 166, IH (Extra Div), 170–171, *per* Lord McCluskey.

decision that the term was reasonable.[99] Transparency is important both to the question of reasonableness and to the effective operation of the "market" in terms.[100]

5.79 **We provisionally propose that the factors to be taken into account in assessing fairness should include whether the contract is transparent, in business-to-business as well as consumer contracts.**

5.80 We also raised in Part III the question whether it should be possible for the court to hold that a term is unfair *simply* because it is not "transparent" – in other words, whether the court should have the power, if it considers it appropriate, to hold the term to be unfair even though, had it been transparent, it would have been fair. We provisionally proposed that "transparency" be incorporated into the list of factors in such a way that it is clear that a term may be unfair principally or even solely because of lack of transparency. Should the same apply in business-to-business contracts? We are hesitant to take this further step, as it seems to us that a business confronted with terms that are unintelligible or hard to read can, unlike consumers, be expected to complain and refuse to contract without clarification. On the other hand confusing presentation, which may equally go to transparency, may confuse business people and consumers alike.

5.81 **We invite views as to whether, for business-to-business as well as consumer contracts, transparency should be incorporated into the list of factors in such a way that a term may be found unfair principally or solely because of lack of transparency.**

(3) The list of factors

5.82 UCTA contains "guidelines" for the application of the reasonableness test.[101] For consumer contracts we have provisionally proposed a rather fuller list than that in UCTA: the list tries to set out what we understand to be the major issues in relation to unfair terms.

5.83 **We consider that a list of factors relevant to the application of the "fair and reasonable" test would be useful in relation to business-to-business contracts as well as consumer contracts, particularly to give guidance to businesses as to how they may ensure that their terms are reasonable. We also think that the list should contain the same factors as that for consumer contracts, though naturally they may apply somewhat differently in a business context.**

[99] Eg *Casson v Ostley PJ Ltd* [2001] BLR 126; *Skipskredittforeningen v Emperor Navigation* [1998] 1 Lloyd's Rep 66; *R W Green Ltd v Cade Bros Farms* [1978] 1 Lloyd's Rep 602 (in relation to the term limiting liability to the contract price).

[100] See para 2.7 above.

[101] The courts apply these to all questions of reasonableness: para 3.50, n 121 above.

(4) An indicative list

5.84 For consumer contracts the legislation must include a list of terms which may be unfair. We have provisionally proposed that the indicative list be reformulated to make it easier to understand and apply in the UK.[102] It should also be expanded to cover certain terms which are commonly considered to be unfair but which are not referred to in the Directive.[103] We propose that the business should have the burden of proving that any term which is so listed is fair and reasonable.[104]

5.85 Should there be a list for business-to-business contracts? We pointed out in Part IV that in relation to consumer contracts the list serves two functions: the first is to give information to businesses and consumers as to what, in an individual case, is likely to be regarded as an unfair clause. The second is to make it easier for the OFT and the other bodies listed in Schedule 1 to ensure that unfair terms are not used by businesses, and for businesses to know what terms are likely to be unacceptable. We discuss below whether any body should be given the power to prevent the use of unfair terms in business-to-business contracts; if this is not done, then clearly the list will not have the second function here. It will still perform the first function.

5.86 Even if there is to be no power to prevent the use of unfair terms in business-to-business contracts, we consider that a list of some sort is important for the first function. At a minimum, it should be made clear that clauses excluding and restricting liability for breach of contract or for negligence are "suspect".[105] As we explain in the next section, we also consider that if a term is on the indicative list the business seeking to rely on it should have the burden of proving that the term is reasonable. This would replicate the effect of UCTA.[106]

5.87 However we doubt whether, in a business-to-business contract, there are other types of clause which are so likely to be unfair that the party relying on them should be obliged to prove that they are reasonable. It may be that experience will prove us wrong.

5.88 **We provisionally propose that the indicative list for business-to-business contracts be limited to clauses excluding and restricting liability for breach of contract or for negligence [breach of duty], but that there should be power to add to the list by Ministerial Order.**

---

[102] Para 4.120 above.

[103] Para 4.117 above.

[104] Para 4.150 above. We present two alternatives: (i) that in respect of terms not so listed the burden of proof should be on the consumer; and (ii) that the burden of proof should be on the business in respect of any term falling within the legislation.

[105] Cf para 3.78 above.

[106] Section 11(5) [s 24(4)].

(5) Burden of proof

5.89 In our view, a business which seeks to rely on a "listed" term should be able to do so only if it shows that the term is fair and reasonable. For consumer contracts, one alternative proposal is that the business should have to prove that any term subject to the legislation is fair and reasonable, whether the term is on the indicative list or not. We do not think that it would be right to impose such a burden in business-to-business contracts; to do so would create unnecessary uncertainty.

5.90 **We provisionally propose that, where a term in a business-to-business contract has not been listed, the burden of proving that the term is not fair and reasonable should be on the party disputing it.**

10. ANCILLARY QUESTIONS

5.91 In this section we deal with a number of ancillary questions that we considered earlier in relation to consumer contracts.

(1) Third parties

5.92 We explained in Part III that third party beneficiaries of a contract who have the right to enforce a term of the contract under the Contracts (Rights of Third Parties) Act 1999 cannot rely on any provisions of UCTA, except section 2(1).[107] In Scots law a third party with a *ius quaesitum tertio* may apparently rely on any part of section 16, so that he may challenge clauses excluding business liability not only for death or personal injury but also for other loss or damage caused by negligence. In Part IV we made the provisional proposal that for consumer contracts this position be maintained.[108]

5.93 **We provisionally propose that the existing position of third party beneficiaries be maintained for business-to-business contracts as well as consumer contracts.**

(2) Secondary contracts

5.94 Just as for consumer contracts, it should not be possible to evade the controls over business-to-business contracts by means of a secondary contract, whether between the same parties or different parties. The issues are the same as they are for consumer contracts and we refer readers to the discussion in Part IV.[109]

(3) Evasion by choice of law

5.95 As for consumer contracts,[110] it should be made clear that the rules on unfair clauses in business-to-business contracts are mandatory, so that if the contract has

---

[107] Which prevents the exclusion or restriction of business liability for death or personal injury caused by negligence. See para 3.101 above.

[108] Para 4.178 above.

[109] Paras 4.187 – 4.192 above.

[110] See para 4.194 above.

a close connection to the UK they will be applied under the Rome Convention despite a choice of another system of law.

(4) Effect if term invalid

5.96 The issues over the effect of a term being invalid because it is not fair and reasonable are the same for business-to-business contracts as they are for consumer contracts. Again we refer readers to the earlier discussion.[111]

5.97 **We propose that the rules on secondary contracts, evasion by choice of law, and the effect of a term being held invalid should be the same for business-to-business contracts as we have proposed for consumer contracts.**

11. PREVENTIVE ACTION

5.98 Though we propose that all business-to-business contracts should be subject to control by the courts whatever the size of the business to whose detriment the term operates, the question of whether there should be provisions to permit authorised bodies to take preventive action against the use or the recommendation of unfair terms in business-to-business contracts needs separate discussion. It is a question of considerable difficulty.

5.99 The preventive powers given by UTCCR regulations 10–15 are designed to correct widespread market failures caused by, on the one hand, insufficient margins of active consumers to police the market and, on the other, the scarcity of organisations able to influence the market by collective action on behalf of consumers. We have indicated already our view that the work of the OFT's Unfair Contract Terms Unit has had a major impact on the market.[112] The OFT has secured the removal of many unfair terms which were almost certainly invalid under UCTA; and this shows that allowing parties to challenge terms in their individual contracts, while invaluable for them, has a limited impact on contracting practice generally.

5.100 Is such a general policing power needed over terms in contracts between businesses? It seems likely that there are many businesses which are sufficiently sophisticated and powerful to be able to bargain for terms that they think suitable, or at least to ensure that terms they consider inappropriate will not in practice be applied against them. To the extent that this leads suppliers to modify their standard terms, this may operate to protect not only the business concerned but also other businesses with similar interests (unless the supplier discriminates between customers and applies different standard terms to different groups, which we think would be costly and therefore unusual). However, it is not always the case that less sophisticated or powerful businesses will benefit.

---

[111] Paras 4.179 – 4.186 above.

[112] Para 3.121 above.

5.101 First, a powerful business may simply insist that its suppliers contract on its own terms. This will leave the supplier's standard terms in place for contracts with less powerful customers.

5.102 Secondly, the powerful business may not be concerned to have the offending term removed from the supplier's conditions. Instead it may simply rely on its market power to ensure that the supplier will not enforce the term against it.[113] The term will still apply to the supplier's contracts and may be enforced against less important customers.

5.103 Thirdly, different customers may have different requirements. For example, a small business is likely to have few reserves to meet contingencies and therefore may be more risk-averse than a larger business. Thus a price variation clause in the supplier's conditions may be acceptable for a larger business but a matter of grave concern for a smaller enterprise. Larger and more powerful businesses may therefore not exercise any pressure on the supplier to remove the term, leaving smaller businesses unprotected.

5.104 Fourthly, it is clear from reported cases that unfair terms do persist in business-to-business contracts and that they are sometimes applied by the suppliers in question.[114]

5.105 A case can be made, therefore, for a body having power to prevent the use of unfair terms by businesses in their contracts with other businesses. Such controls are found in some continental countries. In Sweden it has been reported that the powers have seldom resulted in reported cases, but there may have been informal settlements resulting in unfair terms being withdrawn and the existence of the powers may have had a considerable influence.[115] The relevant legislation in Germany is also seldom used in business-to-business contracts.

5.106 If there were to be such preventive powers, should they be available to protect any size of business? Since the problems are almost certainly greatest for small businesses, it is perhaps arguable that the preventive powers should be slanted in this direction, either by requiring this to be taken into account explicitly by the authority or by giving the powers only to authorities or organisations that are empowered to act on behalf of small businesses.

5.107 The result might be that suppliers would find that they need two sets of conditions, one for small business customers and a second for others. There

---

[113] A similar process is reportedly taking place in relation to late payment of commercial debts: small businesses who under the Late Payment of Commercial Debts (Interest) Act 1998 (see para 5.37 above) are entitled to interest on late payments are simply not claiming it from their more powerful customers for fear of losing the latter's business. See for example V Meek, "Get Interested" (1999) 124 Accountancy 24.

[114] See *Timeload Ltd v British Telecommunications plc* [1995] EMLR 459 (CA); *Stag Line Ltd v Tyne Shiprepair Group Ltd (The "Zinnia")* [1984] 2 Lloyd's Rep 211; *Edmund Murray Ltd v BSP International Foundations Ltd* (1993) 33 Con LR 1.

[115] We are informed that this is the case by Professor J Herre of Stockholm School of Economics.

would obviously be some additional cost involved, but this would be off-set by the increased efficiency in the terms being matched more closely to the needs of different customers.

5.108   However, it seems quite possible that many of the replacement terms will be acceptable to all customers. A parallel may be drawn with the OFT's experience with terms offered to consumers. It appears that frequently businesses whose terms are challenged as being unfair are actually using them without having considered them in much detail. They frequently concede that the terms, at least if applied literally, give them a quite unnecessary degree of protection and might operate unfairly against consumers. They are then quite ready to change the terms to something fairer.[116] It seems plausible that the same is true for business contracts. If so, the gain in efficiency and fairness would be greater still.

5.109   It might be argued that encouraging businesses to improve their standard terms does not alter the reality of the contractual relationship but only the formal position, as in practice the terms are not applied literally but in a fair way. This is admittedly not a justification for allowing the persistence of unfair terms in consumer contracts, since consumers may be put off from claiming by the apparently draconian terms, but, arguably, businesses are unlikely to be deterred in this way. The argument cannot be dismissed out of hand, but it has at least two weak points. The first is that it seems costly to both sides to employ terms that do not fit the reality of their contractual relationship, since there will be considerable scope for disagreement as to what that "reality" is. The second is that it, in effect, leaves a great deal to the discretion of one party, who may apply the terms in what it perceives to be a fair way but which, judged more objectively, is not fair. An example of this is the *Finney Lock Seeds* case,[117] in which a seed company which supplied seed to a farmer limited its liability in the event of the seed being defective to a return of the contract price. The House of Lords held that the clause was unreasonable. One of the principal reasons for doing so was evidence that, in practice, the seed company would normally pay some further compensation when seed was defective; this was taken to show that even the seed company considered the clause to be unreasonable. Put another way, the clause gave the seed company complete discretion to decide whether to pay further compensation according to its own evaluation of whether the fault was primarily its own or that of the farmer, rather than according to a judicial determination of the question. In effect, the clause purported to oust the jurisdiction of the courts over payment of compensation for breach of contract. In these circumstances it is perhaps unsurprising that the clause was held to be unreasonable.

5.110   It seems to us that the decision whether to recommend the extension of the "preventive" powers of UTCCR to business-to-business contracts depends on the answers to at least two questions. The first is whether it is in principle desirable to extend the controls. The second is whether there is some suitable body to take on the task of taking action against businesses that use unfair terms, or trade

---

[116] See Unfair Contract Terms Bulletin 1 (OFT 159, May 1996) para 1.19.

[117] *George Mitchell (Chesterhall) Ltd v Finney Lock Seeds Ltd* [1983] 2 AC 803 (HL).

associations and other bodies that recommend them. It is possible that an association concerned with the interests of businesses, particularly small businesses, might be a candidate. However, to operate an effective unit to police unfair terms would be expensive, and we do not know whether there is any body that would be prepared to meet the necessary expenditure.

5.111 **We invite views on the desirability and the practicability of extending the preventive controls over unfair terms to business-to-business contracts.**

PART VI
SALE OR SUPPLY OF GOODS NOT RELATED TO BUSINESS

6.1 We noted in Part III that UCTA section 6 [s 20] applies not only to consumer and business-to-business contracts but also when the seller or supplier is not making the contract in the course of a business. Thus section 6 [s 20] applies to sales by a consumer to a business (for example a sale of a used car to a car dealer) and to purely "private" sales (for example, a sale of a used car by one private motorist to another). The section imposes controls on clauses affecting the implied obligations as to title and as to description and sample. In this very short Part we consider whether these controls should be retained.

1. OBLIGATIONS AS TO TITLE

6.2 Section 6(1) [s 20(1)] of UCTA prevents any seller or supplier under a hire-purchase agreement from excluding or restricting his obligations under the SGA 1979 section 12 (seller's implied undertakings as to title) or SOGITA section 8.[1]

6.3 We have already said[2] that we consider that these implied obligations reflect a fundamental principle of the law of moveable property, namely, that a seller or supplier of goods should have a good title to pass to the purchaser. We do not see any case for reducing the protection offered by these sections of UCTA. A seller who is unsure whether he has title can limit his liability, provided the fact that the title may be doubtful is brought home to the buyer:

> the seller can contract out of the obligation to transfer *full* title by stipulating for sale with a restricted title; but section 6 of [UCTA] prevents him from excluding or restricting his obligations as to title in any other way.[3]

Moreover, we are not aware of any difficulties over these provisions.

6.4 Maintaining controls over sales by consumers to businesses and other "private" contracts that fall within section 6 [s 20] may have implications for the form of the legislation we envisage. It is likely to mean that the legislation will contain a

---

[1] Section 7, which does the equivalent for other consumer or business-to-business contracts under which possession or ownership of goods passes, does not apply to liability or obligations that do not arise in the course of a business. The same is true of the Scottish equivalent, s 21(3), save that s 21(3A) applies to any kind of contract. This subsection prevents the exclusion or restriction of liability as to title etc that arises under the Supply of Goods and Services Act 1982, s 11B. This difference has not been reproduced in the draft Bill.

[2] Para 5.13 above. As the Law Commissions said in the First Report, para 17, there is "no justification for excluding or varying the implied condition and warranties imposed by section 12, save where it is clear that the seller is purporting to sell only a limited title."

[3] Implied Terms in Contracts for the Supply of Goods (1979) Law Com No 95 ("the 1979 Report") para 70 (emphasis in original).

separate section on sales by consumers and a separate part dealing with "private" contracts.[4] We think the resulting complexity is justified by the importance of these controls.

6.5   We provisionally propose that the existing controls over clauses excluding or restricting implied obligations as to title, etc in contracts for the sale or supply of goods where the seller or supplier is not acting for business purposes should be replicated in the new legislation.

2. CORRESPONDENCE WITH DESCRIPTION OR SAMPLE

6.6   Section 6(3) [s 20(2)] prevents any seller from excluding or restricting liability for breach of the obligations arising under the SGA or (for hire-purchase) SOGITA as to correspondence with description or sample.[5]

6.7   It may seem odd that these controls should apply to "private sellers". We have been unable to discover why it was thought that they should. Section 6 [s 20] is derived from SOGITA, which was passed following the Law Commissions' First Report on Exemption Clauses. Part V of the Report suggested two formulations for legislation to control contracting out of the conditions and warranties implied by sections 13–15 of the SGA. Alternative A would have prohibited exclusion of sections 13–15 in consumer sales only; alternative B would also have prohibited unreasonable exclusion of these sections in other contracts of sale. It is pointed out that alternative B allows for a simpler definition of "consumer sale",[6] but there is no mention of "private" contracts, nor of sales by consumers. Alternative B was preferred by the legislature, and discussion of the resulting Supply of Goods (Implied Terms) Bill in Parliament does not clarify the issue. By the time of the Second Report, the Law Commissions seem to have come to the conclusion that it was only in consumer contracts and business-to-business contracts that controls were needed over other types of contract[7] and other types of exemption clause. No recommendations were made as to the existing provisions that became UCTA section 6 [s 20].[8]

6.8   We are not convinced that there is any need for controls over clauses excluding or restricting the implied obligations as to description or sample in sales by consumers to businesses or as between private parties. We suspect that the controls are of no practical importance. On the other hand we have no evidence that they do any harm.

---

[4]   See para 8.16 below.

[5]   Section 6(3) [s 20(2)] refers also to implied terms as to quality or fitness for purpose, but these do not arise in sales not made in the course of a business.

[6]   See First Report, para 95.

[7]   See Second Report, para 9.

[8]   In the 1979 Report, the Law Commission took the view that exclusion of private contracts from UCTA s 7 stemmed from its decision to make *no* recommendation in the Second Report for controlling exemption clauses in anything other than business contracts.

6.9   However, to keep them in their present form might cause an inconsistency in the new legislation if, as we have provisionally proposed, the controls over such clauses in business-to-business contracts were to be somewhat more limited than at present. It will be recalled that the controls in UCTA section 6 apply whether or not the clause was "negotiated" between the parties. We have provisionally proposed that in business-to-business contracts the controls over negotiated exclusion clauses in UCTA section 6(3) [s 20(2)(ii)] are not needed and that it would suffice for "standard" or "non-negotiated" terms to be subject to the general fairness test.[9] It would be rather paradoxical to provide that, as between one business and another, a negotiated clause is exempt from control but to provide control over even a negotiated clause that is used by a consumer against a business.

6.10   One possibility would be to limit the controls over "private" sales and "sales by consumers" to non-negotiated clauses. It will be seldom if ever that a private seller has a set of standard conditions, but it may be that the seller will sometimes write out a clause that is not negotiated between the parties, and which, had it been in a business-to-business contract, would thus fall within the controls we propose. Another possibility would be simply to remove these controls from "private" sales and sales by consumers to businesses altogether. Or a third is simply to preserve the effect of section 6(3) [s 20(2)(ii)] in respect of sales by consumers and "private" sales, even at the risk of some inconsistency.

6.11   Our provisional view is that the third solution is probably the best one.

6.12   **We provisionally propose that clauses which exclude or restrict liability for breach of the obligations arising under the SGA 1979 or (for hire-purchase) SOGITA as to correspondence with description or sample should remain subject to a "fair and reasonable" test when the sale is between private parties or is by a consumer to a business, irrespective of whether the clause has been negotiated.**

---

[9]   Para 5.47 above.

PART VII
NON-CONTRACTUAL NOTICES EXCLUDING BUSINESS LIABILITY FOR NEGLIGENCE OR BREACH OF DUTY

1. INTRODUCTION

7.1 In Part III we saw that UCTA section 2 [s 16[1]] applies not only to contractual terms that purport to exclude or restrict a business's liability[2] for negligence [breach of duty] but also to notices that purport to do the same in respect of claims in tort [delict]. Notices that purport to exclude or restrict liability for death or personal injury are of no effect; exclusions or restrictions of liability for other loss or damage may be valid if they are fair and reasonable.

2. NON-CONTRACTUAL NOTICES SHOULD BE CONTROLLED

7.2 We have provisionally proposed that any contract term which excludes or restricts liability for death or personal injury caused by negligence [breach of duty] should be of no effect when it is in either a consumer contract[3] or a business-to-business contract.[4] Terms purporting to exclude or restrict business liability for other loss or damage will continue to be subject to a reasonableness test.[5] We believe that it is important to maintain the existing controls over notices which might otherwise exclude a business's liability in tort [delict] to persons with whom it does not have a contractual relationship and who are killed, injured or harmed by its negligence [breach of duty].

7.3 **We provisionally propose that the existing controls over notices which might otherwise exclude a business's liability in tort [delict] to persons with whom it does not have a contractual relationship, and who are killed, injured or harmed by its negligence [breach of duty], should be retained.**

---

[1] In its original form Part II of UCTA did not apply to non-contractual notices disclaiming liability in delict. The relevant amendments were made by the Law Reform (Miscellaneous Provisions) (Scotland) Act 1990, s 68.

[2] There is a difference between England and Scotland as to what counts as business liability. Business liability includes liability arising from the occupation of land for business purposes, but in England there is an exception where the injured party was allowed access to the land for recreational or educational purposes not connected to the occupier's business. This exception does not apply under Scots law. Moreover, under the Occupiers' Liability (Scotland) Act 1960, s 2(1), the statutory obligation to take reasonable care can only be altered by a contractual term: a non-contractual notice is ineffective.

[3] See para 4.35 above.

[4] Para 5.8 above.

[5] See paras 4.40 and 5.42 above.

3. A SEPARATE PROVISION FOR ALL EXCLUSIONS AND RESTRICTIONS OF LIABILITY FOR NEGLIGENCE

7.4 In Part VIII, in which we describe some features of the draft Bill contained in Appendix B, we explain that, because the controls over liability for negligence [breach of duty] apply both to contract terms and non-contractual notices, we have provisionally decided that the new legislation should follow the model of UCTA in having a separate part dealing with exclusions and restrictions of liability for negligence [breach of duty], whether that be in contract or tort [delict] and whether the purported exclusion be by a contract term or a non-contractual notice.

4. PREVENTIVE ACTION

7.5 At present a term of a consumer contract which excludes or restricts liability for negligence [breach of duty] will fall within UTCCR and, if the term is unfair, action can be taken to prevent its use. Non-contractual notices excluding liability in tort [delict] fall outside this.[6]

7.6 Although notices of this kind may be of no effect at all, or of no effect unless they are fair,[7] we believe that they may deter claimants who have suffered injury or loss and who do not know that the notice is invalid. In this respect they are no different to other potentially invalid contract terms.[8] We think that they are likely to continue to be used, despite their ineffectiveness as a matter of law, unless steps can be taken to prevent their use. Therefore we consider that it would be useful if the various bodies listed in UTCCR Schedule 1 (as amended) could act to prevent the use of such notices.[9]

7.7 **We provisionally propose that the preventive powers be extended to cover non-contractual notices which purport to exclude or restrict a business's liability in tort [delict].**

---

[6] Unless the arrangement between the occupier and the claimant is to be treated as a "contract" for the purposes of the Directive; see para 3.107 above.

[7] See para 6.1 above.

[8] Cf para 3.119 above.

[9] This would not of course oblige the bodies authorised to incur expenditure policing such notices. They could merely deal with complaints made to them.

PART VIII
PUTTING THE NEW LEGISLATION INTO CLEAR, ACCESSIBLE TERMS

1. INTRODUCTION

8.1 The third paragraph of our terms of reference requires us to consider the desirability and feasibility of

> Making any replacement legislation clearer and more accessible to the reader, so far as is possible without making the law significantly less certain, by using language which is non-technical with simple sentences, by setting out the law in a simple structure following a clear logic and by using presentation which is easy to follow.

8.2 In Part II we explained the importance that the Law Commissions place on making the substantive law accessible to the businesses and individuals likely to be affected by it on a day-to-day basis, particularly when the relevant legislation is important to them before any question of a dispute arises and when they are not likely to have legal advice. We suggested that we should aim to make the legislation readily understandable, if not to consumers in general, at least to consumer advisers, and to business people with some knowledge of contracting.[1]

8.3 We also explained that we think the only way of testing whether such a project is worthwhile is to draft a sample part of the legislation and expose it to consultation. Therefore we include in Appendix B a draft of a selection of the clauses which would be necessary were the two pieces of existing legislation, UCTA and UTCCR, to be combined.

8.4 Consultees will, we hope, comment not only on the details of the draft but also on whether the overall project to put the new legislation into clear, non-technical terms is worthwhile.[2]

8.5 We would repeat that, in order to prepare the draft, it was necessary to make some assumptions about various decisions on which we are in fact consulting. Inclusion of a particular approach or decision in the draft does not create any presumption that our final report will adopt that decision or approach, nor indeed that it will recommend that the new legislation should be drafted in the way suggested in this consultation paper.[3]

8.6 In this Part of the consultation paper we explain some of the thinking behind the draft provisions. What follows is to some extent similar to the explanatory notes which would normally accompany the draft Bill that we would include in a report in which we recommend legislation. However, it goes a little further than is

---

[1] See para 2.35 above.

[2] Para 8.65 below.

[3] See para 2.38 above.

normal in explanatory notes in explaining the thinking that lies behind the structure of the draft as well as the intention behind each clause.

2. LIMITS TO THE THIRD LIMB OF THE PROJECT

8.7 There are limits to what can be achieved in this limb of the overall project. It would be only fair to admit that, as we tried to put the provisional draft into "clear" and "non-technical" terms, we became more and more aware of these limits.

8.8 One point is that if, as is envisaged, UCTA and UTCCR are to be replaced by a single piece of legislation, that legislation will have to apply to a variety of different contracts – for example, to consumer contracts and business-to-business contracts. It also needs to be in a style that is internally harmonious. This meant that we were not able to pursue one idea, namely to follow the style of many "Plain English" consumer contracts and refer to the parties as "you" (the consumer) and "us" (the business), or (more realistically) as "you" and "the business". That might work for the parts dealing with consumer contracts[4] but it would not work for "business-to-business" contracts. We have, however, used the phrases "the business" and "the consumer".

8.9 A second and more fundamental point is that the legislation is dealing with technical concepts that often are quite complex and cannot be explained in the unfair terms legislation itself. For example, section 6 [s 20] of UCTA prevents the exclusion or restriction of various implied terms under the SGA 1979. It may be that, in an ideal world, a reader would find in the unfair terms legislation itself an explanation of precisely what rights the business may or may not exclude, but in reality that would make the unfair terms legislation unmanageably long. Instead we have to use cross-references to other legislation.

8.10 Thirdly, the legislation has to be precise. We are not drafting a code in the civilian tradition, nor a set of general principles of contract law that can be interpreted liberally by the courts.[5] This is legislation that will be "just another" statute[6] about contract law and will fall to be interpreted in the same way as the existing legislation.[7]

---

[4] Even for consumer contracts it might read rather oddly to business people; they might even feel this to be "anti-business" legislation.

[5] Cf O Lando and H Beale, *Principles of European Contract Law* (1999) art 1:106 (1): "These Principles should be interpreted and developed in accordance with their purposes. In particular, regard should be had to the need to promote good faith and fair dealing, certainty in contractual relationships and uniformity of application."

[6] Or possibly regulations: see para 2.29, n 36 above.

[7] We can envisage legislation on, say, consumer contracts in general that was designed to be interpreted more liberally and which could thus be less precise and more open-textured. We do not think that such a drafting technique is appropriate for legislation applying to only one facet of the contractual relationship. A complete "Consumer Code" might be drafted very differently to the unfair terms legislation with which we are concerned – particularly as it has to apply to other contracts also. See para 8.8 above.

8.11 A fourth point, which as regards legislation that is intended to be "user-friendly" may be more controversial, is that the reader may have to refer to normal rules of statutory interpretation. This is to avoid having to use lengthy phrases that in themselves might make the clauses less clear. Thus the draft does not use "he or she" when referring to individual consumers, not "he, she or it" when referring to legal persons generally. Similarly it uses "persons" to mean both individuals and organisations. The Interpretation Act 1978 provides that "words importing the masculine gender include the feminine"[8] and that "person" includes a corporate or unincorporate body as well as a natural person.[9] After some hesitation we decided that the draft should follow these conventions.

3. SIMPLER STRUCTURE AND LANGUAGE, AND MORE EXPLANATION

8.12 What we think this limb of the project can achieve, by way of making the legislation clearer and more accessible, is twofold. First, we have structured the draft legislation in a less compressed way, so that there are separate parts for each broad type of contract affected. We explain this in more detail in the next section. Secondly, we have tried to keep what might be termed the "principal" sections simple and free from "legal jargon". Consumer contracts are supposed to meet those criteria;[10] it would be ironic if the legislation on unfair terms did not. We have tried to keep "technical detail" to a minimum and to put it into subsidiary provisions, such as definitions sections, where we hope it will be less off-putting to the reader.

8.13 Thirdly, we have tried to amplify the words of the current legislation to make it clearer what it actually requires or forbids. We think this is of particular importance to businesses, which will want to know what they need to do to ensure, so far as possible, that the terms of their contracts with consumers satisfy the legislation; and to help consumers and their advisers.

8.14 Each of these steps has meant using more words. Ultimately a balance has to be struck between clarity and conciseness. Whether the balance we have struck in the draft legislation in Appendix B is appropriate is a question on which we invite consultees to comment.

4. THE PARTS OF THE DRAFT BILL

8.15 As we suggested in Part I,[11] given the complexity of its subject matter, UCTA is in many ways a model of concision. It frequently covers several different types of transaction (for example, consumer contracts, business-to-business contracts and others) within a single section. This makes it hard to understand at first sight, as it is necessary to analyse the provisions closely to see which apply to which situation.

---

[8] Interpretation Act 1978, s 6(a).

[9] Interpretation Act 1978, Sched 1.

[10] See Unfair Contract Terms Bulletin 4 (OFT 170, December 1997) p 14.

[11] Para 1.6 above.

"Consumer", "business" and "private" contracts

8.16 Our first decision was to "unpack" the provisions and make separate provisions for each type of contract, so that the reader, who will normally know which category is in question, can turn straight to the relevant part and ignore those dealing with the other types of contract. This suggested a broad division into Parts dealing respectively with consumer contracts, business-to-business contracts and "private" contracts (that is, contracts between individuals not acting for business purposes[12]). This makes the new legislation longer than the legislation it replaces, but it is our provisional view that this disadvantage is outweighed by the gain in clarity.

8.17 On this model, the "unified regime" to replace UTCCR and those parts of UCTA which deal with consumer contracts would form a separate part of the legislation applying only to consumer contracts. The regime we propose for business-to-business contracts (or, if those proposals are not confirmed, the provisions that would replace the UCTA controls over business contracts) would fall into the business-to-business part; and the few rules which apply to all contracts would be in the "private" contracts part. The draft Bill does not contain provisions dealing with business-to-business contracts.

Exclusions and restrictions of liability for negligence [breach of duty]

8.18 This simple tripartite division (consumer, business-to-business and private) does not cover the whole ground. UCTA applies to clauses which exclude business liability for negligence [breach of duty] irrespective of whether the party who has suffered the harm is a consumer, a business or anyone else; and the provisions apply not only to contractual terms but also, where liability in tort [delict] is concerned, to non-contractual notices (see Part VII above). It would be possible to have clauses which apply to terms that purport to exclude or restrict liability for negligence [breach of duty] in each of the three Parts, but it would still be necessary to have a separate provision for non-contractual notices. After considerable thought we decided provisionally that it would be preferable to keep the "negligence" provisions together in a single, separate Part. Thus the principal provisions would be grouped into four Parts:

(1) Negligence liability [liability for breach of duty]

(2) Consumer contracts

(3) Business-to-business contracts (not included in this draft Bill)

(4) Private contracts.

General provisions

8.19 We think that this division is important for what we might call the principal "operative" clauses. There are in addition, as Parts III, IV and V of this

---

[12] We have asked consultees whether the provisions applying to wholly "private" contracts, and those applying when a consumer sells to a business, should be retained: see paras 6.5 and 6.12 above. For the purposes of the draft Bill we have assumed that they should be, so that consultees can see how they would be fitted into the new legislation.

consultation paper suggest, a number of ancillary questions (such as definitions, the effect of a decision that a term is not "fair and reasonable", and various controls on attempts at evasion of the legislation) which apply "across the board", to each category of contract. It would be possible to insert these provisions into each Part, so that each is complete and free-standing. However, this would involve a good deal of repetition, and we think that it is not necessary. We think that even non-lawyers will readily understand a Part containing general provisions that apply to each of the other Parts. This structure is very common in insurance contracts, which regularly have sections dealing with the various types of cover provided under the policy and then a section of "general conditions". We believe that business people and most consumers are used to that and can therefore be expected to follow a similar structure in the new legislation.

8.20 There are also provisions dealing with what is "fair and reasonable" and the burden of proof. The decision on where these should be placed depends to some extent on whether our provisional proposal that the test of what is "fair and reasonable" should be the same for each type of contract[13] is confirmed, and the recommendation in our final report on the question of the burden of proof.[14] If our final recommendation is that the test of what is "fair and reasonable" and the burden of proof should be the same for both consumer and business-to-business contracts, then these items can also be in the general Part. (There is already a paragraph stating that the factors shall apply to notices with any modifications that are appropriate.[15])

Definitions

8.21 A common technique of drafting statutes is to start with definitions. This is entirely logical but, we think, very off-putting to a person not accustomed to reading legislation. We have used the opposite technique of stating the principal operative provisions first, in language which should be broadly understandable to readers without first having recourse to definitions. The detailed definitions are set out later for use if required.

Form of the legislation

8.22 If there is to be new legislation, it will have to be decided whether it will be a statute or a statutory instrument.[16] For the purposes of this Part we assume that it will be a statute, and so refer to the draft "clauses" of the "Bill".

[13] Paras 4.94 and 5.75 above.

[14] We ask consultees on their views on this at paras 4.150 and 5.90 above.

[15] Sched 1, para 5.

[16] See para 2.29, n 36 above.

5. NEGLIGENCE LIABILITY [LIABILITY FOR BREACH OF DUTY]

Clause 1: Contract terms or notices excluding or restricting business liability for negligence

8.23 Clause 1 is not very different to UCTA section 2 [s 16] but it (or at least its operative part) is placed before the definitions found in UCTA section 1 [or the exceptions found in s 15]. This more direct approach should make it more obvious to the lay reader what the clause is about. For the same reason, the restriction to business liability[17] is introduced into the principal subsections, (1) and (2). Clause 1(4) replaces the cryptic "(whether his own business or another's)" of UCTA section 1(3)(a).[18]

8.24 UCTA section 2(1) [s 16(1)] refers to the exclusion or restriction of liability by a notice "given to persons generally or to particular persons." We have not felt it necessary to reproduce that explanation in the draft Bill; the meaning of the word "notice" seems clear without it.

Clause 2: Exceptions from section 1 for England and Wales

8.25 Clause 2(1) replaces UCTA Schedule 1, paragraph 4, stating the effect of that provision. Clause 2(2) replaces the proviso to UCTA section 1(3).[19] Neither provision of UCTA has an equivalent for Scotland. We see no need to alter that position, hence clause 2(3).

Clause 3: Effect of agreement to, or awareness of, term or notice

8.26 This replaces UCTA section 2(3) [s 16(3)].

6. CONSUMER CONTRACTS

8.27 The draft refers to "consumer contracts", and to "the consumer" and "the business", rather than "a person dealing as consumer". (These terms are defined in clause 15.)

8.28 The principal provisions dealing specifically with consumer contracts fall into two groups. Certain terms are always ineffective. These are covered in clauses 4 and 5. Others are subject to a "fair and reasonable" test. This is provided in clause 6. The headings to the clauses are designed to make this division clear.

Clause 4: Sale to, and hire-purchase by, consumer: terms of no effect

8.29 We have retained the division between contracts of sale and hire-purchase,[20] on the one hand, and other contracts under which possession or ownership of goods

---

[17] UCTA s 1(3) [s 16 does this already].

[18] There is no equivalent phrase for Scotland, but we think it best to include a provision to ensure that employees cannot exclude their own liability in delict and therefore, with it, their employer's vicarious liability for their actions.

[19] Added by Occupiers' Liability Act 1984, s 2.

[20] UCTA s 6 [s 20].

passes,[21] on the other, simply because to combine them would make the relevant clause very long.

8.30 Clause 4(2) uses a different form of words to those in UCTA. For England, UCTA sections 6(2) and 7(2) state that the relevant liabilities "cannot be excluded or restricted by reference to any contract term". For Scotland, sections 20(2)(b)(ii) and 21(1)(a)(ii) provide that the relevant type of clause shall have no effect if it was not fair and reasonable to incorporate it in the contract. The present draft uses the formula that "The business cannot rely on a term of the contract to exclude or restrict its liability" in order to be consistent with clause 6, for which this seems to be the best approach.[22]

8.31 Clause 4(3) sets out the implied terms that cannot be "excluded or restricted" by reference to the sections of the relevant legislation.

8.32 Clause 4(4) replaces UCTA section 12(2) [s 25(1) ("consumer contract" – exemption for contract of sale by auction or competitive tender)]. It is in narrower terms to reflect the requirements of SCGD, under which sellers at other kinds of auctions may not be permitted to exclude or restrict the consumer's rights under the Directive.[23]

Clause 5: Other contracts under which goods pass to consumer: terms of no effect

8.33 Clause 5(3), unlike UCTA section 7 [s 21], refers expressly to the sections of the Supply of Goods and Services Act 1982 that imply terms as to title and as to conformity with description or sample and quality and fitness for purpose into other contracts under which ownership or possession of goods pass. It does not seem necessary to retain the reference currently in UCTA section 7(1) [s 21(3)] to other kinds of "obligation [...] arising by implication of law from the nature of the contract." The terms implied under the 1982 Act seem to occupy the whole of the relevant ground.

Clause 6: Other terms detrimental to consumer of no effect unless fair and reasonable

8.34 All other terms that are subject to control fall under the "fair and reasonable" criterion set out in clause 6. The operative part of this is short;[24] it is the exceptions, such as for "core terms" and terms which are required by statute or which merely reproduce the general law, that are complex. These exceptions are set out in the remainder of clause 6.

---

[21] UCTA s 7 [s 21].

[22] See para 8.38 below.

[23] See paras 4.162 – 4.164 above.

[24] Clause 6(1) and (2).

162

8.35 Clause 6(1) makes it clear that it is only a term that is detrimental to the consumer that may be challenged under this clause, but for reasons explained earlier[25] uses the basic test of whether the clause is "fair and reasonable".

8.36 Clause 6(2) addresses a problem that a single term may include some provisions that are detrimental to the consumer and others that are beneficial to the consumer. The clause is designed so as not to affect the parts of the term that are not detrimental.

8.37 However, within a term or part of a term that is detrimental to the consumer, the clause does not distinguish between parts which are *unfairly* detrimental and parts which, on their own, would be fair and reasonable. To allow the business to enforce any provisions of a detrimental term that could on their own be fair would encourage businesses to include as much "boiler-plate" as possible, knowing that they have nothing to lose because only the unfair parts will be struck out. Under clause 6(2) the court is to decide whether the part of the clause that is detrimental to the consumer is fair and reasonable; if it is not, the whole of the detrimental part will be invalid.

8.38 Clause 6(1) uses the formula that "the business cannot rely on the term" to make it clear that the consumer, if it is in her interest to do so, may enforce a clause that might be seen as unfairly detrimental to her.[26] This is to the same effect as UTCCR regulation 8(1), which provides that "an unfair term ... shall not be binding on the consumer", but is in language that is perhaps more familiar to the reader in the UK.

8.39 The effect of clause 6(3) is that a term which sets out the main subject matter is not subject to review, subject to two provisos. The first proviso is that it is "transparent", the term used to incorporate the "plain, intelligible language" requirement of the Directive. The second proviso rests on the idea that a term cannot represent the main subject matter of the contract if it is substantially different to what the consumer should reasonably have expected, for example in the light of the information given to her.[27]

8.40 Clause 6(4) does the equivalent for the "adequacy of the price". As we explained above, a sum payable under the contract will not qualify as the "price" if it is payable under a "subsidiary term" or is payable in circumstances, or calculated in a way, that is substantially different to what it was reasonable for the consumer to expect. However, the consumer will not be able to challenge the amount of the "principal" price simply on the ground that it was higher than might reasonably have been expected.[28]

---

[25] See paras 4.89 – 4.94 above.

[26] To use the formulation in UCTA ss 6(2) and 7(2) referred to earlier (para 8.30 above) would not be appropriate for terms other than exclusion clauses, while the formulation of the equivalent Scottish provisions would mean that the term was of no effect against either party.

[27] See paras 3.23 – 3.24 and 4.55 above.

[28] See para 4.63 above.

8.41 Recital 13 of the Directive makes it clear that contract terms that do no more than state "rules which, according to the law, shall apply between the contracting parties provided that no other arrangements have been established" need not be subject to review.[29] Clause 6(5) aims at this exemption.[30]

8.42 The OFT has said that in its view the "plain language" requirement is not satisfied if the term is in print that is hard to read, if the terms are not readily accessible to the consumer, or the layout of the contract document is hard to follow. Clause 6(6) imposes explicit requirements to achieve what we have called "transparency".

Clause 7: Sale to, and hire-purchase by, business: effect of certain terms

8.43 Clause 7 deals with the less common type of consumer contract under which a consumer sells goods, or possibly even lets them on hire-purchase, to a business – for example, the consumer who sells a car to a car dealer. UCTA imposes restrictions on the consumer's power to contract out of his obligations as to title and (unless the term is fair and reasonable) description or sample.[31] If these controls are to be continued, it seems sensible to place them under the broad heading of consumer contracts but in a separate section dealing only with these "consumer-to-business" contracts.

7. PRIVATE CONTRACTS

Clause 8: Sale of goods and hire-purchase: effect of certain terms

8.44 We have raised the question whether the rather limited controls over purely "private contract" terms imposed by UCTA and reproduced in this clause are necessary.[32] If they are to be maintained, we consider that they should be placed in a separate Part of the Bill even though the provisions of clause 8(2) and (3) mirror exactly those of clause 7(2) and (3). This is because clause 8 is dealing with a distinct class of contracts, namely contracts where neither party is acting for purposes related to a business. The easiest way to make it clear to the reader is to have a separate provision.

8. BUSINESS-TO-BUSINESS CONTRACTS

8.45 This Part would follow, or possibly precede, the Part dealing with private contracts. As stated above, provisions dealing with business-to-business contracts have not yet been drafted. We would anticipate that they would follow the same style of drafting as is used in the present draft.

[29] See para 3.37 above.

[30] Paras 4.71 – 4.73 above.

[31] In para 6.5 above we ask whether it is necessary to maintain these controls.

[32] See Part VI above.

9. GENERAL PROVISIONS

Clause 9: The fair and reasonable test

8.46 As under UCTA, the test of whether a contract term is fair and reasonable has to be slightly different from that applied to non-contractual notices, because the moment of time at which the fairness of a notice is to be judged must be different from the time at which a contract term is agreed, the test under the Directive.[33] The two tests are set out in subsections (1) and (2) of clause 9.

8.47 Paragraph (b) of each subsection refers to the fact that, on the approach we have provisionally proposed, in determining whether in an individual case the term or notice was fair and reasonable both substantive fairness ("the substance and effect of the term/notice") and procedural fairness ("the circumstances existing when the contract was made / the liability arose") should be taken into account.[34]

8.48 Clause 9(3) refers to the list of factors to be taken into account in deciding whether a term or notice is fair and reasonable which, we have provisionally proposed, should be included in the legislation. As the list is rather lengthy, it has been placed in a separate Schedule.[35] If our final report recommends that there should be separate lists for the different types of contract (we have provisionally proposed that the same list can apply to both consumer and business-to-business contracts[36]), there may have to be separate lists in separate Schedules.

8.49 Clause 9(4) refers to the Schedule containing the new indicative list and the examples that we propose the list should contain. We have provisionally proposed that there should be different lists for consumer and business-to-business contracts. Each Part can simply refer the reader to the relevant Schedule.[37]

Clause 10: Savings for mandatory and regulatory provisions

8.50 Terms which are required by other legislation or rules of law, or by regulators, will continue to be exempt from control.[38] So will terms that are required or authorised by international conventions to which the UK is party. This exemption follows UCTA section 29(1); it is narrower than the exemption that UTCCR seems to give.[39]

Clause 11: Secondary contracts

8.51 UCTA contains provisions designed to prevent evasion of the Act's controls over a contract by a second contract taking away rights that are secured by UCTA under

---

[33] See para 3.52 above.

[34] Paras 4.95 – 4.103 above.

[35] See the draft Bill, Sched 1, which is explained in para 8.61 below.

[36] Para 5.83 above.

[37] The (partial) list for consumer contracts is in the draft Bill, Sched 2.

[38] See paras 4.73 – 4.76 above.

[39] Paras 3.38 and 4.70 above.

the first contract.[40] The provisions in Part I (England) have proved difficult to apply.[41] They and the equivalent sections for Scotland would be replaced by this clause. It would have the result that, if the term in the first contract would be of no effect at all under clause 1(1), 4, 5, 7(2) or 8(2), the term in the secondary contract will equally be of no effect; if the term in the first contract would be subject to the "fair and reasonable" test, the same will apply to the term of the secondary contract. As the latter term will be treated as if it were part of the main contract, it will not be exempted from control on the ground that it is a "core term".[42] The clause will apply whether the parties to the two contracts are the same or different.[43] As under UCTA Part II,[44] there is an explicit saving for settlements of existing disputes.

Clause 12: Effect on contract of term having no effect

8.52   This replaces UTCCR regulation 8(2).[45]

Clause 13: Burden of proof

8.53   Clause 13(1) replaces UCTA section 12(3) [s 25(1)].

8.54   In Part IV we asked for consultees' views on whether the burden of proving that a clause is "fair and reasonable" should be on the business in all cases, or only in cases in which the term is to be found on the "indicative list". We have drafted alternative versions of the relevant clause: thus the first version of clause 13(2) and (3) (under "AND") represents the first alternative, and the second version of clause 13(2)–(4) (under "OR") the second.

10. INTERPRETATION

Clause 14: "Negligence" and "breach of duty"

8.55   This replaces UCTA section 1(1) [s 25(1)].

Clause 15: "Consumer contract", "the consumer" and "the business"

8.56   This replaces UCTA section 12 [s 25(1)] but uses the rather wider test of whether the activity of either party was "related to" business, as found in SCGD.[46] It does not require that any goods supplied be of a type ordinarily supplied for private use or consumption if the contract is to count as a consumer contract, as this restriction cannot survive SCGD.[47]

---

[40]   Section 10 [s 23].

[41]   See paras 3.114 – 3.115 above.

[42]   See para 4.189 above.

[43]   Clause 11(2). Cf paras 3.114 – 3.115 above.

[44]   See para 3.114, n 232 above.

[45]   See paras 4.179 – 4.180 above.

[46]   Art 2(a): see paras 3.81 – 3.85 and 4.152 above.

[47]   Paras 3.86 and 4.161 above.

8.57   The last phrase of the clause exempts employment contracts from the controls over consumer contracts in general. This follows the approach of UTCCR, which seem not to apply to employment contracts.[48] For the purposes of this draft we have assumed that employment contracts will not be brought within the controls over consumer contracts.[49]

Clause 16: "Exclusion or restriction of liability"

8.58   This clause replaces UCTA section 13 [s 25(3) and (5)]. Examples of "exclusions and restrictions" are given in the next clause. Clause 16 also defines the meaning of "exclude or restrict liability" in Schedule 2, paragraph 1.

Clause 17: Examples of "exclusion or restriction of liability"

8.59   This clause contains examples to show more clearly what is meant by "exclusion or restriction of liability" when that is referred to in clauses 1, 4, 5, 7 and 8. The examples are also referred to in Schedule 2, paragraph 1, as examples of terms that are presumed to be unfair under clause 9(4).

Clause 18: Interpretation of other expressions

8.60   The list of definitions in clause 17 is largely derived from UCTA section 14 [s 25]. It contains some additional definitions which in UCTA were contained in the relevant clauses but which seemed to "clutter" those clauses unnecessarily.

11. THE SCHEDULES

Schedule 1: Factors relevant to fairness

8.61   The various factors that seem relevant to whether a term or notice is fair and reasonable[50] are set out in Schedule 1. They are grouped into paragraphs in order to make it clearer how each one is likely to be relevant.

Schedule 2: Terms that are presumed to be unfair

8.62   Schedule 2 replaces the "indicative and non-exhaustive list of terms that may be regarded as unfair" presently in Schedule 2 to UTCCR. We have provisionally proposed that the list be reformulated, "translating" the examples into terms which are recognisable to readers from the UK. To give consultees an idea of how this might be done, the draft Bill contains four paragraphs that are intended to replace UTCCR Schedule 1, paragraph 1(b)–(e). An explanation for each one will be found in Part IV above.[51]

---

[48]   See para 3.45 above.

[49]   We have invited views on whether contracts of employment should be exempted: see paras 4.80 – 4.81 above.

[50]   See paras 4.95 – 4.103 above.

[51]   See paras 4.125 – 4.142 above.

12. Questions for Consultees

8.63 Given the limitations of this third limb of the project that are set out above, we believe that we have made the draft Bill about as clear and non-technical as is likely to be possible. We would of course be very glad to receive suggestions from consultees on how the draft might be further simplified. The principal question we would ask, however, is whether the simpler structure that we have adopted and the amplification of its intended meaning that we have included in the draft (for example by using expanded lists of factors and examples) offer any real improvement over the legislation that this draft is intended to replace.

8.64 **Do consultees have any suggestions as to how the draft Bill might be further simplified or made more accessible, particularly to those without a legal training?**

8.65 **Do consultees consider that the techniques of using a simplified structure and amplifying what is meant by the clauses should be pursued in any legislation that is finally recommended?**

PART IX
PROVISIONAL PROPOSALS AND QUESTIONS FOR CONSULTEES

9.1 We set out below our provisional proposals and the questions on which we invite the views of consultees. Some consultees may not wish to comment on all issues; their views are no less welcome. We would be grateful for comments not only on the matters specifically listed below, but also on any other points raised by this consultation paper. It would be very helpful if, when responding, consultees could indicate either the paragraph of this Part to which their remarks relate, or the paragraph of this consultation paper in which the issue was originally raised.

THE IMPACT OF OUR PROPOSALS

9.2 We invite comments on the practical and economic impact that our proposals would have on both consumers and businesses. (Paragraph 2.41)

CONSUMER CONTRACTS

Models for the replacement regime

9.3 There should be a single piece of legislation for the whole of the UK. (Paragraph 4.17)

9.4 So far as possible, the new unified regime should be clearer and more accessible to the reader than the present instruments. (Paragraph 4.19)

No reduction of consumer protection

9.5 With the exception of UCTA section 5 [s 19], the additional protection given by UCTA to consumers, beyond that given by UTCCR, should be maintained. If consultees disagree, which other additional protection would they do away with? (Paragraph 4.29)

Incorporation of other statutory and common law rules

9.6 To incorporate other statutory and common law rules applying to potentially "unfair" terms in consumer contracts into the proposed legislation would not be appropriate as part of this exercise, with the exception of any changes necessitated by SCGD. (Paragraph 4.32)

Terms of no effect

9.7 The terms set out below, at least in substance, should continue to be of no effect under the new regime:

(1) exclusions or restrictions of business liability for death or personal injury caused by negligence [breach of duty] (in any type of contract);

(2) exclusions or restrictions of liability for breach of the implied terms as to title in contracts for sale, hire-purchase or other transfer of property in goods;

(3) exclusions or restrictions of liability for breach of the implied terms as to description, quality etc in contracts for the supply of goods to a consumer; and

(4) terms which, in relation to any of the kinds of liability in (1)–(3) above,

    (a) make the liability or its enforcement subject to restrictive or onerous conditions;

    (b) exclude or restrict any right or remedy in respect of the liability, or subject a person to any prejudice in consequence of his pursuing any such right or remedy; or

    (c) exclude or restrict rules of evidence or procedure. (Paragraph 4.35)

9.8 In relation to consumers, the terms listed in paragraph 9.7 should be of no effect even if they relate to the creation, transfer or termination of an interest in land, and would therefore be exempt from control under UCTA. (Paragraph 4.37)

9.9 If consultees believe that there is a case for any other kind of term found in a consumer contract to be made automatically of no effect, they are invited to submit a reasoned case for its inclusion in the list. (Paragraph 4.39)

Terms which must be "fair" or "fair and reasonable"

9.10 Other terms in consumer contracts will be required to satisfy a "fairness" test. (Paragraph 4.40)

Individually negotiated terms

9.11 The new regime should apply to both negotiated and non-negotiated terms. We particularly invite comments on the practical and economic impact that this proposal would have. (Paragraph 4.54)

Terms not subject to control

"Core terms"

9.12 (1) The new legislation should exclude the main subject matter from the scope of review, but

(2) only in so far as

    (a) it is not substantially different from what the consumer should reasonably expect, and

    (b) it is stated in plain language (and is otherwise "transparent": see paragraph 9.24 below). (Paragraph 4.60)

9.13 The adequacy of the price should not be reviewable under the legislation, where

(1) having to make the payment, or the way in which it is calculated, is not substantially different from what the consumer, in the light of what he was told when or before the contract was made and all the other circumstances, should reasonably expect, and

(2) the price is not one contained in a subsidiary term,

provided that the price is stated in plain language (and is otherwise "transparent": see paragraph 9.24 below). (Paragraph 4.68)

9.14 Terms required or authorised by an international convention to which the UK is party should be exempt from the new "reasonableness" regime, but not terms which merely reflect the principles of such a convention. (Paragraph 4.70)

Mandatory and permitted terms

9.15 The exemption for terms which reflect what would be the law in the absence of contrary agreement should not apply unless the terms are in plain language (and are otherwise "transparent": see paragraph 9.24 below). (Paragraph 4.73)

9.16 A term should not be exempt merely because it represents the law of another Member State. (Paragraph 4.74)

9.17 Terms required by regulators should be exempt, but not those merely approved by a regulator. (Paragraph 4.76)

Excluded contracts

9.18 The new legislation should make it clear that it applies where the consumer is the seller or supplier. (Paragraph 4.78)

9.19 We invite views on

(1) whether contracts of employment should be covered by the new regime at all; and

(2) if so, whether they should count as consumer contracts, or as business-to-business contracts, or as a separate category subject to some (but not necessarily all) of the controls that apply to consumer contracts. (Paragraph 4.81)

9.20 The controls should apply to terms in cross-border contracts for the supply of goods to consumers in the same way as they would apply to the same terms in a domestic contract. (Paragraph 4.82)

9.21 There should be no special treatment of consumer contracts to which English or Scots law applies only through the choice of the parties. (Paragraph 4.86)

The test to be applied

The basic test

9.22 The basic test in the new legislation should be whether, judged by reference to the time the contract was made, the term is a fair and reasonable one; it is not necessary to include an explicit reference to good faith. We ask consultees whether they agree with this and, if not, what test they think should be used. (Paragraph 4.94)

9.23 We ask for consultees' views on our provisional proposal that the new legislation should contain detailed guidelines on the application of the "fair and reasonable" test, and on the contents of those guidelines proposed at paragraphs 4.96 and 4.99 – 4.101 above. (Paragraph 4.103)

Plain and intelligible language

9.24 (1) The factors to be taken into account in assessing fairness should include whether the contract is "transparent", in the sense of being expressed in plain language, presented in a clear manner and accessible to the consumer.

(2) Transparency should also be a condition of exemption for "core" and default terms (see paragraphs 9.12, 9.13 and 9.15 above). (Paragraph 4.106)

9.25 Whilst lack of transparency should not automatically render a term unfair, it should be made clear that a term may be found unfair principally or solely on that ground. (Paragraph 4.109)

9.26 The rule of interpretation in favour of the consumer should be stated in the new instrument. We would welcome consultees' views on what form this statement should take. (Paragraph 4.111)

Indicative lists

9.27 The legislation should include a new version of the indicative list, containing not only what is required by the Directive but the additional terms set out in paragraphs 4.113 and 4.116 above. We ask consultees if they agree with these additions and if there are any other terms which should be listed. (Paragraph 4.117)

9.28 The indicative list should be reformulated in terms which are more directly applicable to UK law and more readily comprehensible to UK readers. (Paragraph 4.121)

9.29 We invite views as to whether the list, and therefore the preventive powers under UTCCR regulations 10-15, should be extended so as explicitly to include contract terms which are automatically of no effect under other parts of the new legislation. (Paragraph 4.124)

9.30 We invite views on whether the reformulated list should refer to any clause which purports to exclude or restrict a business's liability for the death of or personal injury to a consumer and is not covered by the part of the list dealing with clauses that are automatically of no effect. (Paragraph 4.127)

9.31 Paragraph 1(d) of the indicative list should be replaced by a reference to a term entitling the business, on withdrawal by the consumer or termination of the contract because of the consumer's breach, to retain a pre-payment which is not reasonable in amount. (Paragraph 4.139)

9.32 The list should contain examples. We invite comments on this general question as well as on the individual examples discussed at paragraphs 4.125 – 4.142 above, and on the relevant parts of the draft Bill,[1] in terms of both substance and style. (Paragraph 4.143)

9.33 We invite views as to whether the types of terms listed in paragraph 2 of UTCCR Schedule 2 should continue to be set out as exceptions to the indicative list. (Paragraph 4.145)

Burden of showing that term is reasonable

9.34 We invite views on the question whether (a) the burden of proving that a term is fair should always rest on the business, or (b) the consumer should have to show that the term is unfair unless the term in question is on the indicative list. (The draft in Appendix B contains alternative formulations on this point.) (Paragraph 4.150)

Ancillary questions

Definitions

9.35 There should be no provision for "mixed" transactions in the new legislation, and it should be left to the determination of the judge according to the predominant purpose of each transaction. (Paragraph 4.157)

9.36 The present requirement that, for a contract for the supply of goods to qualify as a consumer contract, the goods supplied under the contract should be of a type ordinarily supplied for private use or consumption should not be retained – whether or not the contract is one of sale (in which case this requirement must in any event be abandoned so as to comply with SCGD). (Paragraph 4.161)

9.37 Sales by auction of second-hand goods, where the consumer can be present at the sale, should continue to be exempted from the absolute ban on contracting out which applies to other consumer sales. (Paragraph 4.164)

9.38 Sales by competitive tender should no longer be exempted from counting as "consumer" contracts. (Paragraph 4.165)

9.39 (1) The absolute ban on contracting out in consumer contracts should apply in favour of a person who is in fact a consumer even if he has held himself out as making the contract in the course of a business – whether or not the contract is one of sale (in which case this is required by SCGD) – and

(2) for the purpose of determining whether a contract other than one for the sale or supply of goods is a consumer contract, and is therefore subject to the fair and reasonable test, the definition of a consumer should include such a person. (Paragraph 4.167)

9.40 It should be made clear in the new legislation that a contract will be made in the course of a business if it "relates" to the business, even if it is a contract for the sale of an item not normally sold. (Paragraph 4.169)

---

[1] Sched 2.

9.41 The new legislation should make it clear that contracts with government departments or local or public authorities may count as consumer contracts. (Paragraph 4.171)

9.42 The new legislation should refer simply to "contracts", so that it may be interpreted in line with any ECJ interpretation of what constitutes a contract for the purposes of the Directive. (Paragraph 4.175)

Third party beneficiaries

9.43 We propose no change in any of the UK jurisdictions as to the rules governing the right of third party beneficiaries to challenge unfair terms in the contracts from which they derive their rights. (Paragraph 4.178)

Effect of invalid exclusion or restriction

9.44 An equivalent is needed to UTCCR regulation 8 (effect of unfair term). (Paragraph 4.180)

9.45 The new legislation should state that, where part of a term is detrimental to the consumer and the rest is not, it is only the detrimental part that is of no effect if it is unfair. (Paragraph 4.186)

Evasion of the controls

9.46 There should be a provision subjecting terms in "secondary contracts" to the same controls as if they appeared in the main contract. Genuine agreements to settle an existing dispute should be exempted. (Paragraph 4.192)

9.47 It should be made clear that the rules on unfair clauses in consumer contracts are mandatory so that, if the contract has a close connection to the UK, they will be applied under the Rome Convention despite a choice of another system of law. (Paragraph 4.194)

Prevention

9.48 To avoid any doubt, the legislation should provide that the authorised bodies may take steps to prevent a business purporting to use a term which in practice the business does not effectively incorporate into the contract, and also any term which is unfair because it is not transparent even if in substance the term is fair. (Paragraph 4.198)

9.49 We invite views on whether and to what extent the omission of important information from terms should be subject to preventive control in the new legislation. (Paragraph 4.200)

9.50 We invite views on the question of who should bear the burden of proof in preventive proceedings. (Paragraph 4.202)

9.51 The listed bodies should have power to act against the use or proposal of any non-negotiated term which either would be of no effect or would be unreasonable under the proposed new regime. We invite views as to whether they should also have powers to act against practices of *negotiating* terms which are nonetheless unfair. (Paragraph 4.204)

Provisions no longer required

9.52 Section 5 [s 19] of UCTA should not be reproduced in the new legislation. (Paragraph 4.207)

9.53 Neither part of section 9 [s 22(a), (b)] of UCTA is still required. (Paragraph 4.209)

9.54 Section 28 of UCTA can now be repealed without replacement. (Paragraph 4.211)

BUSINESS-TO-BUSINESS CONTRACTS

Terms which are of no effect

9.55 A person who makes a contract to obtain goods or services "related to", even if not "in the course of", his business should be treated as dealing as a business and not as a consumer. (Paragraph 5.12)

9.56 The substance of UCTA sections 6(1) and 7(3A) [ss 20(1), 21(3A)] should be incorporated into the new legislation. (Paragraph 5.14)

The case for extending the range of terms subject to a "fairness" test

9.57 A good case can be made for extending the power to challenge unfair terms in at least some individual business-to-business contracts from the types of term subject to the reasonableness test of UCTA to the wider range covered (for consumer contracts) by UTCCR. (Paragraph 5.25)

The range of businesses to be protected

9.58 Our provisional view is that it would be better to treat all businesses alike in being able to benefit from the protection, allowing the courts to take into account the size of the business, and whether it makes transactions of the kind in question regularly or only occasionally, in assessing the fairness of the terms complained of. We ask consultees whether they agree. If not, how would they prefer to see the protection limited? (Paragraph 5.40)

"Standard" or "non-negotiated" terms, or all terms?

Should any controls apply to negotiated contracts?

9.59 For business-to-business contracts, the "fairness test" should be extended to cover the same range of terms as would be subject to the fairness test under our proposals for consumer contracts, but only where the term in question "has not been negotiated" or is "standard". (Paragraph 5.44)

9.60 We would welcome evidence from consultees on whether in practice there are significant numbers of terms which were not standard, or which were negotiated, and which are seen as unfair. Our provisional conclusion is that the controls over negotiated exclusion clauses in UCTA sections 6 and 7 [ss 20(2)(ii), 21(1)(ii)] are not needed and that it would suffice to have the general fairness test over "standard" or "non-negotiated" terms. (Paragraph 5.47)

"Standard terms" or "not individually negotiated terms"?

9.61 If controls are to be limited to standard terms, the question should be whether the particular term is standard rather than whether any of the standard terms have been subject to negotiation. (Paragraph 5.56)

9.62 If controls are to be limited to terms that are in some way standard, they should apply to any term which has been drafted in advance and has not been negotiated, whether or not the term is one regularly used by the proponent. (Paragraph 5.59)

Exemptions from the new regime

"Core" terms

9.63 The same formulation of the "core terms" should apply to business-to-business contracts as to consumer contracts. (Paragraph 5.61)

Mandatory and permitted terms

9.64 The same rules on mandatory and permitted terms should apply to business-to-business contracts as to consumer contracts. (Paragraph 5.63)

Excluded contracts

9.65 We are not aware of calls for business-to-business contracts of the types excluded from UCTA to be brought within the scope of the unfair terms legislation. We would be interested to hear any evidence suggesting that any of them should be covered, but provisionally we propose to maintain the existing exemptions. (Paragraph 5.66)

9.66 We invite views on the question whether international business-to-business contracts should be exempt from the controls proposed for domestic contracts. (Paragraph 5.70)

9.67 We invite views on whether the exemption for contracts subject to the law of a part of the UK only by choice of the parties should continue to apply to the new regime for business-to-business contracts. (Paragraph 5.72)

9.68 The new regime need not extend to non-contractual agreements between utility suppliers and businesses. (Paragraph 5.73)

The test to be applied

The basic test

9.69 The same "fair and reasonable" test should apply to business-to-business contracts as we propose for consumer contracts. (Paragraph 5.75)

Plain and intelligible language

9.70 The factors to be taken into account in assessing fairness should include whether the contract is transparent, in business-to-business as well as consumer contracts. (Paragraph 5.79)

9.71 We invite views as to whether, for business-to-business as well as consumer contracts, transparency should be incorporated into the list of factors in such a way that a term may be found unfair principally or solely because of lack of transparency. (Paragraph 5.81)

The list of factors

9.72 A list of factors relevant to the application of the "fair and reasonable" test would be useful in relation to business-to-business contracts as well as consumer contracts, particularly to give guidance to businesses as to how they may ensure that their terms are reasonable. The list should contain the same factors as that for consumer contracts, though naturally they may apply somewhat differently in a business context. (Paragraph 5.83)

An indicative list

9.73 The indicative list for business-to-business contracts should be limited to clauses excluding and restricting liability for breach of contract or for negligence [breach of duty], but there should be power to add to the list by Ministerial Order. (Paragraph 5.88)

Burden of proof

9.74 Where a term in a business-to-business contract has not been listed, the burden of proving that the term is not fair and reasonable should be on the party disputing it. (Paragraph 5.90)

Ancillary questions

9.75 The existing position of third party beneficiaries should be maintained for business-to-business contracts as well as consumer contracts. (Paragraph 5.93)

9.76 The rules on secondary contracts, evasion by choice of law, and the effect of a term being held invalid should be the same for business-to-business contracts as we have proposed for consumer contracts. (Paragraph 5.97)

Preventive action

9.77 We invite views on the desirability and the practicability of extending the preventive controls over unfair terms to business-to-business contracts. (Paragraph 5.111)

SALE OR SUPPLY OF GOODS NOT RELATED TO BUSINESS

9.78 The existing controls over clauses excluding or restricting implied obligations as to title, etc in contracts for the sale or supply of goods where the seller or supplier is not acting for business purposes should be replicated in the new legislation. (Paragraph 6.5)

9.79 Clauses which exclude or restrict liability for breach of the obligations arising under the SGA 1979 or (for hire-purchase) SOGITA as to correspondence with description or sample should remain subject to a "fair and reasonable" test when the sale is between private parties or is by a consumer to a business, irrespective of whether the clause has been negotiated. (Paragraph 6.12)

NON-CONTRACTUAL NOTICES EXCLUDING BUSINESS LIABILITY FOR NEGLIGENCE OR BREACH OF DUTY

9.80 The existing controls over notices which might otherwise exclude a business's liability in tort [delict] to persons with whom it does not have a contractual relationship, and who are killed, injured or harmed by its negligence [breach of duty], should be retained. (Paragraph 7.3)

9.81 The preventive powers should be extended to cover non-contractual notices which purport to exclude or restrict a business's liability in tort [delict]. (Paragraph 7.7)

PUTTING THE NEW LEGISLATION INTO CLEAR, ACCESSIBLE TERMS

9.82 Do consultees have any suggestions as to how the draft Bill might be further simplified or made more accessible, particularly to those without a legal training? (Paragraph 8.64)

9.83 Do consultees consider that the techniques of using a simplified structure and amplifying what is meant by the clauses should be pursued in any legislation that is finally recommended? (Paragraph 8.65)

APPENDIX A
PROTECTION FROM UNFAIR TERMS AFFORDED TO BUSINESSES IN OTHER JURISDICTIONS

A.1　This appendix identifies some notable examples of protection afforded to businesses from unfair contractual terms in other jurisdictions. The systems of the following countries are considered: Australia, New Zealand, Canada, the USA, France, Germany, the Netherlands and Sweden. This is not a comprehensive study and is intended simply to highlight some of the various methods of protection that exist.

A.2　There are three approaches taken to unfair terms in business-to-business contracts:

    (1)　the business is treated as a consumer for the purposes of legislation;

    (2)　there are discrete controls governing business-to-business contracts; and

    (3)　pro-active preventive measures exist to reduce the need for litigation.

Most countries appear to utilise at least two of these methods of control.

1. AUSTRALIA

A.3　There are controls on unfair terms in business-to-business contracts at both federal and state level in Australia. Certain sections of the federal Trade Practices Act 1974 treat businesses as consumers in certain circumstances, and some states have enacted the relevant sections in their own legislation. There are also provisions in the federal Act that deal specifically with unconscionable conduct in business-to-business contracts and include mechanisms to prevent such conduct continuing.

Businesses treated as consumers

A.4　At federal level, the Trade Practices Act 1974 (the "1974 federal Act") implies various provisions into consumer contracts for sale, exchange, lease-hire or hire-purchase that are similar in effect to those implied by SOGITA in the UK.[1] Any

---

[1]　There are implied undertakings relating to title, encumbrances and quiet possession (s 69); in contracts of sale by description, to conformance with that description (s 70); to quality or fitness (s 71); in contracts of sale by sample, to conformance with the sample (s 72); and in contracts for the supply of services, to care and skill (s 74). Under subsection (3), s 74 does not apply to

    services that are, or are to be, provided, granted or conferred under:

        (a) a contract for or in relation to the transportation or storage of goods for the purposes of a business, trade, profession or occupation carried on or engaged in by the person for whom the goods are transported or stored; or

        (b) a contract of insurance.

term that attempts to exclude these provisions is void.[2] Some businesses will fall within the definition of a "consumer" because that definition is framed in terms of the goods or services concerned, their price and the use for which they are intended, rather than the status of the parties to the contract. Section 4B(1) provides:

> For the purposes of this Act, unless the contrary intention appears:
>
> (a)   a person shall be taken to have acquired goods as a consumer if, and only if:
>
>   (i)   the price of the goods did not exceed the prescribed amount [currently $40,000[3]]; or
>
>   (ii)   where that price exceeded the prescribed amount – the goods were of a kind ordinarily acquired for personal, domestic or household use or consumption or the goods consisted of a commercial vehicle;
>
> and the person did not acquire the goods, or hold himself or herself out as acquiring the goods, for the purpose of re-supply or for the purpose of using them up or transforming them, in trade or commerce, in the course of a process of production or manufacture or of repairing or treating other goods or fixtures on land; and
>
> (b)   a person shall be taken to have acquired particular services as a consumer if, and only if:
>
>   (i)   the price of the services did not exceed the prescribed amount [$40,000[4]]; or
>
>   (ii)   where that price exceeded the prescribed amount – the services were of a kind ordinarily acquired for personal, domestic or household use or consumption.[5]

A.5   With the exception of the provisions as to title, encumbrances and quiet possession, corporations[6] can limit liability for breach of the warranties or conditions provided for by the Act to certain remedies.[7] However, any limitation

---

[2]   Section 68.

[3]   Trade Practices Act 1974, s 4B(2)(a).

[4]   *Ibid.*

[5]   Trade Practices Act 1974, s 4B(1).

[6]   Section 4 defines a corporation as any body corporate that
   (a)   is a foreign corporation;
   (b)   is a trading corporation formed within the limits of Australia or is a financial corporation so formed;
   (c)   is incorporated in a Territory; or
   (d)   is the holding company of a body corporate of a kind referred to in paragraph (a), (b) or (c).

[7]   In the case of goods, replacement or cost of replacement (of the same goods or an equivalent) or the repair or cost of repair of the goods. In the case of services, the supplying of the service again or the cost of having the service supplied again. See s 68A(1)(a) and (b).

must be reasonable and cannot apply to contracts for the supply of goods or services ordinarily acquired for personal, domestic or household use or consumption.

A.6   In September 1983 the state and federal Ministers for Consumer Affairs agreed to uniform legislation. However, only the resulting legislation of Western Australia[8] and the Northern Territory[9] incorporated regulation of implied warranties.[10] In Western Australia the approach is identical to that of the federal Act.[11] In the Northern Territory, there is no value threshold; a contract will be a consumer contract (in relation to warranties) if the goods are not acquired, or held out as being acquired, for the purpose of re-supplying them, using them up or transforming them in the course of a business, or in connection with the repair or treatment of other goods or fixtures on land.[12] The relevant implied undertakings, and the prohibition on their exclusion, are the same as in the federal statute,[13] but reasonable limitation is not confined to contracts where a corporation is the supplier.[14]

A.7   One further method of protection is contained in the Contracts Review Act 1980 of New South Wales, which protects persons from using unjust[15] contracts or provisions. Under section 7 there are various avenues available to the court on a finding of an unjust contract or contractual provision,[16] but relief will only be granted in relation to contracts that are not entered into in the course of or for the purpose of a trade, business or profession. The one exception is persons involved in farming undertakings, who are afforded protection under the Act if the undertaking is carried on wholly or principally in New South Wales.[17]

---

[8]   Fair Trading Act 1987, Part III, ss 33–41, which incorporates the relevant parts of the federal Act into the state's law.

[9]   Consumer Affairs and Fair Trading Act 1990, Part V, Div 2, ss 61–71.

[10]   Victoria's Goods Act 1958 contains similar provisions to those of the federal Act, but the prescribed amount is $15,000 rather than $40,000, and commercial vehicles are not included (see s 85). The relevant exclusionary provisions are ss 95 (terms excluding the warranties are void) and 97(3) (terms reasonably limiting recovery), which apply to all contracts of sale.

[11]   Fair Trading Act 1987, s 6.

[12]   Consumer Affairs and Fair Trading Act 1990, s 5.

[13]   Sections 62–68.

[14]   Section 69.

[15]   The Contracts Review Act 1980, s 4(1), defines unjust as including "unconscionable, harsh or oppressive".

[16]   The court can refuse to enforce any or all of the provisions of the contract; declare the contract void, in whole or in part; make an order varying the contract, in whole or in part; or make an order for execution of a land instrument, either varying the provisions of the instrument or terminating or otherwise affecting its operation or effect (s 7(1)(a)–(d)).

[17]   Contracts Review Act 1980, s 6(2).

Discrete controls on business-to-business contracts

A.8   Section 51AC(1)[18] of the 1974 federal Act prohibits unconscionable conduct[19] in business transactions that are worth less than $1 million,[20] but applies only to contracts for the supply or acquisition of goods or services to or from a person other than a public limited company.[21]

A.9   Section 51AC(3) provides a non-exhaustive list of factors relevant to the consideration of unconscionability,[22] and in theory the scope of the section is quite wide.[23] However, in practice it appears to be limited to situations where the business is in a position comparable to that of a consumer – for example, where unfair pressure or tactics are exerted on a party not in a position to protect its interests.[24]

A.10   On finding unconscionable conduct the court can either grant an injunction,[25] or it can make certain other orders if it considers that they will compensate a party, in whole or in part, for loss or damage or will prevent or reduce any loss or damage.[26]

2. NEW ZEALAND

A.11   There is no general protection from unfair terms in New Zealand. Instead there is legislation targeting specific contracts such as hire-purchase, insurance, lay-by sales, door-to-door sales and unsolicited goods. Businesses are given protection by

(1)   legislation relating to guarantees in contracts for the sale or supply of goods and services, where the definition of a consumer is extended to include businesses acting in certain capacities;[27]

---

[18]   There are equivalent provisions to s 51AC in the state legislation.

[19]   Inserted by the Trade Practices Amendment (Fair Trading) Act 1998.

[20]   Or an amount prescribed by regulations under s 51AC(7).

[21]   See s 51AC(1)(a) and (b).

[22]   Among these are the relative strength of the bargaining positions of the supplier and business consumer; whether there were conditions imposed on the business consumer that were not reasonably necessary for the protection of the legitimate interests of the supplier; whether the business consumer could understand any documents involved; whether there was any undue influence or pressure; and the extent to which the supplier was willing to negotiate with the consumer. See s 51AC(3).

[23]   It can apply to any contract or term that the court considers to fall within the scope of the considerations listed at s 51AC(3).

[24]   See, eg, *Australian Competition and Consumer Commission v Simply No-Knead (Franchising) Pty Ltd* [2000] FCA 1365, paras 39–51.

[25]   See s 80.

[26]   See s 87(1). Section 87(2) lists the various orders available. The court can declare the contract void, in full or in part; vary the contract; refuse to enforce any or all provisions; order a refund of money or return of property; order a payment of damages; order that a party pay for repair or new parts for goods supplied by them; or order the supply of specified services.

[27]   Consumer Guarantees Act 1993.

(2)   legislation regulating credit contracts, which treats certain businesses and consumers alike;[28] and

(3)   legislation relating to unfair trading practices, which offers pro-active prevention of such practices by means of application to the court.[29]

Businesses treated as consumers

A.12   The Consumer Guarantees Act 1993 implies, in contracts for the supply of goods, guarantees of title, quality, fitness for particular purpose, compliance with description or sample, reasonable price, and availability of repair facilities and spare parts;[30] and, in contracts for the supply of services, guarantees of reasonable care, skill, fitness for purpose, time of completion, and price.[31] Contracting out of these guarantees is prohibited.[32] The definition of a consumer focuses on the intended use of the goods or services rather than the nature of the purchaser. A business will therefore benefit from protection under the Act if it

(a)   Acquires from a supplier goods or services of a kind ordinarily acquired for personal, domestic, or household use or consumption; and

(b)   Does not acquire the goods or services, or hold [itself] out as acquiring the goods or services, for the purpose of –

(i)   Resupplying them in trade; or

(ii)   Consuming them in the course of a process of production or manufacture; or

(iii) In the case of goods, repairing or treating in trade other goods or fixtures on land.[33]

A.13   The guarantees provided by the Act cannot normally be excluded.[34] However, if goods or services are acquired (or expressed to be acquired) by a consumer for the purposes of a business,[35] the supplier can contract out of the guarantees provided that the agreement is in writing, or, if this is not possible because the supplier is unaware of the purchaser's acceptance, the supplier has "clearly displayed the

---

[28]   Credit Contracts Act 1981.

[29]   Fair Trading Act 1986.

[30]   See ss 5–13.

[31]   See ss 28–31.

[32]   Except in business transactions: see para A.13 below.

[33]   Consumer Guarantees Act 1993, s 2(1) (definition of a consumer).

[34]   Section 43(1).

[35]   Under s 2(1), "business" means

(a) Any undertaking whether carried on for gain or reward or not; or

(b) Any undertaking in the course of which –

(i)   Goods or services are acquired or supplied; or

(ii) Any interest in land is acquired or disposed of –

whether free of charge or not.

terms and conditions of the service at every place of the supplier's business".[36] As a result, instances of protection actually extending to a business in practice are likely to be few and far between.

A.14 The Credit Contracts Act 1981 contains protection for debtors in certain types of credit contracts. Part I offers protection from oppressive terms[37] in all credit contracts, whether between a creditor and a consumer or a creditor and a business. If the court finds a contract to be oppressive, it can re-open the contract and make various orders as to how the parties must proceed.[38]

A.15 Part II of the Act requires disclosure in "controlled credit contracts"[39] and provides penalties for non-disclosure.[40] This part appears to be aimed at protecting small businesses, or those inexperienced in the credit finance industry, as section 15(d)–(m) excludes various types of contracts from the definition of a "controlled credit contract". Many of these exclusions focus on situations where the debtor is either large enough, experienced enough in credit contracts, or entitled to assume that the creditor will protect the debtor's interests.[41]

---

[36] Section 43(2). If any of the guarantees are excluded other than in accordance with this section, the supplier or manufacturer will be committing an offence under s 13(i) of the Fair Trading Act 1986.

[37] Section 9 of the Act defines oppressive as "oppressive, harsh, unjustly burdensome, unconscionable, or in contravention of reasonable standards of commercial practice".

[38] Sections 10–14. The powers of the court (contained in s 14) include an order that an account be taken; a direction that property that is the subject of the contract be transferred, assigned or delivered; and a direction that a party to the contract pay a sum to the other party.

[39] Section 15 defines a controlled credit contract as a credit contract

  (a) Where the creditor, or one of the creditors, for the time being is a financier acting in the course of his business; or

  (b) Which results from an introduction of one of the parties to the contract to another such party by a paid adviser; or

  (c) That has been prepared by a paid adviser.

[40] Sections 24–30. These include extinguishing various liabilities of the debtor, depending on which class of disclosure has been omitted.

[41] Eg a company with paid up capital exceeding $1 million (s 15(d)(iii)); where the credit outstanding is, or will be, $250,000 or more (s 15(f)); where the debtor is a financier (carrying on the business of providing credit or entering into credit contracts in his own name as creditor, or on behalf of or as trustee or nominee for another) (s 15(d)(i)); where the debtor is the Crown, or a local authority or government agency (s 15(d)(ii)); or where the debtor and creditor are part of the same body corporate (s 15(e)).

Pro-active preventive measures

A.16 The Fair Trading Act 1986 prohibits misleading and deceptive conduct in trade[42] generally,[43] and in relation to the "nature, manufacturing process, characteristics, suitability for a purpose, or quantity of goods",[44] the "nature, characteristics, suitability for a purpose, or quantity of services"[45] and the "availability, nature, terms or conditions, or any other matter" relating to offers of employment.[46] There are similar provisions prohibiting false representations in relation to the supply of goods or services, or land.[47]

A.17 Contravention of the Act is a criminal offence[48] but a civil remedy is also available. On an application from the Commerce Commission, the court can grant an injunction to prevent both further breaches and future possible breaches of the Act.[49] The Commission can also seek an order that a person in contravention of any of the parts of the Act disclose or publicise information relating to the unfair practice,[50] and the court has further powers to declare contracts void or partially enforceable.[51]

3. CANADA

A.18 Protection from unfair terms in Canada is either incorporated into consumer protection legislation or only applies to businesses that are in a comparable position to the consumer. There is also some legislation providing pro-active prevention, but it is similarly limited in its scope.

Businesses treated as consumers

A.19 A number of provinces imply terms into consumer contracts similar to those in the SGA 1979[52] and prohibit their exclusion. In some of these statutes the definitions used create protection for certain narrow categories of business-to-business transactions. Saskatchewan treats family farming corporations, and individuals buying goods for agricultural or fishing purposes, as consumers under

---

[42] Trade is defined in s 2 as

> any trade, business, industry, profession, occupation, activity of commerce, or undertaking relating to the supply or acquisition of goods or services or to the disposition or acquisition of any interest in land.

[43] Trade Practices Act 1986, 9.

[44] Section 10.

[45] Section 11.

[46] Section 12.

[47] Sections 13 and 14.

[48] Section 40.

[49] Section 41.

[50] Section 42.

[51] Section 43.

[52] Implied terms as to title, quiet enjoyment, freedom from encumbrance, merchantable quality, correspondence with description or sample, and fitness for particular purpose.

its Consumer Protection Act 1996.[53] The North West Territories' 1998 legislation of the same name[54] protects businesses party to all contracts for goods or services except

> (a) a contract of sale of goods that are intended for resale by the buyer in the course of his or her business,
>
> (b) a contract of sale to a retailer of a vending machine or a bottle cooler to be installed in his or her retail establishment,
>
> (c) a contract of sale to a corporation, and
>
> (d) a sale in which the cash price of the goods or services or both exceeds $7,500. [55]

Discrete controls on business-to-business contracts

A.20 In Ontario, the Unconscionable Transactions Relief Act 1990 empowers the courts to re-open a transaction or former settlement and take account; order repayment of excess; or set aside or revise any security given or agreement made in respect of money-lending.[56] Any such transaction can fall within the scope of the Act; but it would appear that only businesses which are in positions comparable to that of a consumer can benefit from the protection, because the Act applies only "where the terms of the bargain are grossly unfair and were procured by the one party as a result of the other's weakness or necessity being taken advantage of."[57]

Pro-active preventive measures

A.21 Preventive measures exist in legislation prohibiting unfair trade practices in a number of provinces.[58] In this section we focus on the legislation in Saskatchewan and British Columbia.

---

[53] See Consumer Protection Act 1996, c S-50.11, Part III, s 39(d) and (e).

[54] Consumer Protection Act 1998 (RSNWT 1998 c 21) Part VI, s 70(1).

[55] See the definition of "retail sales" in s 1. There are similar exclusions from the definition of "retail hire purchase", which is also covered by the Act. There are similar Acts in Nova Scotia, Manitoba, New Brunswick and British Columbia, but the definitions are more restrictive and, it is suggested, apply to even fewer (if any) business-to-business contracts: see Consumer Protection Act 1989, RS c 92m, s 26(1) (Nova Scotia); Consumer Protection Act 1987, RSM c C200, ss 1 and 58 (Manitoba); Consumer Product Warranty and Liability Act 1980, SNB c-18.1, ss 1 and 8 (New Brunswick); and Sale of Goods Act RS 1996, c 410, s 20 (British Columbia).

[56] Unconscionable Transactions Relief Act RSO 1990, c U-2, s 2.

[57] *Adams v Fahrngruber* (1976) 10 OR (2d) 96, 102, *per* Grant J. The court held that the transaction was not harsh or unconscionable because there was no inequality of bargaining power between the two parties and the money was not needed urgently by the borrower.

[58] For example, in British Columbia and Newfoundland (Trade Practices Acts: RSBC 1996 c 457 and RSN 1990 c T-7 respectively); in Alberta (Fair Trading Act 1999 c F-1.05); in Ontario and Prince Edward Island (Business Practices Acts: 1990 c B-18 and RSPEI 1988 c B-7 respectively); and in Saskatchewan (Consumer Protection Act 1996 c C-30.1).

A.22   In Saskatchewan, Part II of the Consumer Protection Act prohibits "unfair practices"[59] and lists the "taking advantage of a consumer by including in a consumer agreement terms or conditions that are harsh, oppressive or excessively one-sided" as an unfair practice.[60] Business-to-business contracts will gain protection under the Act if the goods involved are "ordinarily used for personal, family or household purposes".[61]

A.23   The Act provides for the appointment of a Director,[62] who has powers to investigate possible contraventions of Part II,[63] and section 17 allows a person to enter into a "voluntary compliance agreement" if the Director's provisional finding is that an unfair practice is being committed or is about to be committed.

A.24   British Columbia's Trade Practices Act[64] similarly protects consumers from deceptive or unconscionable practices.[65] However, only one form of business is affected by the Act: the protection applies to any form of disposition of personal or real property to an individual for purposes relating to a first time business opportunity scheme. This is a scheme

    (a)   in which the individual has not been previously engaged,

    (b)   for which the initial payment does not exceed $50,000 or another amount prescribed by the Lieutenant Governor in Council, and

    (c)   which requires

        (i)   the expenditure of money and management services by the consumer, and

        (ii)   the performance of personal services by the consumer or another person.[66]

A.25   There are provisions in the Act (similar to those in the Saskatchewan legislation) establishing a Director and his or her duties and powers.[67] Contravention of the provisions relating to deceptive or unconscionable conduct is an offence.[68]

---

[59]   See s 7.

[60]   Section 6(q).

[61]   See s 3(d), which defines goods. Section 3(a) states that a consumer is "an individual that participates or may participate in a transaction involving goods or services".

[62]   Section 9.

[63]   Sections 10–13.

[64]   RSBC 1996 c 457.

[65]   See ss 3 (deceptive acts or practices) and 4 (unconscionable acts or practices). Section 4(3)(e) lists terms or conditions that are so harsh or adverse to the consumer, at the time the contract is entered into, as to be inequitable.

[66]   Section 1.

[67]   Sections 5–17.1.

[68]   Section 25(3).

4. THE USA

A.26 Control of unfair terms in the USA is contained in section 2-302 of the Uniform Commercial Code (the "UCC"), which has been enacted in various forms by all states except Louisiana. The protection is not limited to any particular form of contract, but the approach taken by the courts to business contracts is stricter and more rigorous than the approach taken to consumer contracts.

Businesses treated as consumers

A.27 Section 2-302 of the UCC extends the common law doctrine of unconscionability. It provides:

> If the court as a matter of law finds the contract or any clause of the contract to have been unconscionable at the time it was made the court may refuse to enforce the contract, or it may enforce the remainder of the contract without the unconscionable clause, or it may so limit the application of any unconscionable clause as to avoid any unconscionable result.[69]

A.28 In principle, the section applies to all contracts for the sale of goods, whether between businesses or involving a consumer. However, when applying the section to business contracts the courts examine the relative strengths and vulnerabilities of the parties, finding unconscionability only when one party is in a position of weakness. Examples include large-scale business dealing with uneducated, individual concerns;[70] a party who is inexperienced within the industry in question or with the technical language involved;[71] a lack of any realistic alternatives to the contract;[72] an inability of one party to assess the commercial risk involved;[73] and acceptance of a degree of risk beyond the boundaries of commercial reasonableness.[74]

A.29 Whilst the section could potentially apply to any term of the contract – or indeed the contract as a whole – it has not been invoked (except in a few anomalous

---

[69] UCC s 2-302(1).

[70] *Johnson v Mobile Oil Corp* 415 F Supp 264 (1976) (ED Mich). The case involved an unconscionable exclusion clause in a franchise agreement between a large oil company and a poorly educated petrol station owner.

[71] *Weaver v American Oil Co* 276 NE 2d 144 (1971) (Ind), a similar situation to *Johnson v Mobile Oil Corp* (see previous footnote). Arterburn CJ noted the petrol station owner's limited experience of the industry and that he should not be "expected to know the law or understand the meaning of technical terms": p 145.

[72] *Martin v The Joseph Harris Co Inc* 767 F 2d 296 (1985) (6th Cir). The objectionable clause (which limited damages to the price of the seeds purchased) was used by all national distributors of seed, giving the farmer little option but to accept it.

[73] *Trinkle v Schumacher Co* 301 NW 2d 255 (1980) (Wis Ct App). In a contract for the sale of fabric, a clause preventing any claims after the fabric had been cut was unconscionable when a latent defect made it impossible to discover whether any claim was necessary until after the fabric had been cut.

[74] *Martin v The Joseph Harris Co Inc*, n 72 above. The farmer was forced to accept the risk of the loss of his crop to a fungus, when the supplier could have easily (and cheaply) treated the seeds to prevent any such risk.

cases[75]) in any situations that would go beyond the protection afforded in the UK under common law principles or UCTA.

5. FRANCE

A.30 The Code de la Consommation regulates unfair terms in contracts between "professionals" and "non-professionals or consumers". These terms are not defined in the Code, but until the enactment of Directive 93/13/EEC the French courts treated businesses as consumers if they were engaged in contracts where they had the same level of knowledge as a consumer. For example, the Cour de Cassation held that an estate agent contracting for the installation of a burglar alarm on its premises was a consumer, and a clause that purported to limit the installer's liability was subject to review under the law on abusive clauses.[76]

A.31 After 1993, the courts took a more restrictive approach, influenced by the definition of "consumer" in the Directive, which includes only "personne physique".[77] The current approach appears to be that set out by the Cour de Cassation in a 1995 case.[78] The court held that a printing company could not challenge a clause in its contract with EDF (the French electricity company) which limited EDF's liability for power failures. The court stated that the legislation did not apply to contracts for goods or services which are directly related to the business activities of the parties.[79]

A.32 The French system has not expressly rejected the notion of treating certain classes of traders on the same footing as consumers for the purposes of protection from unfair terms.

6. GERMANY

A.33 Protection from unfair terms is contained in the German Civil Code (das Bürgerliches Gesetzbuch, the "BGB"). There are provisions relating to general contractual conduct, which treat businesses as consumers,[80] as well as specific provisions relating to standard terms,[81] of which some treat businesses the same as

---

[75] Eg *Bank of India, Nat Assn v Holyfield* 563 SW 2d 438 (1978) (Ark), where an agreement for the hire-purchase of a number of dairy cattle was unconscionable because all the risk passed to the farmer on the day the cattle were delivered.

[76] Civ 1ere, 28 April 1987.

[77] Article 2.

[78] Civ 1ere, 24 January 1995.

[79] This formulation has been used in Civ 1ere, 3 January 1996 and 30 January 1996.

[80] BGB, Book 1: General Part, s 3: Legal Transactions, Arts 138 and 157. English translations are taken from S L Goren, *The German Civil Code* (revised ed 1994).

[81] Book 2: The Law of Obligations, s 2: Shaping contractual obligations by means of standard business terms. These provisions replaced the Standard Contract Terms Act 1976 (die Gesetz zur Regelung des Rechts der Allegemeinen Geschaftsbedingunged) from 1 January 2002. English translations are taken from *http://www.iuscomp.org/gla/statutes/BGB.htm#b2s2*.

consumers and others deal with businesses separately.[82] There are also pro-active preventive measures in separate legislation.[83]

Businesses treated as consumers

General contractual conduct

A.34   Article 157 of the BGB contains a requirement that "Contracts shall be interpreted according to the requirements of good faith, giving consideration to common usage."

A.35   Article 138 states that a legal transaction is void if it is against public policy[84] or if a person gains a disproportionate pecuniary advantage by "exploiting the need, inexperience, lack of sound judgment or substantial lack of will power of another".[85] This article will probably affect only small or inexperienced businesses.

Standard terms

A.36   Section 2 of Book 2 of the BGB only applies to standard business terms that have not been individually negotiated. Standard business terms are terms which are "pre-established for a multitude of contracts which one party to the contract (the user) presents to the other party upon the conclusion of the contract".[86]

A.37   Specific protection from unfair terms is contained in Articles 305(2), 305c and 307–309. However, Articles 305(2),[87] 308[88] and 309[89] do not apply to "standard business terms which are proffered to a businessperson, a legal person governed by public law or a special fund governed by public law."[90] The articles applicable to business-to-business contracts are therefore Articles 305c and 307.

---

[82]   The closest analogy to this paper is that there are discrete controls on business contracts, but the BGB actually excludes businesses from sections that apply to specific contractual clauses. The relevant considerations in a business-to-business contract containing such clauses are therefore different from those in a consumer contract containing the same clauses.

[83]   The Act on Enjoinment Actions for Violations of Consumer and Other Rights (Gesetz über Unterlassungsklagen bei Verbraucherrechts- und anderen Verstößen (the Unterlassungs-klagengesetz or "UKlaG")).

[84]   Art 138(1).

[85]   Art 138(2).

[86]   Art 305(1).

[87]   Art 305(2) provides that a standard term is incorporated into a contract only if the user expressly brings it to the other party's attention (either directly or by means of a clearly visible sign at the place where the contract is made) and gives the other party a reasonable opportunity to find out what it says, and the other party agrees that it is to apply.

[88]   Art 308 sets out various types of term which, in standard business terms, are subject to an appraisal of validity.

[89]   Art 309 sets out various types of term which, in standard business terms, are always invalid.

[90]   Art 310. "Business person" is defined by Art 14 as

> any natural or legal person, or partnership with legal capacity, which, on entering into a legal transaction, acts in exercise of its trade or self-employed professional activity.

A.38 Article 305c prevents surprise clauses from forming part of the contract. These are clauses which

> in the circumstances, in particular in view of the outward appearance of the contract, are so unusual that the contractual partner of the user could not be expected to have reckoned with them.[91]

A.39 Article 307(1) provides that standard business terms are invalid if,

> contrary to the requirement of good faith, they place the contractual partner of the user at an unreasonable disadvantage. An unreasonable disadvantage may also result from the fact that the provision is not clear and comprehensible.

Article 307(2) goes on to provide that, in case of doubt, unreasonable disadvantage is assumed if a provision cannot be reconciled with the essential basic principles of the statutory rule from which it deviates, or so restricts the essential rights or duties arising from the nature of the contract that there is a risk that it will jeopardise the purpose of the contract.

Discrete controls on business-to-business contracts

A.40 Although Articles 308 and 309 do not apply to businesses,[92] terms that fall within these provisions are still subject to Article 307, and can be struck down, even in business-to-business contracts, if the test in that article is satisfied.[93]

Pro-active preventive measures

A.41 Under section 1 of the UKlaG,[94] a party using standard terms which are void under Articles 307–309 of the BGB, or recommending the use of such terms, can be required to stop using them or to retract any such recommendation. Sections 3–4 of the UKlaG define the organisations and institutions which can bring proceedings under section 1.[95]

7. THE NETHERLANDS

A.42 There are two specific forms of protection from unfair terms extended to businesses in the Netherlands: legislation which requires disclosure of standard terms (even if they are not potentially unfair) and legislation which polices the

---

> A "partnership with legal capacity" is a partnership which possesses the capacity to acquire rights and to enter into obligations.

[91] Art 305c(1). Art 305c(2) provides that, in case of doubt, standard business terms are to be interpreted against the user.

[92] See para A.37 above.

[93] Art 310(1).

[94] See n 83 above.

[95] There is currently no English translation of the UKlaG; the relevant sections of the Act replace the relevant provisions of the Standard Contract Terms Act 1976 (ss 13–22), which were to similar effect. We are grateful to Dr Gerhard Dannemann for the information provided.

reasonableness of standard terms. (There is also a list of terms that are presumed to be unfair, but this is only of direct application to consumers.) Both forms of protection are extended only to small businesses. Larger businesses are protected only by a general requirement of good faith.[96]

Businesses treated as consumers

A.43   Section 3 of Title 5 of Book 6 of the Dutch Civil Code affords protection from unreasonably onerous and surprising written[97] stipulations in standard form contracts.[98] Article 6:233 grants power to annul terms if they are unreasonably onerous to the other party or the user of the standard form contract has not "afforded the other party a reasonable opportunity to take cognisance of the general conditions".[99] To afford such reasonable opportunity, the user of the term simply needs to ensure that the other party has a copy of the terms before or at the time the contract is made,[100] or at least that the other party has been informed of the term before the formation of the contract, and that it is open for inspection on request. The user can either provide a copy personally or else deposit it with the relevant chamber of commerce and industry, or with the registrar of a court, for collection by the other party.[101]

A.44   Application of this protection in business-to-business contracts appears to be limited to small businesses or businesses with little experience in the industry in question, because Article 6:235 excludes medium and large businesses (those that employ 50 or more persons, or are obliged to publish their annual accounts[102]) and businesses which regularly use the same or similar general conditions in other contracts. However, businesses which are not protected by section 6:233 may, in exceptional cases, be able to rely on Article 6:248, which provides for a general

---

[96]   Contained in Article 6:248 (s 4 of title 5 of Book 6) of the Dutch Civil Code. All English translations are taken from P P C Haanappel and E Mackaay, *New Netherlands Civil Code* (1990).

[97]   It is generally accepted that in consumer cases protection should be extended to oral agreements as a result of the courts' obligation to interpret national law in conformity with directives.

[98]   Art 6:231. Stipulations that go to the essence of the contract (the translation given is the essence of the prestations, which literally means a payment of money or performance of a service) are expressly excluded from the article, except in consumer contracts if they are unclear.

[99]   Art 6:233. The latter ground applies even where the standard terms are absolutely reasonable; they can be annulled "en bloc".

[100]   Art 6:234(1)(a).

[101]   Art 6:234(1)(b). In 1999 the *Hoge Raad* decided (Geurtzen/Kampstaal) that it may be contrary to good faith to invoke Arts 6:233(b) and 6:234(1) in cases where the other party nonetheless knew the contents of the standard terms. In this case (a business-to-business case) the other party, a subcontractor, had previously concluded similar contracts with other parties in which the same conditions (which were the standard conditions of a branch organisation) had applied.

[102]   See Art 2:360 (company law). The exclusion also extends to companies which are part of a group and are exempted by Art 2:403(1) from the obligation to publish their accounts separately.

requirement of good faith in all contracts. It may be contrary to good faith in certain circumstances to invoke a (valid) standard term, and the courts may look to Articles 6:233, 6:236 and 6:237[103] for guidance when applying Article 6:248 to standard terms in such contracts.[104]

Discrete controls on business-to-business contracts

A.45   As in the German system, the Dutch Civil Code also includes lists of clauses that are either automatically unfair[105] or presumed to be unfair[106] in consumer contracts. However, it appears that (as in the German system) terms falling within these lists can still be held invalid in business-to-business contracts under Article 6:233, and the courts will look to these lists for guidance when applying Article 6:233 to business-to-business contracts.

Pro-active preventive measures

A.46   Certain interest groups can seek a declaration that a stipulation is unreasonably onerous.[107] Such claims lie against either the user of the term or any legal person who promotes its use, but actions can only be brought if the interest group has given the user an opportunity to modify the general conditions after mutual consultation so as to remove the objectionable term.[108] The Court of Appeal in the Hague has exclusive jurisdiction to hear actions,[109] and the judge has authority to indicate the method by which the unreasonably onerous stipulation should be removed.[110] The methods available include prohibiting the use or promotion of the stipulation; ordering revocation of a recommendation to use it; and publication of the decision at the expense of one or more parties.[111]

A.47   Furthermore, a party cannot seek to enforce terms that are so closely associated with terms already held onerous that the result would be unreasonable; and a party can seek an order preventing the use of a term that is the subject of declaration proceedings if such use would be unreasonable.[112]

---

[103] See para A.45 below.

[104] The extent to which large businesses need such protection is seen as a controversial issue.

[105] The "black list"; see Art 6:236.

[106] The "grey list"; see Art 6:237.

[107] Art 6:240(1). The interest groups involved are defined in Art 6:240(3).

[108] Art 6:240(4).

[109] Art 6:241(1).

[110] Art 6:241(4).

[111] Art 6:241(3).

[112] Art 6:244.

8. SWEDEN[113]

A.48   There are two forms of protection afforded to businesses in Sweden.[114] The main provision is section 36 of the Contracts Act,[115] which provides a general prohibition against unreasonable terms in contracts. There is also the Terms of Contract between Tradesmen Act,[116] which provides for a pro-active regime to prevent the use of improper terms in contracts between tradesmen.

A.49   All of the Swedish legislation is set against a background of consultation and co-operation between interest groups, big business and government. As a result many disputes are resolved before they reach court.

Businesses treated as consumers

A.50   Section 36 of the Contracts Act was introduced in 1976,[117] and provides that a contract term[118] can be modified or set aside if it is unreasonable. The section also provides that, in considering whether a term is unreasonable, the court should have regard not only to the contents of the agreement and the circumstances at the time it was formed but also to "subsequent circumstances, and circumstances in general".[119] Furthermore, where the term is "of such significance for the agreement that it would be unreasonable to demand the continued enforceability of the remainder of the agreement with its terms unchanged,"[120] the court has the power to modify other parts of the agreement or set it aside completely.

A.51   Whilst not ruling out application to other contractual situations, the section is clearly aimed at protecting parties who are in the weaker position in the contract, and recognises that businesses can often be in such a position. Paragraph 2 provides that, when considering the application of the section,

---

[113]   The regulation of contracts in the other Scandinavian countries is broadly the same. Note that the law on collective regulation of contract terms has not been restricted to standard form contracts. See, eg, T Wilhelmsson, "The Implementation of the EC Directive on Unfair Contract Terms in Finland" (1997) 5 ERPL 151.

[114]   English translations are taken from Bernitz and Draper, *Consumer Protection in Sweden: Legislation, Institutions and Practice* (2nd ed 1986).

[115]   SFS 1915:218.

[116]   SFS 1984:292.

[117]   See C Hultmark, "Obligations, Contracts and Sales" in M Bogdan, *Swedish Law in the New Millennium* (2000) 273, 280.

[118]   The section also applies to "terms of any other legal relationships than that of contract": s 36.3.

[119]   Section 36.1.

[120]   *Ibid.*

particular attention shall be paid to the need to protect those parties who, in their capacity as consumers or otherwise, hold an inferior bargaining position in the contractual relationship.[121]

Pro-active preventive measures

A.52 The Terms of Contract between Tradesmen Act[122] empowers the Market Court, an administrative body, to grant injunctions preventing a tradesman who demands the inclusion of an "improper" term in a contract from using the term, or a term of similar effect, in future contracts.[123] Both associations of tradesmen and the tradesman against whom the term in question was directed can bring a claim,[124] and once again the Act expressly provides that special consideration be given to the need to protect the "person who assumes an inferior position in the contract relationship".[125] However, an injunction should only be granted if it is in the public interest to do so.[126] The court will issue an injunction under the penalty of a fine unless there are special reasons not to do so, and the onus is then on the party who brought the claim to bring proceedings in the ordinary courts for imposition of the fine.[127] Finally, the Market Court is entitled to review a decision to grant an injunction if circumstances have changed or if some other special reason exists.[128]

A.53 This Act has rarely been used and there is only one reported case on its effects. In this case, the Market Court prevented the City of Gothenburg from using a clause in a contract for the delivery of energy that gave the city the right unilaterally to alter the price and other terms during the ongoing contractual period.[129]

---

[121] Professor Herre has indicated to us that the section has not been invoked very often by businesses, but has probably influenced a change in business practices and has had a greater impact than the Terms of Contract between Tradesmen Act 1984 (discussed below).

[122] SFS 1984:292.

[123] Section 1.

[124] Section 3.

[125] Section 2.1.

[126] Section 2.2.

[127] Section 5.

[128] Section 4.

[129] MD 1985:16.

APPENDIX B
Unfair Terms

CONTENTS

PART 1

BUSINESS LIABILITY FOR NEGLIGENCE

1 Contract terms or notices excluding or restricting business liability for negligence

(1) Business liability for death or personal injury which results from negligence cannot be excluded or restricted by a contract term or notice.

(2) Business liability for other loss or damage which results from negligence cannot be excluded or restricted by a contract term or notice unless (as the case may be)—

    (a) the term is fair and reasonable, or

    (b) it is fair and reasonable to allow reliance on the notice.

(3) "Business liability" means liability for breach of an obligation or duty that arises—

    (a) from anything that was done or should have been done for purposes related to a business, or

    (b) from the occupation of premises used for purposes related to the business of the occupier.

(4) "Anything done for purposes related to a business" includes anything done by an employee of the business which is within the scope of his employment.

2 Exceptions from section 1 for England and Wales

(1) Section 1 does not prevent an employee from excluding or restricting his liability for negligence towards his employer.

(2) Section 1 does not apply to the business liability of an occupier of premises towards a person who obtains access to the premises for recreational or educational purposes if—

    (a) granting him access for those purposes falls outside the purposes of the business, and

    (b) he suffers loss or damage by reason of the dangerous state of the premises.

(3) This section does not apply to Scotland.

3 Effect of agreement to, or awareness of, term or notice

The defence that a person voluntarily accepted any risk is not to be available against that person merely because he agreed to, or was aware of, a contract term or notice excluding or restricting business liability for negligence.

PART 2

CONSUMER CONTRACTS

4   Sale to, and hire-purchase by, consumer: terms of no effect

(1)   This section applies to a consumer contract for the sale of goods to, or hire-purchase of goods by, the consumer.

(2)   The business cannot rely on a term of the contract to exclude or restrict its liability to the consumer for breach of the obligations arising under any of the following provisions of the Sale of Goods Act 1979 (c. 54) ("the 1979 Act") or the Supply of Goods (Implied Terms) Act 1973 (c. 13) ("the 1973 Act").

(3)   Those provisions are—
    (a)   section 12 of the 1979 Act or section 8 of the 1973 Act (implied terms as to title and other similar matters),
    (b)   section 13 of the 1979 Act or section 9 of the 1973 Act (implied terms as to conformity of goods with description),
    (c)   section 14 of the 1979 Act or section 10 of the 1973 Act (implied terms as to quality of goods or fitness of goods for a particular purpose),
    (d)   section 15 of the 1979 Act or section 11 of the 1973 Act (implied terms as to conformity of goods with sample).

(4)   In the case of a contract for the sale of second-hand goods which is made at a public auction which the consumer has the opportunity of attending in person, subsection (2) does not apply to the provisions of the 1979 Act mentioned in subsection (3)(b) to (d).

5   Other contracts under which goods pass to consumer: terms of no effect

(1)   This section applies to a consumer contract for the transfer of the possession or ownership of goods to the consumer otherwise than by sale or hire-purchase.

(2)   The business cannot rely on a term of the contract to exclude or restrict its liability to the consumer for breach of the obligations arising under any of the following provisions of the Supply of Goods and Services Act 1982 (c. 29).

(3)   Those provisions are—
    (a)   section 2, 7, 11B or 11H (implied terms as to title and other similar matters),
    (b)   section 3, 8, 11C or 11I (implied terms as to conformity of goods with description),
    (c)   section 4, 9, 11D or 11J (implied terms as to quality of goods or fitness of goods for a particular purpose),
    (d)   section 5, 10, 11E or 11K (implied terms as to conformity of goods with sample).

6   Other terms detrimental to consumer of no effect unless fair and reasonable

(1)   Where a term of a consumer contract is detrimental to the consumer, the business cannot rely on the term unless the term is fair and reasonable.

(2) Where part of a term of a consumer contract is detrimental to the consumer but the rest of the term is not, this section is to apply only to the part of the term which is detrimental.

(3) This section does not apply to a term—
    (a) which is transparent,
    (b) which sets out the main subject matter of the contract, and
    (c) which is not substantially different from what the consumer reasonably expected.

(4) Nothing in this section enables the adequacy of the price or remuneration payable under a contract to be questioned in any legal proceedings if the price or remuneration—
    (a) is transparent,
    (b) is not payable under or because of a subsidiary term of the contract,
    (c) is not payable in circumstances which are substantially different from what the consumer reasonably expected, and
    (d) is not calculated in a way which is substantially different from that.

(5) This section does not apply to a term—
    (a) which is transparent, and
    (b) which is the same as, or not substantially different from, what would apply as a matter of law in the absence of the term.

(6) "Transparent" means—
    (a) expressed in plain language,
    (b) presented in a clear manner, and
    (c) accessible to the consumer.

7 Sale to, and hire-purchase by, business: effect of certain terms

(1) This section applies to a consumer contract for the sale of goods to, or hire-purchase of goods by, the business.

(2) The consumer cannot rely on a term of the contract to exclude or restrict his liability to the business for breach of the obligations arising under section 12 of the 1979 Act or section 8 of the 1973 Act (implied terms as to title and other similar matters).

(3) Unless the term is fair and reasonable, the consumer cannot rely on a term of the contract to exclude or restrict his liability to the business for breach of the obligations arising under—
    (a) section 13 of the 1979 Act or section 9 of the 1973 Act (implied terms as to conformity of goods with description), or
    (b) section 15 of the 1979 Act or section 11 of the 1973 Act (implied terms as to conformity of goods with sample).

PART 3

PRIVATE CONTRACTS

8   Sale of goods and hire-purchase: effect of certain terms

    (1)   This section applies to a contract for the sale or hire-purchase of goods if neither party makes the contract for purposes related to any business of his.

    (2)   The seller or supplier cannot rely on a term of the contract to exclude or restrict his liability for breach of the obligations arising under section 12 of the 1979 Act or section 8 of the 1973 Act (implied terms as to title and other similar matters).

    (3)   Unless the term is fair and reasonable, the seller or supplier cannot rely on a term of the contract to exclude or restrict his liability for breach of the obligations arising under—

        (a)   section 13 of the 1979 Act or section 9 of the 1973 Act (implied terms as to conformity of goods with description), or

        (b)   section 15 of the 1979 Act or section 11 of the 1973 Act (implied terms as to conformity of goods with sample).

PART 4

MISCELLANEOUS AND SUPPLEMENTAL

The fair and reasonable test

9   The fair and reasonable test

    (1)   Whether a contract term is fair and reasonable is to be determined—

        (a)   by reference to the time when the contract was made, and

        (b)   by taking into account the substance and effect of the term and all the circumstances existing when the contract was made.

    (2)   Whether it is fair and reasonable to allow reliance on a notice is to be determined—

        (a)   by reference to the time when the liability arose, and

        (b)   by taking into account the substance and effect of the notice and all the circumstances existing when the liability arose.

    (3)   Any matters specified in Schedule 1 which are relevant must be taken into account for the purposes of subsection (1) or (2).

    (4)   Schedule 2 contains a list (and some examples) of consumer contract terms which (subject to section 13) are to be regarded for the purposes of section 6 as not being fair and reasonable.

Miscellaneous

10   Savings for mandatory and regulatory provisions

    (1)   This Act does not apply to a contract term—

        (a)   which is required by any enactment or rule of law,

    (b)   which is required or authorised by the provisions of any international convention to which the United Kingdom is a party, or

    (c)   which is required by, or incorporated pursuant to a decision or ruling of, a competent authority acting in the exercise of any statutory jurisdiction or function.

(2)   Subsection (1)(c) does not apply if the competent authority is itself a party to the contract.

11   Secondary contracts

(1)   A term of a contract ("the secondary contract") which reduces the rights or remedies, or increases the obligations, of a person under another contract ("the main contract") is to be subject to the same provisions of this Act as would apply to the term if it were included in the main contract.

(2)   It does not matter for the purposes of this section whether the parties to the secondary contract are the same as the parties to the main contract.

(3)   This section does not apply if the secondary contract is a settlement of a dispute which has arisen under the main contract.

12   Effect on contract of term having no effect

Where a contract term has no effect because of this Act, the rest of the contract is to continue to bind the parties if the contract is capable of continuing in existence without that term.

13   Burden of proof

(1)   It is for a person claiming that a contract is not a consumer contract to prove that that is the case.

AND

(2)   It is for a person claiming—
    (a)   that a term is fair and reasonable, or
    (b)   that it is fair and reasonable to allow reliance on a notice,
to prove that that is the case.

(3)   Nothing in subsection (2) prevents a court, tribunal, arbitrator or arbiter from holding—
    (a)   that a term is not fair and reasonable, or
    (b)   that it is not fair and reasonable to allow reliance on a notice,
even though the issue has not been raised.

OR

(2)   Subject to subsection (3), it is for a person claiming—
    (a)   that a term is not fair and reasonable, or
    (b)   that it is not fair and reasonable to allow reliance on a notice,
to prove that that is the case.

(3)   It is for a person claiming that a consumer contract term falling within Schedule 2 is fair and reasonable to prove that that is the case.

(4) Nothing in subsection (2) or (3) prevents a court, tribunal, arbitrator or arbiter from holding—

    (a) that a term is not fair and reasonable, or

    (b) that it is not fair and reasonable to allow reliance on a notice,

even though the issue has not been raised.   *5*

Interpretation

14 **"Negligence" and "breach of duty"**

(1) "Negligence" means the breach—

    (a) of any obligation to take reasonable care or exercise reasonable skill in the performance of a contract where the obligation arises from the *10* express or implied terms of the contract,

    (b) of any common law duty to take reasonable care or exercise reasonable skill, or

    (c) of the common duty of care imposed by the Occupiers' Liability Act 1957 (c. 31).   *15*

(2) In the application of sections 1 to 3 to Scotland, any reference to negligence is to be read as a reference to breach of duty.

(3) "Breach of duty" means the breach—

    (a) of any such obligation as is mentioned in subsection (1)(a),

    (b) of any such duty as is mentioned in subsection (1)(b), or   *20*

    (c) of the duty of reasonable care imposed by section 2(1) of the Occupiers' Liability (Scotland) Act 1960 (c. 30).

15 **"Consumer contract", "the consumer" and "the business"**

"Consumer contract" means a contract between—

    (a) an individual ("the consumer") who makes the contract for purposes *25* which are not related to any business of his, and

    (b) a person ("the business") who makes the contract for purposes which are related to his business,

but a contract of employment is not a consumer contract.

16 **"Exclusion or restriction of liability"**   *30*

(1) Any reference in this Act to the exclusion or restriction of any liability includes a reference to—

    (a) making any right or remedy in respect of the liability subject to restrictive or onerous conditions,

    (b) excluding or restricting any right or remedy in respect of the liability,   *35*

    (c) subjecting a person to any prejudice for pursuing any such right or remedy,

    (d) excluding or restricting rules of evidence or procedure,

    (e) excluding or restricting liability by excluding or restricting any obligation or duty which gives rise to that liability.   *40*

(2) But an agreement in writing to submit present or future differences to arbitration is not to be treated as excluding or restricting any liability.

17   Examples of "exclusion or restriction of liability"

(1)   These are examples of a contract term falling within section 16(1)(a)—

   (a)   a term which requires claims to be made within a short period of time,

   (b)   a term which provides that defective goods will be replaced only if a person returns them to a particular place at his own expense.   *5*

(2)   These are examples of a contract term falling within section 16(1)(b)—

   (a)   a term which restricts a person's right to terminate a contract,

   (b)   a term which limits the damages which may be claimed by a person,

   (c)   a term which prevents a person from deducting compensation due to him from payments due by him.   *10*

(3)   These are examples of a contract term falling within section 16(1)(c)—

   (a)   a term which provides for a deposit paid by a person to be forfeited if he pursues any remedy,

   (b)   a term which provides that a purchaser who exercises a right to have defective goods repaired by a third party will invalidate any rights he has against the seller.   *15*

(4)   This is an example of a contract term falling within section 16(1)(d)—

   a term which provides that a decision of the seller, or a third party, that goods are or are not defective is to be conclusive.

(5)   This is an example of a contract term falling within section 16(1)(e)—   *20*

   a term which excludes "all conditions or warranties".

18   Interpretation of other expressions

(1)   In this Act—

   "business" includes a profession and the activities of a government department or local or public authority,   *25*

   "business liability" is to be construed in accordance with section 1(3) and (4),

   "competent authority" means a court, tribunal, arbitrator or arbiter, government department or public authority,

   "enactment" includes a provision of, or of an instrument made under, an Act of the Scottish Parliament and a provision of subordinate legislation (within the meaning of the Interpretation Act 1978 (c. 30)) ,   *30*

   "goods" has the same meaning as in the 1979 Act,

   "hire-purchase agreement" has the same meaning as in the Consumer Credit Act 1974 (c. 39), and "hire-purchase" is to be construed accordingly,   *35*

   "notice" includes an announcement, whether or not in writing, and any other communication,

   "personal injury" includes any disease and any impairment of physical or mental condition,   *40*

   "statutory" means conferred by an enactment,

   "supplier" means the person by whom goods are bailed or (in Scotland) hired under a hire-purchase agreement,

   "the 1973 Act" means the Supply of Goods (Implied Terms) Act 1973 (c. 13),   *45*

   "the 1979 Act" means the Sale of Goods Act 1979 (c. 54),

"transparent" has the meaning given by section 6(6).

(2) Any reference in this Act to a contract for the hire-purchase of goods by a person is to be read as a reference to a hire-purchase agreement under which goods are bailed or (in Scotland) hired to that person.

(3) It is immaterial for the purposes of this Act—

5

(a) whether any breach of duty or obligation was inadvertent or intentional, or

(b) whether liability for any such breach arises directly or vicariously.

SCHEDULES

SCHEDULE 1

Section 9

MATTERS REFERRED TO IN SECTION 9(3)

Matters relating to the substance and effect of a term

1   The following are matters which relate to the substance and effect of a term—   *5*

     (a)   the balance of the interests of the parties,

     (b)   the risks to the party adversely affected by the term,

     (c)   the possibility and likelihood of insurance,

     (d)   any other way in which his interest might be protected,   *10*

     (e)   the extent to which the term (whether alone or with other terms) differs from what would have applied in the absence of the term.

Matters relating to the circumstances existing when a contract was made

2   The following are matters which relate to the circumstances existing when a contract was made—   *15*

     (a)   the knowledge and understanding of the party adversely affected by the term,

     (b)   the strength of the bargaining positions of the parties,

     (c)   the nature of the goods or services for which the contract was concluded,   *20*

     (d)   the other terms of the contract,

     (e)   the terms of any other contract on which the contract is dependent.

3   (1)   The following matters are relevant to the knowledge and understanding of the party adversely affected by the term—

     (a)   any previous course of dealing between the parties,   *25*

     (b)   whether the party adversely affected knew of the term,

     (c)   whether he understood the meaning and implications of the term,

     (d)   what other persons in a similar position to him would normally expect in the case of a similar transaction,

     (e)   the complexity of the transaction,   *30*

     (f)   the information given to him before or when the contract was made,

     (g)   whether the contract was transparent,

     (h)   the way that the contract was explained to him,

     (i)   whether he had a reasonable opportunity to absorb any information given,   *35*

     (j)   whether he took professional advice, or it was reasonable to expect that he should have taken such advice,

    (k)   whether he had a realistic opportunity to cancel the contract without charge.

 (2)   The matters mentioned in sub-paragraph (1)(f) to (k) are particularly relevant where the transaction is complex.

4   The following matters are relevant to the strength of the bargaining positions of the parties—

    (a)   whether the transaction was an unusual one for either of the parties,

    (b)   whether the party adversely affected by the term was offered a choice over the term,

    (c)   whether he had an opportunity to seek a more favourable term,

    (d)   whether he had an opportunity to enter into a similar contract with other persons, but without that term,

    (e)   whether there were alternative means by which his requirements could have been met,

    (f)   whether it was reasonable, given his abilities, for him to have taken advantage of any offer, opportunity or alternative mentioned in sub-paragraphs (b) to (e).

Application of Schedule to notices

5   In its application to a notice, this Schedule is to have effect with such modifications as may be appropriate.

SCHEDULE 2

Section 9

TERMS REFERRED TO IN SECTION 9(4)

1   Terms which attempt to exclude or restrict liability to the consumer for breach of contract.

Section 17 contains some examples of such terms.

2   Terms which have the object or effect of imposing obligations on the consumer in circumstances where the obligations on the part of the business are dependent on the satisfaction of conditions which are wholly within the control of the business.

For example

        a term of a loan agreement which obliges the consumer to take the loan in circumstances where the other party is under an obligation to make the loan only with the approval of one of its managers.

3   Terms which entitle the business—

    (a)   when the consumer exercises a right to withdraw from the contract, or

    (b)   when the contract is terminated because of the consumer's breach,

to retain any payment made by way of deposit or otherwise if the payment is not reasonable in amount.

For example

a term of a contract for the sale of a house by a developer to a consumer which requires the consumer to pay a 25 per cent. deposit to the developer in circumstances where there is no reasonable justification for the deposit being larger than the customary 10 per cent. deposit.

5

4   Terms which require the consumer, when in breach of contract, to pay a sum which significantly exceeds a genuine and reasonable estimate, calculated at the time the contract was made, of the loss the business is likely to suffer.

For example

  (i)   a term of a contract (other than a loan agreement) which requires the consumer, when late in making any payment, to pay a default rate of interest which is substantially more than the business has to pay when borrowing money,

10

  (ii)   a term of a loan agreement which requires the consumer, when late in making any payment, to pay a default rate of interest which is substantially above the rate payable before default,

15

  (iii)   a term of a contract for the sale of goods which requires the consumer, if he wrongfully terminates the contract, to compensate the business for the full loss of profit it suffers, without making any allowance for the amount which the business should be able to recover by taking reasonable steps to resell the goods.

20

APPENDIX C
THE UNFAIR CONTRACT TERMS ACT 1977

PART I

AMENDMENT OF LAW FOR ENGLAND AND WALES AND NORTHERN IRELAND

Introductory

1 Scope of Part I

(1) For the purposes of this Part of this Act, "negligence" means the breach –

    (a) of any obligation, arising from the express or implied terms of a contract, to take reasonable care or exercise reasonable skill in the performance of the contract;

    (b) of any common law duty to take reasonable care or exercise reasonable skill (but not any stricter duty);

    (c) of the common duty of care imposed by the Occupiers' Liability Act 1957 or the Occupiers' Liability Act (Northern Ireland) 1957.

(2) This Part of this Act is subject to Part III; and in relation to contracts, the operation of sections 2 to 4 and 7 is subject to the exceptions made by Schedule 1.

(3) In the case of both contract and tort, sections 2 to 7 apply (except where the contrary is stated in section 6(4)) only to business liability, that is liability for breach of obligations or duties arising –

    (a) from things done or to be done by a person in the course of a business (whether his own business or another's); or

    (b) from the occupation of premises used for business purposes of the occupier;

and references to liability are to be read accordingly but liability of an occupier of premises for breach of an obligation or duty towards a person obtaining access to the premises for recreational or educational purposes, being liability for loss or damage suffered by reason of the dangerous state of the premises, is not a business liability of the occupier unless granting that person such access for the purposes concerned falls within the business purposes of the occupier.

(4) In relation to any breach of duty or obligation, it is immaterial for any purpose of this Part of this Act whether the breach was inadvertent or intentional, or whether liability for it arises directly or vicariously.

Avoidance of liability for negligence, breach of contract, etc

2 Negligence liability

(1) A person cannot by reference to any contract term or to a notice given to persons generally or to particular persons exclude or restrict his liability for death or personal injury resulting from negligence.

(2) In the case of other loss or damage, a person cannot so exclude or restrict his liability for negligence except in so far as the term or notice satisfies the requirement of reasonableness.

(3) Where a contract term or notice purports to exclude or restrict liability for negligence a person's agreement to or awareness of it is not of itself to be taken as indicating his voluntary acceptance of any risk.

3 Liability arising in contract

(1) This section applies as between contracting parties where one of them deals as consumer or on the other's written standard terms of business.

(2) As against that party, the other cannot by reference to any contract term –

    (a) when himself in breach of contract, exclude or restrict any liability of his in respect of the breach; or

(b) claim to be entitled –

    (i) to render a contractual performance substantially different from that which was reasonably expected of him, or

    (ii) in respect of the whole or any part of his contractual obligation, to render no performance at all,

except in so far as (in any of the cases mentioned above in this subsection) the contract term satisfies the requirement of reasonableness.

4 Unreasonable indemnity clauses

(1) A person dealing as consumer cannot by reference to any contract term be made to indemnify another person (whether a party to the contract or not) in respect of liability that may be incurred by the other for negligence or breach of contract, except in so far as the contract term satisfies the requirement of reasonableness.

(2) This section applies whether the liability in question –

    (a) is directly that of the person to be indemnified or is incurred by him vicariously;

    (b) is to the person dealing as consumer or to someone else.

Liability arising from sale or supply of goods

5 "Guarantee" of consumer goods

(1) In the case of goods of a type ordinarily supplied for private use or consumption, where loss or damage –

    (a) arises from the goods proving defective while in consumer use; and

    (b) results from the negligence of a person concerned in the manufacture or distribution of the goods,

liability for the loss or damage cannot be excluded or restricted by reference to any contract term or notice contained in or operating by reference to a guarantee of the goods.

(2) For these purposes –

    (a) goods are to be regarded as "in consumer use" when a person is using them, or has them in his possession for use, otherwise than exclusively for the purposes of a business; and

    (b) anything in writing is a guarantee if it contains or purports to contain some promise or assurance (however worded or presented) that defects will be made good by complete or partial replacement, or by repair, monetary compensation or otherwise.

(3) This section does not apply as between the parties to a contract under or in pursuance of which possession or ownership of the goods passed.

6 Sale and hire-purchase

(1) Liability for breach of the obligations arising from –

    (a) section 12 of the Sale of Goods Act 1979 (seller's implied undertakings as to title, etc);

    (b) section 8 of the Supply of Goods (Implied Terms) Act 1973 (the corresponding thing in relation to hire-purchase),

cannot be excluded or restricted by reference to any contract term.

(2) As against a person dealing as consumer, liability for breach of the obligations arising from –

    (a) section 13, 14 or 15 of the 1979 Act (seller's implied undertakings as to conformity of goods with description or sample, or as to their quality or fitness for a particular purpose);

    (b) section 9, 10 or 11 of the 1973 Act (the corresponding things in relation to hire-purchase),

cannot be excluded or restricted by reference to any contract term.

(3) As against a person dealing otherwise than as consumer, the liability specified in subsection (2) above can be excluded or restricted by reference to a contract term, but only in so far as the term satisfies the requirement of reasonableness.

(4) The liabilities referred to in this section are not only the business liabilities defined by section 1(3), but include those arising under any contract of sale of goods or hire-purchase agreement.

(5) *For the purposes of this section, so far as relating to section 13 or 14 or 15 of the 1979 Act or section 9 or 10 or 11 of the 1973 Act a party to a contract deals as consumer where –*

    (a) he is a natural person who makes the contract otherwise than in the course of a business, and

    (b) the other party does make the contract in the course of a business,

and accordingly section 12(1) and (2) does not have effect for those purposes so far as so relating.

(6) *A person shall not by virtue of subsection (5) above be regarded as dealing as consumer if –*

    (a) the goods in question are second-hand goods, and

    (b) the contract is made at public auction where persons dealing as consumers have the opportunity of attending in person.[1]

7 Miscellaneous contracts under which goods pass

(1) Where the possession or ownership of goods passes under or in pursuance of a contract not governed by the law of sale of goods or hire-purchase, subsections (2) to (4) below apply as regards the effect (if any) to be given to contract terms excluding or restricting liability for breach of obligation arising by implication of law from the nature of the contract.

(2) As against a person dealing as consumer, liability in respect of the goods' correspondence with description or sample, or their quality or fitness for any particular purpose, cannot be excluded or restricted by reference to any such term.

(3) As against a person dealing otherwise than as consumer, that liability can be excluded or restricted by reference to such a term, but only in so far as the term satisfies the requirement of reasonableness.

(3A) Liability for breach of the obligations arising under section 2 of the Supply of Goods and Services Act 1982 (implied terms about title etc in certain contracts for the transfer of the property in goods) cannot be excluded or restricted by references to any such term.

(4) Liability in respect of –

    (a) the right to transfer ownership of the goods, or give possession; or

    (b) the assurance of quiet possession to a person taking goods in pursuance of the contract,

cannot (in a case to which subsection (3A) above does not apply) be excluded or restricted by reference to any such term except in so far as the term satisfies the requirement of reasonableness.

(5) This section does not apply in the case of goods passing on a redemption of trading stamps within the Trading Stamps Act 1964 or the Trading Stamps Act (Northern Ireland) 1965.

(6) *For the purposes of this section so far as relating to any obligation arising in respect of –*

    (a) the goods' correspondence with description or sample, or

    (b) their quality or fitness for any purpose,

---

[1] The words in italics would be added by the DTI's draft Sale and Supply of Goods to Consumers Regulations 2002, reg 6(2).

references to a person dealing as consumer shall be construed in accordance with subsections (5) and (6) of section 6 (and section 12(1) and (2) accordingly does not have effect for those purposes so far as so relating).[2]

Other provisions about contracts

. . .

9 Effect of breach

(1) Where for reliance upon it a contract term has to satisfy the requirement of reasonableness, it may be found to do so and be given effect accordingly notwithstanding that the contract has been terminated either by breach or by a party electing to treat it as repudiated.

(2) Where on a breach the contract is nevertheless affirmed by a party entitled to treat it as repudiated, this does not of itself exclude the requirement of reasonableness in relation to any contract term.

10 Evasion by means of secondary contract

A person is not bound by any contract term prejudicing or taking away rights of his which arise under, or in connection with the performance of, another contract, so far as those rights extend to the enforcement of another's liability which this Part of this Act prevents that other from excluding or restricting.

Explanatory provisions

11 The "reasonableness" test

(1) In relation to a contract term, the requirement of reasonableness for the purposes of this Part of this Act, section 3 of the Misrepresentation Act 1967 and section 3 of the Misrepresentation Act (Northern Ireland) 1967 is that the term shall have been a fair and reasonable one to be included having regard to the circumstances which were, or ought reasonably to have been, known to or in the contemplation of the parties when the contract was made.

(2) In determining for the purposes of section 6 or 7 above whether a contract term satisfies the requirement of reasonableness, regard shall be had in particular to the matters specified in Schedule 2 to this Act; but this subsection does not prevent the court or arbitrator from holding, in accordance with any rule of law, that a term which purports to exclude or restrict any relevant liability is not a term of the contract.

(3) In relation to a notice (not being a notice having contractual effect), the requirement of reasonableness under this Act is that it should be fair and reasonable to allow reliance on it, having regard to all the circumstances obtaining when the liability arose or (but for the notice) would have arisen.

(4) Where by reference to a contract term or notice a person seeks to restrict liability to a specified sum of money, and the question arises (under this or any other Act) whether the term or notice satisfies the requirement of reasonableness, regard shall be had in particular (but without prejudice to subsection (2) above in the case of contract terms) to –

    (a) the resources which he could expect to be available to him for the purpose of meeting the liability should it arise; and

    (b) how far it was open to him to cover himself by insurance.

(5) It is for those claiming that a contract term or notice satisfies the requirement of reasonableness to show that it does.

12 "Dealing as consumer"

(1) A party to a contract "deals as consumer" in relation to another party if –

---

[2] The words in italics would be added by the DTI's draft Sale and Supply of Goods to Consumers Regulations 2002, reg 6(3).

(a) he neither makes the contract in the course of a business nor holds himself out as doing so; and

(b) the other party does make the contract in the course of a business; and

(c) in the case of a contract governed by the law of sale of goods or hire-purchase, or by section 7 of this Act, the goods passing under or in pursuance of the contract are of a type ordinarily supplied for private use or consumption.

(2) But on a sale by auction or by competitive tender the buyer is not in any circumstances to be regarded as dealing as consumer.

(3) Subject to this, it is for those claiming that a party does not deal as consumer to show that he does not.

13 Varieties of exemption clause

(1) To the extent that this Part of this Act prevents the exclusion or restriction of any liability it also prevents –

(a) making the liability or its enforcement subject to restrictive or onerous conditions;

(b) excluding or restricting any right or remedy in respect of the liability, or subjecting a person to any prejudice in consequence of his pursuing any such right or remedy;

(c) excluding or restricting rules of evidence or procedure;

and (to that extent) sections 2 and 5 to 7 also prevent excluding or restricting liability by reference to terms and notices which exclude or restrict the relevant obligation or duty.

(2) But an agreement in writing to submit present or future differences to arbitration is not to be treated under this Part of this Act as excluding or restricting any liability.

14 Interpretation of Part I

In this Part of this Act –

"business" includes a profession and the activities of any government department or local or public authority;

"goods" has the same meaning as in the Sale of Goods Act 1979:

"hire-purchase agreement" has the same meaning as in the Consumer Credit Act 1974;

"negligence" has the meaning given by section 1(1);

"notice" includes an announcement, whether or not in writing, and any other communication or pretended communication; and

"personal injury" includes any disease and any impairment of physical or mental condition.

PART II

AMENDMENT OF LAW FOR SCOTLAND

15 Scope of Part II

(1) This Part of this Act . . ., is subject to Part III of this Act and does not affect the validity of any discharge or indemnity given by a person in consideration of the receipt by him of compensation in settlement of any claim which he has.

(2) Subject to subsection (3) below, sections 16 to 18 of this Act apply to any contract only to the extent that the contract –

(a) relates to the transfer of the ownership or possession of goods from one person to another (with or without work having been done on them);

(b) constitutes a contract of service or apprenticeship;

(c) relates to services of whatever kind, including (without prejudice to the foregoing generality) carriage, deposit and pledge, care and custody, mandate, agency, loan and services relating to the use of land;

(d) relates to the liability of an occupier of land to persons entering upon or using that land;

(e) relates to a grant of any right or permission to enter upon or use land not amounting to an estate or interest in the land.

(3) Notwithstanding anything in subsection (2) above, section 16 to 18 –

    (a) do not apply to any contract to the extent that the contract –

        (i) is a contract of insurance (including a contract to pay an annuity on human life);

        (ii) relates to the formation, constitution or dissolution of any body corporate or unincorporated association or partnership;

    (b) apply to –

        a contract of marine salvage or towage;

        a charter party of a ship or hovercraft;

        a contract for the carriage of goods by ship or hovercraft; or,

        a contract to which subsection (4) below relates,

    only to the extent that –

        (i) both parties deal or hold themselves out as dealing in the course of a business (and then only in so far as the contract purports to exclude or restrict liability for breach of duty in respect of death or personal injury); or

        (ii) the contract is a consumer contract (and then only in favour of the consumer).

(4) This subsection relates to a contract in pursuance of which goods are carried by ship or hovercraft and which either –

    (a) specifies ship or hovercraft as the means of carriage over part of the journey to be covered; or

    (b) makes no provision as to the means of carriage and does not exclude ship or hovercraft as that means,

in so far as the contract operates for and in relation to the carriage of the goods by that means.

16 Liability for breach of duty

(1) Subject to subsection (1A) below, where a term of a contract, or a provision of a notice given to persons generally or to particular persons, purports to exclude or restrict liability for breach of duty arising in the course of any business or from the occupation of any premises used for business purposes of the occupier, that term or provision –

    (a) shall be void in any case where such exclusion or restriction is in respect of death or personal injury;

    (b) shall, in any other case, have no effect if it was not fair and reasonable to incorporate the term in the contract or, as the case may be, if it is not fair and reasonable to allow reliance on the provision.

(1A) Nothing in paragraph (b) of subsection (1) above shall be taken as implying that a provision of a notice has effect in circumstances where, apart from that paragraph, it would not have effect.

(2) Subsection (1)(a) above does not affect the validity of any discharge and indemnity given by a person, on or in connection with an award to him of compensation for pneumoconiosis attributable to employment in the coal industry, in respect of any further claim arising from his contracting that disease.

(3) Where under subsection (1) above a term of a contract or a provision of a notice is void or has no effect, the fact that a person agreed to, or was aware of, the term or provision shall not of itself be sufficient evidence that he knowingly and voluntarily assumed any risk.

17 Control of unreasonable exemptions in consumer or standard form contracts

(1) Any term of a contract which is a consumer contract or a standard form contract shall have no effect for the purpose of enabling a party to the contract –

    (a) who is in breach of a contractual obligation, to exclude or restrict any liability of his to the consumer or customer in respect of the breach;

(b) in respect of a contractual obligation, to render no performance, or to render a performance substantially different from that which the consumer or customer reasonably expected from the contract;

if it was not fair and reasonable to incorporate the term in the contract.

(2) In this section "customer" means a party to a standard form contract who deals on the basis of written standard terms of business of the other party to the contract who himself deals in the course of a business.

18 Unreasonable indemnity clauses in consumer contracts

(1) Any term of a contract which is a consumer contract shall have no effect for the purpose of making the consumer indemnify another person (whether a party to the contract or not) in respect of liability which that other person may incur as a result of breach of duty or breach of contract, if it was not fair and reasonable to incorporate the term in the contract.

(2) In this section "liability" means liability arising in the course of any business or from the occupation of any premises used for business purposes of the occupier.

19 "Guarantee of consumer goods"

(1) This section applies to a guarantee –

(a) in relation to goods which are of a type ordinarily supplied for private use or consumption; and

(b) which is not a guarantee given by one party to the other party to a contract under or in pursuance of which the ownership or possession of the goods to which the guarantee relates is transferred.

(2) A term of a guarantee to which this section applies shall be void in so far as it purports to exclude or restrict liability for loss or damage (including death or personal injury) –

(a) arising from the goods proving defective while –

(i) in use otherwise than exclusively for the purposes of a business; or

(ii) in the possession of a person for such use; and

(b) resulting from the breach of duty of a person concerned in the manufacture or distribution of the goods.

(3) For the purposes of this section, any document is a guarantee if it contains or purports to contain some promise or assurance (however worded or presented) that defects will be made good by complete or partial replacement, or by repair, monetary compensation otherwise.

20 Obligations implied by law in sale and hire-purchase contracts

(1) Any term of a contract which purports to exclude or restrict liability for breach of the obligations arising from –

(a) section 12 of the Sale of Goods Act 1979 (seller's implied undertakings as to title etc.);

(b) section 8 of the Supply of Goods (Implied Terms) Act 1973 (implied terms as to title in hire-purchase agreements),

shall be void.

(2) Any term of a contract which purports to exclude or restrict liability for breach of the obligations arising from –

(a) section 13, 14 or 15 of the said Act of 1979 (seller's implied undertakings as to conformity of goods with description or sample, or as to their quality or fitness for a particular purpose);

(b) section 9, 10 or 11 of the said Act of 1973 (the corresponding provisions in relation to hire-purchase),

shall –

(i) in the case of a consumer contract, be void against the consumer;

(ii) in any other case, have no effect if it was not fair and reasonable to incorporate the term in the contract.

21 Obligations implied by law in other contracts for the supply of goods

(1) Any term of a contract to which this section applies purporting to exclude or restrict liability for breach of an obligation –

(a) such as is referred to in subsection (3)(a) below –

(i) in the case of a consumer contract, shall be void against the consumer, and

(ii) in any other case, shall have no effect if it was not fair and reasonable to incorporate the term in the contract;

(b) such as is referred to in subsection (3)(b) below, shall have no effect if it was not fair and reasonable to incorporate the term in the contract.

(2) This section applies to any contract to the extent that it relates to any such matter as is referred to in section 15(2)(a) of this Act, but does not apply to –

(a) a contract of sale of goods or a hire-purchase agreement; or

(b) a charter party of a ship or hovercraft unless it is a consumer contract (and then only in favour of the consumer).

(3) An obligation referred to in this subsection is an obligation incurred under a contract in the course of a business and arising by implication of law from the nature of the contract which relates –

(a) to the correspondence of goods with description or sample, or to the quality or fitness of goods for any particular purpose; or

(b) to any right to transfer ownership or possession of goods, or to the enjoyment of quiet possession of goods.

(4) Nothing in this section applies to the supply of goods on a redemption of trading stamps within the Trading Stamps Act 1964.

22 Consequence of breach

For the avoidance of doubt, where any provision of this Part of this Act requires that the incorporation of a term in a contract must be fair and reasonable for that term to have effect –

(a) if that requirement is satisfied, the term may be given effect to notwithstanding that the contract has been terminated in consequence of breach of that contract;

(b) for the term to be given effect to, that requirement must be satisfied even where a party who is entitled to rescind the contract elects not to rescind it.

23 Evasion by means of secondary contract

Any term of any contract shall be void which purports to exclude or restrict, or has the effect of excluding or restricting –

(a) the exercise, by a party to any other contract, of any right or remedy which arises in respect of that other contract in consequence of breach of duty, or of obligation, liability for which could not by virtue of the provisions of this Part of this Act be excluded or restricted by a term of that other contract;

(b) the application of the provisions of this Part of this Act in respect of that or any other contract.

24 The "reasonableness" test

(1) In determining for the purposes of this Part of this Act whether it was fair and reasonable to incorporate a term in a contract, regard shall be had only to the circumstances which were, or ought reasonably to have been, known to or in the contemplation of the parties to the contract at the time the contract was made.

(2) In determining for the purposes of section 20 or 21 of this Act whether it was fair and reasonable to incorporate a term in a contract, regard shall be had in particular to the

matters specified in Schedule 2 to this Act; but this subsection shall not prevent a court or arbiter from holding, in accordance with any rule of law, that a term which purports to exclude or restrict any relevant liability is not a term of the contract.

(2A) In determining for the purposes of this Part of this Act whether it is fair and reasonable to allow reliance on a provision of a notice (not being a notice having contractual effect), regard shall be had to all the circumstances obtaining when the liability arose or (but for the provision) would have arisen.

(3) Where a term in a contract or a provision of a notice purports to restrict liability to a specified sum of money, and the question arises for the purposes of this Part of this Act whether it was fair and reasonable to incorporate the term in the contract or whether it is fair and reasonable to allow reliance on the provision, then, without prejudice to subsection (2) above in the case of a term in a contract, regard shall be had in particular to –

(a) the resources which the party seeking to rely on that term or provision could expect to be available to him for the purpose of meeting the liability should it arise;

(b) how far it was open to that party to cover himself by insurance.

(4) The onus of proving that it was fair and reasonable to incorporate a term in a contract or that it is fair and reasonable to allow reliance on a provision of a notice shall lie on the party so contending.

25 Interpretation of Part II

(1) In this Part of this Act –

"breach of duty" means the breach –

(a) of any obligation, arising from the express or implied terms of a contract, to take reasonable care or exercise reasonable skill in the performance of the contract;

(b) of any common law duty to take reasonable care or exercise reasonable skill;

(c) of the duty of reasonable care imposed by section 2(1) of the Occupiers' Liability (Scotland) Act 1960;

"business" includes a profession and the activities of any government department or local or public authority;

"consumer" has the meaning assigned to that expression in the definition in this section of "consumer contract";

"consumer contract" means a contract (not being a contract of sale by auction or competitive tender) in which –

(a) one party to the contract deals, and the other party to the contract ("the consumer") does not deal or hold himself out as dealing, in the course of a business, and

(b) in the case of a contract such as is mentioned in section 15(2)(a) of this Act, the goods are of a type ordinarily supplied for private use or consumption;

and for the purposes of this Part of this Act the onus of proving that a contract is not to be regarded as a consumer contract shall lie on the party so contending;

"goods" has the same meaning as in the Sale of Goods Act 1979;

"hire-purchase agreement" has the same meaning as in section 189(1) of the Consumer Credit Act 1974;

"notice" includes an announcement, whether or not in writing, and any other communication or pretended communication;

"personal injury" includes any disease and any impairment of physical or mental condition.

(2) In relation to any breach of duty or obligation, it is immaterial for any purpose of this Part of this Act whether the act or omission giving rise to that breach was inadvertent or intentional, or whether liability for it arises directly or vicariously.

(3) In this Part of this Act, any reference to excluding or restricting any liability includes--

    (a) making the liability or its enforcement subject to any restrictive or onerous conditions;

    (b) excluding or restricting any right or remedy in respect of the liability, or subjecting a person to any prejudice in consequence of his pursuing any such right or remedy;

    (c) excluding or restricting any rule of evidence or procedure;

    (d) . . .

but does not include an agreement to submit any question to arbitration.

(4) . . .

(5) In sections 15 and 16 and 19 to 21 of this Act, any reference to excluding or restricting liability for breach of an obligation or duty shall include a reference to excluding or restricting the obligation or duty itself.

PART III

PROVISIONS APPLYING TO WHOLE OF UNITED KINGDOM

Miscellaneous

26 International supply contracts

(1) The limits imposed by this Act on the extent to which a person may exclude or restrict liability by reference to a contract term do not apply to liability arising under such a contract as is described in subsection (3) below.

(2) The terms of such a contract are not subject to any requirement of reasonableness under section 3 or 4: and nothing in Part II of this Act shall require the incorporation of the terms of such a contract to be fair and reasonable for them to have effect.

(3) Subject to subsection (4), that description of contract is one whose characteristics are the following –

    (a) either it is a contract of sale of goods or it is one under or in pursuance of which the possession or ownership of goods passes; and

    (b) it is made by parties whose places of business (or, if they have none, habitual residences) are in the territories of different States (the Channel Islands and the Isle of Man being treated for this purpose as different States from the United Kingdom).

(4) A contract falls within subsection (3) above only if either –

    (a) the goods in question are, at the time of the conclusion of the contract, in the course of carriage, or will be carried, from the territory of one State to the territory of another; or

    (b) the acts constituting the offer and acceptance have been done in the territories of different States; or

    (c) the contract provides for the goods to be delivered to the territory of a State other than that within whose territory those acts were done.

27 Choice of law clauses

(1) Where the law applicable to a contract is the law of any part of the United Kingdom only by choice of the parties (and apart from that choice would be the law of some country outside the United Kingdom) sections 2 to 7 and 16 to 21 of this Act do not operate as part of the law applicable to the contract.

(2) This Act has effect notwithstanding any contract term which applies or purports to apply the law of some country outside the United Kingdom, where (either or both) –

    (a) the term appears to the court, or arbitrator or arbiter to have been imposed wholly or mainly for the purpose of enabling the party imposing it to evade the operation of this Act; or

(b) in the making of the contract one of the parties dealt as consumer, and he was then habitually resident in the United Kingdom, and the essential steps necessary for the making of the contract were taken there, whether by him or by others on his behalf.

(3) In the application of subsection (2) above to Scotland, for paragraph (b) there shall be substituted –

"(b) the contract is a consumer contract as defined in Part II of this Act, and the consumer at the date when the contract was made was habitually resident in the United Kingdom, and the essential steps necessary for the making of the contract were taken there, whether by him or by others on his behalf.".

28 Temporary provision for sea carriage of passengers

(1) This section applies to a contract for carriage by sea of a passenger or of a passenger and his luggage where the provisions of the Athens Convention (with or without modification) do not have, in relation to the contract, the force of law in the United Kingdom.

(2) In a case where –

(a) the contract is not made in the United Kingdom, and

(b) neither the place of departure nor the place of destination under it is in the United Kingdom,

a person is not precluded by this Act from excluding or restricting liability for loss or damage, being loss or damage for which the provisions of the Convention would, if they had the force of law in relation to the contract, impose liability on him.

(3) In any other case, a person is not precluded by this Act from excluding or restricting liability for that loss or damage –

(a) in so far as the exclusion or restriction would have been effective in that case had the provisions of the Convention had the force of law in relation to the contract; or

(b) in such circumstances and to such extent as may be prescribed, by reference to a prescribed term of the contract.

(4) For the purposes of subsection (3) (a), the values which shall be taken to be the official values in the United Kingdom of the amounts (expressed in gold francs) by reference to which liability under the provisions of the Convention is limited shall be such amounts in sterling as the Secretary of State may from time to time by order made by statutory instrument specify.

(5) In this section, –

(a) the references to excluding or restricting liability include doing any of those things in relation to the liability which are mentioned in section 13 or section 25 (3) and (5); and

(b) "the Athens Convention" means the Athens Convention relating to the Carriage of Passengers and their Luggage by Sea, 1974; and

(c) "prescribed" means prescribed by the Secretary of State by regulations made by statutory instrument;

and a statutory instrument containing the regulations shall be subject to annulment in pursuance of a resolution of either House of Parliament.

29 Saving for other relevant legislation

(1) Nothing in this Act removes or restricts the effect of, or prevents reliance upon, any contractual provision which –

(a) is authorised or required by the express terms or necessary implication of an enactment; or

(b) being made with a view to compliance with an international agreement to which the United Kingdom is a party, does not operate more restrictively than is contemplated by the agreement.

(2) A contract term is to be taken –

    (a) for the purposes of Part I of this Act, as satisfying the requirement of reasonableness; and

    (b) for those of Part II, to have been fair and reasonable to incorporate,

if it is incorporated or approved by, or incorporated pursuant to a decision or ruling of, a competent authority acting in the exercise of any statutory jurisdiction or function and is not a term in a contract to which the competent authority is itself a party.

(3) In this section –

"competent authority" means any court, arbitrator or arbiter, government department or public authority;

"enactment" means any legislation (including subordinate legislation) of the United Kingdom or Northern Ireland and any instrument having effect by virtue of such legislation; and

"statutory" means conferred by an enactment.

30 . . .

31 Commencement; amendments; repeals

(1) This Act comes into force on 1st February 1978.

(2) Nothing in this Act applies to contracts made before the date on which it comes into force; but subject to this, it applies to liability for any loss or damage which is suffered on or after that date.

(3) The enactments specified in Schedule 3 to this Act are amended as there shown.

(4) The enactments specified in Schedule 4 to this Act are repealed to the extent specified in column 3 of that Schedule.

32 Citation and extent

(1) This Act may be cited as the Unfair Contract Terms Act 1977.

(2) Part I of this Act extends to England and Wales and to Northern Ireland; but it does not extend to Scotland.

(3) Part II of this Act extends to Scotland only.

(4) This Part of this Act extends to the whole of the United Kingdom.

SCHEDULE 1

SCOPE OF SECTIONS 2 TO 4 AND 7

Section 1(2)

1. Sections 2 to 4 of this Act do not extend to –

    (a) any contract of insurance (including a contract to pay an annuity on human life);

    (b) any contract so far as it relates to the creation or transfer of an interest in land, or to the termination of such an interest, whether by extinction, merger, surrender, forfeiture or otherwise;

    (c) any contract so far as it relates to the creation or transfer of a right or interest in any patent, trade mark, copyright or design right, registered design, technical or commercial information or other intellectual property, or relates to the termination of any such right or interest;

    (d) any contract so far as it relates –

        (i) to the formation or dissolution of a company (which means any body corporate or unincorporated association and includes a partnership), or

        (ii) to its constitution or the rights or obligations of its corporators or members;

(e) any contract so far as it relates to the creation or transfer of securities or of any right or interest in securities.

2. Section 2(1) extends to –

    (a) any contract of marine salvage or towage;

    (b) any charterparty of a ship or hovercraft; and

    (c) any contract for the carriage of goods by ship or hovercraft;

but subject to this sections 2 to 4 and 7 do not extend to any such contract except in favour of a person dealing as consumer.

3. Where goods are carried by ship or hovercraft in pursuance of a contract which either –

    (a) specifies that as the means of carriage over part of the journey to be covered, or

    (b) makes no provision as to the means of carriage and does not exclude that means,

then sections 2(2), 3 and 4 do not, except in favour of a person dealing as consumer, extend to the contract as it operates for and in relation to the carriage of the goods by that means.

4. Section 2(1) and (2) do not extend to a contract of employment, except in favour of the employee.

5. Section 2(1) does not affect the validity of any discharge and indemnity given by a person, on or in connection with an award to him of compensation for pneumoconiosis attributable to employment in the coal industry, in respect of any further claim arising from his contracting that disease.

SCHEDULE 2

"GUIDELINES" FOR APPLICATION OF REASONABLENESS TEST

Sections 11(2), 24(2)

The matters to which regard is to be had in particular for the purposes of sections 6(3), 7(3) and (4), 20 and 21 are any of the following which appear to be relevant –

    (a) the strength of the bargaining positions of the parties relative to each other, taking into account (among other things) alternative means by which the customer's requirements could have been met;

    (b) whether the customer received an inducement to agree to the term, or in accepting it had an opportunity of entering into a similar contract with other persons, but without having to accept a similar term;

    (c) whether the customer knew or ought reasonably to have known of the existence and extent of the term (having regard, among other things, to any custom of the trade and any previous course of dealing between the parties);

    (d) where the term excludes or restricts any relevant liability if some condition is not complied with, whether it was reasonable at the time of the contract to expect that compliance with that condition would be practicable;

    (e) whether the goods were manufactured, processed or adapted to the special order of the customer.

APPENDIX D
THE UNFAIR TERMS IN CONSUMER
CONTRACTS REGULATIONS 1999[1]

1 Citation and commencement

These Regulations may be cited as the Unfair Terms in Consumer Contracts Regulations 1999 and shall come into force on 1st October 1999.

2 Revocation

The Unfair Terms in Consumer Contracts Regulations 1994 are hereby revoked.

3 Interpretation

(1) In these Regulations –

"the Community" means the European Community;

"consumer" means any natural person who, in contracts covered by these Regulations, is acting for purposes which are outside his trade, business or profession;

"court" in relation to England and Wales and Northern Ireland means a county court or the High Court, and in relation to Scotland, the Sheriff or the Court of Session;

"Director" means the Director General of Fair Trading;

"EEA Agreement" means the Agreement on the European Economic Area signed at Oporto on 2nd May 1992 as adjusted by the protocol signed at Brussels on 17th March 1993;

"Member State" means a State which is a contracting party to the EEA Agreement;

"notified" means notified in writing;

"qualifying body" means a person specified in Schedule 1;

"seller or supplier" means any natural or legal person who, in contracts covered by these Regulations, is acting for purposes relating to his trade, business or profession, whether publicly owned or privately owned;

"unfair terms" means the contractual terms referred to in regulation 5.

(2) In the application of these Regulations to Scotland for references to an "injunction" or an "interim injunction" there shall be substituted references to an "interdict" or "interim interdict" respectively.

4 Terms to which these Regulations apply

(1) These Regulations apply in relation to unfair terms in contracts concluded between a seller or a supplier and a consumer.

(2) These Regulations do not apply to contractual terms which reflect –

(a) mandatory statutory or regulatory provisions (including such provisions under the law of any Member State or in Community legislation having effect in the United Kingdom without further enactment);

(b) the provisions or principles of international conventions to which the Member States or the Community are party.

5 Unfair terms

(1) A contractual term which has not been individually negotiated shall be regarded as unfair if, contrary to the requirement of good faith, it causes a significant imbalance in the parties' rights and obligations arising under the contract, to the detriment of the consumer.

---

[1] As amended by the Unfair Terms in Consumer Contracts (Amendment) Regulations 2001, SI 2001 No 1186.

(2) A term shall always be regarded as not having been individually negotiated where it has been drafted in advance and the consumer has therefore not been able to influence the substance of the term.

(3) Notwithstanding that a specific term or certain aspects of it in a contract has been individually negotiated, these Regulations shall apply to the rest of a contract if an overall assessment of it indicates that it is a pre-formulated standard contract.

(4) It shall be for any seller or supplier who claims that a term was individually negotiated to show that it was.

(5) Schedule 2 to these Regulations contains an indicative and non-exhaustive list of the terms which may be regarded as unfair.

6 Assessment of unfair terms

(1) Without prejudice to regulation 12, the unfairness of a contractual term shall be assessed, taking into account the nature of the goods or services for which the contract was concluded and by referring, at the time of conclusion of the contract, to all the circumstances attending the conclusion of the contract and to all the other terms of the contract or of another contract on which it is dependent.

(2) In so far as it is in plain intelligible language, the assessment of fairness of a term shall not relate –

(a) to the definition of the main subject matter of the contract, or

(b) to the adequacy of the price or remuneration, as against the goods or services supplied in exchange.

7 Written contracts

(1) A seller or supplier shall ensure that any written term of a contract is expressed in plain, intelligible language.

(2) If there is doubt about the meaning of a written term, the interpretation which is most favourable to the consumer shall prevail but this rule shall not apply in proceedings brought under regulation 12.

8 Effect of unfair term

(1) An unfair term in a contract concluded with a consumer by a seller or supplier shall not be binding on the consumer.

(2) The contract shall continue to bind the parties if it is capable of continuing in existence without the unfair term.

9 Choice of law clauses

These Regulations shall apply notwithstanding any contract term which applies or purports to apply the law of a non-Member State, if the contract has a close connection with the territory of the Member States.

10 Complaints – consideration by Director

(1) It shall be the duty of the Director to consider any complaint made to him that any contract term drawn up for general use is unfair, unless –

(a) the complaint appears to the Director to be frivolous or vexatious; or

(b) a qualifying body has notified the Director that it agrees to consider the complaint.

(2) The Director shall give reasons for his decision to apply or not to apply, as the case may be, for an injunction under regulation 12 in relation to any complaint which these Regulations require him to consider.

(3) In deciding whether or not to apply for an injunction in respect of a term which the Director considers to be unfair, he may, if he considers it appropriate to do so, have regard to any undertakings given to him by or on behalf of any person as to the continued use of such a term in contracts concluded with consumers.

11 Complaints – consideration by qualifying bodies

(1) If a qualifying body specified in Part One of Schedule 1 notifies the Director that it agrees to consider a complaint that any contract term drawn up for general use is unfair, it shall be under a duty to consider that complaint.

(2) Regulation 10(2) and (3) shall apply to a qualifying body which is under a duty to consider a complaint as they apply to the Director.

12 Injunctions to prevent continued use of unfair terms

(1) The Director or, subject to paragraph (2), any qualifying body may apply for an injunction (including an interim injunction) against any person appearing to the Director or that body to be using, or recommending use of, an unfair term drawn up for general use in contracts concluded with consumers.

(2) A qualifying body may apply for an injunction only where –

   (a) it has notified the Director of its intention to apply at least fourteen days before the date on which the application is made, beginning with the date on which the notification was given; or

   (b) the Director consents to the application being made within a shorter period.

(3) The court on an application under this regulation may grant an injunction on such terms as it thinks fit.

(4) An injunction may relate not only to use of a particular contract term drawn up for general use but to any similar term, or a term having like effect, used or recommended for use by any person.

13 Powers of the Director and qualifying bodies to obtain documents and information

(1) The Director may exercise the power conferred by this regulation for the purpose of –

   (a) facilitating his consideration of a complaint that a contract term drawn up for general use is unfair; or

   (b) ascertaining whether a person has complied with an undertaking or court order as to the continued use, or recommendation for use, of a term in contracts concluded with consumers.

(2) A qualifying body specified in Part One of Schedule 1 may exercise the power conferred by this regulation for the purpose of –

   (a) facilitating its consideration of a complaint that a contract term drawn up for general use is unfair; or

   (b) ascertaining whether a person has complied with –

      (i) an undertaking given to it or to the court following an application by that body, or

      (ii) a court order made on an application by that body,

   as to the continued use, or recommendation for use, of a term in contracts concluded with consumers.

(3) The Director may require any person to supply to him, and a qualifying body specified in Part One of Schedule 1 may require any person to supply to it –

   (a) a copy of any document which that person has used or recommended for use, at the time the notice referred to in paragraph (4) below is given, as a pre-formulated standard contract in dealings with consumers;

   (b) information about the use, or recommendation for use, by that person of that document or any other such document in dealings with consumers.

(4) The power conferred by this regulation is to be exercised by a notice in writing which may –

   (a) specify the way in which and the time within which it is to be complied with; and

(b) be varied or revoked by a subsequent notice.

(5) Nothing in this regulation compels a person to supply any document or information which he would be entitled to refuse to produce or give in civil proceedings before the court.

(6) If a person makes default in complying with a notice under this regulation, the court may, on the application of the Director or of the qualifying body, make such order as the court thinks fit for requiring the default to be made good, and any such order may provide that all the costs or expenses of and incidental to the application shall be borne by the person in default or by any officers of a company or other association who are responsible for its default.

14 Notification of undertakings and orders to Director

A qualifying body shall notify the Director –

(a) of any undertaking given to it by or on behalf of any person as to the continued use of a term which that body considers to be unfair in contracts concluded with consumers;

(b) of the outcome of any application made by it under regulation 12, and of the terms of any undertaking given to, or order made by, the court;

(c) of the outcome of any application made by it to enforce a previous order of the court.

15 Publication, information and advice

(1) The Director shall arrange for the publication in such form and manner as he considers appropriate, of –

(a) details of any undertaking or order notified to him under regulation 14;

(b) details of any undertaking given to him by or on behalf of any person as to the continued use of a term which the Director considers to be unfair in contracts concluded with consumers;

(c) details of any application made by him under regulation 12, and of the terms of any undertaking given to, or order made by, the court;

(d) details of any application made by the Director to enforce a previous order of the court.

(2) The Director shall inform any person on request whether a particular term to which these Regulations apply has been –

(a) the subject of an undertaking given to the Director or notified to him by a qualifying body; or

(b) the subject of an order of the court made upon application by him or notified to him by a qualifying body;

and shall give that person details of the undertaking or a copy of the order, as the case may be, together with a copy of any amendments which the person giving the undertaking has agreed to make to the term in question.

(3) The Director may arrange for the dissemination in such form and manner as he considers appropriate of such information and advice concerning the operation of these Regulations as may appear to him to be expedient to give to the public and to all persons likely to be affected by these Regulations.

16 The functions of the Financial Services Authority

The functions of the Financial Services Authority under these Regulations shall be treated as functions of the Financial Services Authority under the Financial Services and Markets Act 2000.

Schedule 1

Qualifying bodies

Part One

1 The Information Commissioner.

2 The Gas and Electricity Markets Authority.

3 The Director General of Electricity Supply for Northern Ireland.

4 The Director General of Gas for Northern Ireland.

5 The Director General of Telecommunications.

6 The Director General of Water Services.

7 The Rail Regulator.

8 Every weights and measures authority in Great Britain.

9 The Department of Enterprise, Trade and Investment in Northern Ireland.

10 The Financial Services Authority.

Part Two

11 Consumers' Association

Schedule 2

Indicative and non-exhaustive list of terms which may be regarded as unfair

1 Terms which have the object or effect of –

(a) excluding or limiting the legal liability of a seller or supplier in the event of the death of a consumer or personal injury to the latter resulting from an act or omission of that seller or supplier;

(b) inappropriately excluding or limiting the legal rights of the consumer vis-à-vis the seller or supplier or another party in the event of total or partial non-performance or inadequate performance by the seller or supplier of any of the contractual obligations, including the option of offsetting a debt owed to the seller or supplier against any claim which the consumer may have against him;

(c) making an agreement binding on the consumer whereas provision of services by the seller or supplier is subject to a condition whose realisation depends on his own will alone;

(d) permitting the seller or supplier to retain sums paid by the consumer where the latter decides not to conclude or perform the contract, without providing for the consumer to receive compensation of an equivalent amount from the seller or supplier where the latter is the party cancelling the contract;

(e) requiring any consumer who fails to fulfil his obligation to pay a disproportionately high sum in compensation;

(f) authorising the seller or supplier to dissolve the contract on a discretionary basis where the same facility is not granted to the consumer, or permitting the seller or supplier to retain the sums paid for services not yet supplied by him where it is the seller or supplier himself who dissolves the contract;

(g) enabling the seller or supplier to terminate a contract of indeterminate duration without reasonable notice except where there are serious grounds for doing so;

(h) automatically extending a contract of fixed duration where the consumer does not indicate otherwise, when the deadline fixed for the consumer to express his desire not to extend the contract is unreasonably early;

(i) irrevocably binding the consumer to terms with which he had no real opportunity of becoming acquainted before the conclusion of the contract;

(j) enabling the seller or supplier to alter the terms of the contract unilaterally without a valid reason which is specified in the contract;

(k) enabling the seller or supplier to alter unilaterally without a valid reason any characteristics of the product or service to be provided;

(l) providing for the price of goods to be determined at the time of delivery or allowing a seller of goods or supplier of services to increase their price without in both cases giving the consumer the corresponding right to cancel the contract if the final price is too high in relation to the price agreed when the contract was concluded;

(m) giving the seller or supplier the right to determine whether the goods or services supplied are in conformity with the contract, or giving him the exclusive right to interpret any term of the contract;

(n) limiting the seller's or supplier's obligation to respect commitments undertaken by his agents or making his commitments subject to compliance with a particular formality;

(o) obliging the consumer to fulfil all his obligations where the seller or supplier does not perform his;

(p) giving the seller or supplier the possibility of transferring his rights and obligations under the contract, where this may serve to reduce the guarantees for the consumer, without the latter's agreement;

(q) excluding or hindering the consumer's right to take legal action or exercise any other legal remedy, particularly by requiring the consumer to take disputes exclusively to arbitration not covered by legal provisions, unduly restricting the evidence available to him or imposing on him a burden of proof which, according to the applicable law, should lie with another party to the contract.

2 Scope of paragraphs 1(g), (j) and (l)

(a) Paragraph 1(g) is without hindrance to terms by which a supplier of financial services reserves the right to terminate unilaterally a contract of indeterminate duration without notice where there is a valid reason, provided that the supplier is required to inform the other contracting party or parties thereof immediately.

(b) Paragraph 1(j) is without hindrance to terms under which a supplier of financial services reserves the right to alter the rate of interest payable by the consumer or due to the latter, or the amount of other charges for financial services without notice where there is a valid reason, provided that the supplier is required to inform the other contracting party or parties thereof at the earliest opportunity and that the latter are free to dissolve the contract immediately.

Paragraph 1(j) is also without hindrance to terms under which a seller or supplier reserves the right to alter unilaterally the conditions of a contract of indeterminate duration, provided that he is required to inform the consumer with reasonable notice and that the consumer is free to dissolve the contract.

(c) Paragraphs 1(g), (j) and (l) do not apply to:

– transactions in transferable securities, financial instruments and other products or services where the price is linked to fluctuations in a stock exchange quotation or index or a financial market rate that the seller or supplier does not control;

– contracts for the purchase or sale of foreign currency, traveller's cheques or international money orders denominated in foreign currency.

(d) Paragraph 1(l) is without hindrance to price indexation clauses, where lawful, provided that the method by which prices vary is explicitly described.

APPENDIX E
COUNCIL DIRECTIVE 93/13/EEC ON UNFAIR TERMS IN CONSUMER CONTRACTS

THE COUNCIL OF THE EUROPEAN COMMUNITIES,

Having regard to the Treaty establishing the European Economic Community, and in particular Article 100 A thereof,

Having regard to the proposal from the Commission,[1]

In cooperation with the European Parliament,[2]

Having regard to the opinion of the Economic and Social Committee,[3]

1. Whereas it is necessary to adopt measures with the aim of progressively establishing the internal market before 31 December 1992; whereas the internal market comprises an area without internal frontiers in which goods, persons, services and capital move freely;

2. Whereas the laws of Member States relating to the terms of contract between the seller of goods or supplier of services, on the one hand, and the consumer of them, on the other hand, show many disparities, with the result that the national markets for the sale of goods and services to consumers differ from each other and that distortions of competition may arise amongst the sellers and suppliers, notably when they sell and supply in other Member States;

3. Whereas, in particular, the laws of Member States relating to unfair terms in consumer contracts show marked divergences;

4. Whereas it is the responsibility of the Member States to ensure that contracts concluded with consumers do not contain unfair terms;

5. Whereas, generally speaking, consumers do not know the rules of law which, in Member States other than their own, govern contracts for the sale of goods or services; whereas this lack of awareness may deter them from direct transactions for the purchase of goods or services in another Member State;

6. Whereas, in order to facilitate the establishment of the internal market and to safeguard the citizen in his role as consumer when acquiring goods and services under contracts which are governed by the laws of Member States other than his own, it is essential to remove unfair terms from those contracts;

7. Whereas sellers of goods and suppliers of services will thereby be helped in their task of selling goods and supplying services, both at home and throughout the internal market; whereas competition will thus be stimulated, so contributing to increased choice for Community citizens as consumers;

[1]   OJ No C 73, 24.3.1992, p 7.

[2]   OJ No C 326, 16.12.1991, p 108 and OJ No C 21, 25.1.1993.

[3]   OJ No C 159, 17.6.1991, p 34.

8. Whereas the two Community programmes for a consumer protection and information policy[4] underlined the importance of safeguarding consumers in the matter of unfair terms of contract; whereas this protection ought to be provided by laws and regulations which are either harmonized at Community level or adopted directly at that level;

9. Whereas in accordance with the principle laid down under the heading "Protection of the economic interests of the consumers", as stated in those programmes: "acquirers of goods and services should be protected against the abuse of power by the seller or supplier, in particular against one-sided standard contracts and the unfair exclusion of essential rights in contracts";

10. Whereas more effective protection of the consumer can be achieved by adopting uniform rules of law in the matter of unfair terms; whereas those rules should apply to all contracts concluded between sellers or suppliers and consumers; whereas as a result inter alia contracts relating to employment, contracts relating to succession rights, contracts relating to rights under family law and contracts relating to the incorporation and organization of companies or partnership agreements must be excluded from this Directive;

11. Whereas the consumer must receive equal protection under contracts concluded by word of mouth and written contracts regardless, in the latter case, of whether the terms of the contract are contained in one or more documents;

12. Whereas, however, as they now stand, national laws allow only partial harmonization to be envisaged; whereas, in particular, only contractual terms which have not been individually negotiated are covered by this Directive; whereas Member States should have the option, with due regard for the Treaty, to afford consumers a higher level of protection through national provisions that are more stringent than those of this Directive;

13. Whereas the statutory or regulatory provisions of the Member States which directly or indirectly determine the terms of consumer contracts are presumed not to contain unfair terms; whereas, therefore, it does not appear to be necessary to subject the terms which reflect mandatory statutory or regulatory provisions and the principles or provisions of international conventions to which the Member States or the Community are party; whereas in that respect the wording "mandatory statutory or regulatory provisions" in Article 1(2) also covers rules which, according to the law, shall apply between the contracting parties provided that no other arrangements have been established;

14. Whereas Member States must however ensure that unfair terms are not included, particularly because this Directive also applies to trades, business or professions of a public nature;

15. Whereas it is necessary to fix in a general way the criteria for assessing the unfair character of contract terms;

16. Whereas the assessment, according to the general criteria chosen, of the unfair character of terms, in particular in sale or supply activities of a public nature providing collective services which take account of solidarity among users, must

---

[4]   OJ No C 92, 25.4.1975, p 1 and OJ No C 133, 3.6.1981, p 1.

be supplemented by a means of making an overall evaluation of the different interests involved; whereas this constitutes the requirement of good faith; whereas, in making an assessment of good faith, particular regard shall be had to the strength of the bargaining positions of the parties, whether the consumer had an inducement to agree to the term and whether the goods or services were sold or supplied to the special order of the consumer; whereas the requirement of good faith may be satisfied by the seller or supplier where he deals fairly and equitably with the other party whose legitimate interests he has to take into account;

17. Whereas, for the purposes of this Directive, the annexed list of terms can be of indicative value only and, because of the cause of the minimal character of the Directive, the scope of these terms may be the subject of amplification or more restrictive editing by the Member States in their national laws;

18. Whereas the nature of goods or services should have an influence on assessing the unfairness of contractual terms;

19. Whereas, for the purposes of this Directive, assessment of unfair character shall not be made of terms which describe the main subject matter of the contract nor the quality/price ratio of the goods or services supplied; whereas the main subject matter of the contract and the price/quality ratio may nevertheless be taken into account in assessing the fairness of other terms; whereas it follows, inter alia, that in insurance contracts, the terms which clearly define or circumscribe the insured risk and the insurer's liability shall not be subject to such assessment since these restrictions are taken into account in calculating the premium paid by the consumer;

20. Whereas contracts should be drafted in plain, intelligible language, the consumer should actually be given an opportunity to examine all the terms and, if in doubt, the interpretation most favourable to the consumer should prevail;

21. Whereas Member States should ensure that unfair terms are not used in contracts concluded with consumers by a seller or supplier and that if, nevertheless, such terms are so used, they will not bind the consumer, and the contract will continue to bind the parties upon those terms if it is capable of continuing in existence without the unfair provisions;

22. Whereas there is a risk that, in certain cases, the consumer may be deprived of protection under this Directive by designating the law of a non-Member country as the law applicable to the contract; whereas provisions should therefore be included in this Directive designed to avert this risk;

23. Whereas persons or organizations, if regarded under the law of a Member State as having a legitimate interest in the matter, must have facilities for initiating proceedings concerning terms of contract drawn up for general use in contracts concluded with consumers, and in particular unfair terms, either before a court or before an administrative authority competent to decide upon complaints or to initiate appropriate legal proceedings; whereas this possibility does not, however, entail prior verification of the general conditions obtaining in individual economic sectors;

24. Whereas the courts or administrative authorities of the Member States must have at their disposal adequate and effective means of preventing the continued application of unfair terms in consumer contracts,

HAS ADOPTED THIS DIRECTIVE:

Article 1

1. The purpose of this Directive is to approximate the laws, regulations and administrative provisions of the Member States relating to unfair terms in contracts concluded between a seller or supplier and a consumer.

2. The contractual terms which reflect mandatory statutory or regulatory provisions and the provisions or principles of international conventions to which the Member States or the Community are party, particularly in the transport area, shall not be subject to the provisions of this Directive.

Article 2

For the purposes of this Directive:

(a) "unfair terms" means the contractual terms defined in Article 3;

(b) "consumer" means any natural person who, in contracts covered by this Directive, is acting for purposes which are outside his trade, business or profession;

(c) "seller or supplier" means any natural or legal person who, in contracts covered by this Directive, is acting for purposes relating to his trade, business or profession, whether publicly owned or privately owned.

Article 3

1. A contractual term which has not been individually negotiated shall be regarded as unfair if, contrary to the requirement of good faith, it causes a significant imbalance in the parties' rights and obligations arising under the contract, to the detriment of the consumer.

2. A term shall always be regarded as not individually negotiated where it has been drafted in advance and the consumer has therefore not been able to influence the substance of the term, particularly in the context of a pre-formulated standard contract.

The fact that certain aspects of a term or one specific term have been individually negotiated shall not exclude the application of this Article to the rest of a contract if an overall assessment of the contract indicates that it is nevertheless a pre-formulated standard contract.

Where any seller or supplier claims that a standard term has been individually negotiated, the burden of proof in this respect shall be incumbent on him.

3. The Annex shall contain an indicative and non-exhaustive list of the terms which may be regarded as unfair.

Article 4

1. Without prejudice to Article 7, the unfairness of a contractual term shall be assessed, taking into account the nature of the goods or services for which the contract was concluded and by referring, at the time of conclusion of the contract, to all the circumstances attending the conclusion of the contract and to all the other terms of the contract or of another contract on which it is dependent.

2. Assessment of the unfair nature of the terms shall relate neither to the definition of the main subject matter of the contract nor to the adequacy of the price and remuneration, on the one hand, as against the services or goods supplied in exchange, on the other, in so far as these terms are in plain intelligible language.

Article 5

In the case of contracts where all or certain terms offered to the consumer are in writing, these terms must always be drafted in plain, intelligible language. Where there is doubt about the meaning of a term, the interpretation most favourable to the consumer shall prevail. This rule on interpretation shall not apply in the context of the procedures laid down in Article 7(2).

Article 6

1. Member States shall lay down that unfair terms used in a contract concluded with a consumer by a seller or supplier shall, as provided for under their national law, not be binding on the consumer and that the contract shall continue to bind the parties upon those terms if it is capable of continuing in existence without the unfair terms.

2. Member States shall take the necessary measures to ensure that the consumer does not lose the protection granted by this Directive by virtue of the choice of the law of a non-Member country as the law applicable to the contract if the latter has a close connection with the territory of the Member States.

Article 7

1. Member States shall ensure that, in the interests of consumers and of competitors, adequate and effective means exist to prevent the continued use of unfair terms in contracts concluded with consumers by sellers or suppliers.

2. The means referred to in paragraph 1 shall include provisions whereby persons or organizations, having a legitimate interest under national law in protecting consumers, may take action according to the national law concerned before the courts or before competent administrative bodies for a decision as to whether contractual terms drawn up for general use are unfair, so that they can apply appropriate and effective means to prevent the continued use of such terms.

3. With due regard for national laws, the legal remedies referred to in paragraph 2 may be directed separately or jointly against a number of sellers or suppliers from the same economic sector or their associations which use or recommend the use of the same general contractual terms or similar terms.

Article 8

Member States may adopt or retain the most stringent provisions compatible with the Treaty in the area covered by this Directive, to ensure a maximum degree of protection for the consumer.

Article 9

The Commission shall present a report to the European Parliament and to the Council concerning the application of this Directive five years at the latest after the date in Article 10(1).

Article 10

1. Member States shall bring into force the laws, regulations and admi[n] provisions necessary to comply with this Directive no later than 31 Dec[ember] 1994. They shall forthwith inform the Commission thereof.

These provisions shall be applicable to all contracts concluded after 31 December 1994.

2. When Member States adopt these measures, they shall contain a reference to this Directive or shall be accompanied by such reference on the occasion of their official publication. The methods of making such a reference shall be laid down by the Member States.

3. Member States shall communicate the main provisions of national law which they adopt in the field covered by this Directive to the Commission.

Article 11

This Directive is addressed to the Member States.

Done at Luxembourg, 5 April 1993.

For the Council

The President

N. HELVEG PETERSEN

[The Annex is effectively identical to Schedule 2 to UTCCR. See Appendix D above.]

	UTCCR	Provisional proposals
App... • Separate Parts for England and Scotland.	• Apply to the UK as a whole.	• There should be a single piece of legislation for the whole of the UK.
Parties protected • Most sections apply to both consumer and non-consumer contracts. • Sections 4 and 5 [ss 18, 19] apply only to consumer contracts. • Section 6(1) and (3) [s 20(1), (2)(ii)] apply to any party whatever their status.	• Apply only to contracts between a business seller or supplier and a consumer.	• Should apply to both consumer and business-to-business contracts. • UCTA s 6(1) and (3) [s 20(1), (2)(ii)] should be incorporated into the new legislation.
Terms of no effect • Exclusion or restriction of liability for death or personal injury caused by negligence [breach of duty]. • Exclusion or restriction of liability for breach of the implied terms as to title in contracts for sale, hire-purchase or (except in Scotland) other transfer of property in goods. • Exclusion or restriction of liability for breach of the implied terms as to description, quality etc in contracts for the supply of goods to a person dealing as consumer.	• There are no terms that are automatically of no effect. All terms are subject to the test of fairness.	• Maintain present rules rendering some exclusions and restrictions of no effect (except in relation to guarantees); other terms to be subject to a reasonableness test.

UCTA	UTCCR	Provisional proposals
• Exclusion or restriction of liability, by means of a term or notice in a "guarantee", of a manufacturer's or distributor's liability in tort [delict] to a person injured by goods proving defective while in consumer use.		
Range of terms controlled • Applies only to terms excluding or restricting liability (except s 4 [s 18]).	• Apply to any contractual term except "core" terms (see below).	• Should apply to all terms (except "core" terms) both in consumer and in business-to-business contracts.
Terms not individually negotiated • Controls over specific types of term (ss 2, 4–7 [ss 16, 18–21]) apply whether or not clause was negotiated. Section 3 [s 17] applies (a) to all consumer contracts; (b) in non-consumer contracts, only to written standard terms of business. • Some exclusions are of no effect against any party; others are of no effect against consumers, but against non-consumers only if unreasonable (ss 6 and 7 [ss 20, 21]).	• Only apply to terms that have been drafted in advance and not individually negotiated.	• In business-to-business contracts, controls should apply to terms that have been drafted in advance and not individually negotiated. • We ask whether the present protection afforded to businesses under UCTA ss 6 and 7 [ss 20, 21] (which apply to all terms, whether negotiated or not) should be retained.

UCTA	UTCCR	Provisional proposals
Terms not subject to controls *(1) "Definitional" and "core" terms* • Generally applies only to terms excluding or restricting liability (see above). Section 3(2)(b) applies to a term entitling a party to render a performance "substantially different from that which was reasonably expected", or no performance at all.	• Terms that define the main subject matter of the contract, provided they are in plain intelligible language.	• The legislation should exclude the main subject matter from the scope of review, but only in so far as a) it is not substantially different from what the consumer should reasonably expect, in the light of what he or she was told when or before the contract was made and all the other circumstances; and b) it is stated transparently.
• Terms setting the price to be paid are beyond the scope of the legislation.	• No control over the adequacy of the price, provided the relevant terms are in plain and intelligible language.	• The adequacy of the price should not be subject to review where the price a) is not payable in circumstances substantially different from what the consumer reasonably expected, or calculated in a way which is substantially different from that; and b) is not one contained in a subsidiary term; and c) is transparent.

UCTA	UTCCR	Provisional proposals
(2) "Mandatory" and "permitted" terms • Terms required or authorised by an enactment.	• Terms required or (probably) authorised in any Member State or in Community legislation of immediate direct effect in the UK.	• Terms complying with mandatory statutory rules should be exempt; also terms which are not substantially different from the default rules, provided they are in plain language.
Terms required or authorised by regulators • Terms required or approved by competent authorities, acting in the course of any statutory jurisdiction or function.	• Possible that terms required or approved by regulatory agencies may be exempt.	• Only terms that are required by regulators should be exempt.
International instruments • Terms made with a view to compliance with an international treaty to which the UK is a party, provided the term does not operate more restrictively than was contemplated by the agreement.	• Terms which reflect provisions and principles of international treaties to which Member States or the Community are party.	• Only terms which reflect what is required or authorised by international conventions (not those which merely reflect the principles of such conventions) should be exempt.
Excluded contracts **(1) Domestic contracts** *Consumers as suppliers* • Section 3 [s 17] applies to contracts irrespective of whether the consumer is the buyer or seller, supplier or recipient.	• Unclear whether UTCCR apply to contracts where the consumer is the seller or supplier.	• The legislation should apply where the consumer is the seller or supplier.

UCTA	UTCCR	Provisional proposals
• Contracts of insurance.	• Apply to all consumer contracts without any such exclusions.	• In relation to consumer contracts, there should be no exclusion of insurance, land or securities contracts (required by Directive 93/13/EEC).
• Contracts relating to land, securities, or (in Scotland) guarantees.		• All of the exemptions should be maintained so far as they relate to business-to-business contracts.
• In business-to-business contracts: a) contracts relating to intellectual property or company matters; b) unless the contract attempts to exclude or restrict liability for negligence [breach of duty] in respect of death or personal injury: i) any contract of marine salvage ii) any charterparty of a ship or hovercraft iii) any contract for the carriage of goods by ship or hovercraft.		
• Contracts of employment are not excluded, except that s 2 applies only in favour of the employee.	• Contracts of employment are beyond the scope of the legislation.	• We ask whether contracts of employment should be covered by the new regime, and, if so, whether they should count as consumer contracts, as business-to-business contracts, or as a separate category subject to some but not all of the controls.

UCTA	UTCCR	Provisional proposals
(2) International contracts • Certain sections do not apply to contracts for the supply of goods made by parties in different States which involve the carriage of goods between States, offer and acceptance across State borders, or delivery in a State other than that in which the contract was made.	• No such exception; apply whenever the law of a part of the UK applies.	• Terms restricting liability for breaches of SGA 1979 ss 13–15 in cross-border consumer contracts should be subject to the legislation (required by SCGD). • Rules making other exclusions of no effect should also apply to cross-border contracts ("fairness" test at least required by Directive 93/13/EEC). • We ask whether international business-to-business contracts should be exempted from the controls proposed for domestic contracts.
(3) Choice of UK law • Contracts in which English or Scots law applies only because the parties have chosen that law to govern their contract.	• No such exclusion.	• No such exclusion for consumer contracts (partly required by Directive 93/13/EEC and SCGD).
The test of validity • Whether the term was a fair and reasonable one to include in the contract.	• A term is unfair if, contrary to good faith, it causes a significant imbalance in the parties' rights and obligations arising under the contract, to the detriment of the consumer.	• Whether, judged by reference to the time the contract was made, the term is fair and reasonable.

UCTA	UTCCR	Provisional proposals
• In case of doubt, terms are interpreted against the party relying on them.	• In case of doubt, the interpretation most favourable to the consumer prevails.	• In both consumer and business-to-business contracts, it should be a separate ground of unfairness that the term is not "transparent" – ie plainly expressed, clearly presented and accessible.
Factors to be taken into account in applying the test • Circumstances which were, or ought reasonably to have been, known to or in the contemplation of the parties when the contract was made. • Factors listed in Schedule 2 guidelines and s 11(4). **Burden of showing unfairness** • Burden of showing that the term is fair and reasonable is on the party claiming that it is.	• All the circumstances attending the conclusion of the contract. • All the other terms of the contract, or of another contract on which it is dependent. • No other factors listed in the regulations (though some in the Recitals to the Directive). • No statement of which party bears the burden; probably on the consumer.	• There should be detailed guidelines relating both to fairness in substance and to procedural fairness. • We ask whether the burden should either i) be on the party claiming that the term is fair and reasonable to show that it is; or ii) be on the party claiming that it is *not* fair and reasonable to show that it is not, unless it falls within Schedule 2, in which case it is for the party claiming that the term *is* fair and reasonable to show that it is.

UCTA	UTCCR	Provisional proposals
		• In business-to-business contracts, where a term is not included in the indicative list, the burden of proving that it is not fair and reasonable should be on the party disputing it.
Definition of consumer • One party neither makes the contract in the course of a business nor holds himself out as doing so; and • The other party does make the contract in the course of a business. • Whether goods passing under the contract are of a type ordinarily supplied for private use or consumption. *Auction sales* • The buyer in a sale by auction or by competitive tender is not considered a consumer.	• Any natural person who, in contracts covered by the regulations, is acting for purposes outside his trade, business or profession.	• Limited to an individual who makes the contract for purposes which are not related to any business of his. The requirement that the person does not hold himself out as making the contract in the course of a business will not be included. (Required by SCGD) • In the case of contracts governed by the law of sale of goods or hire-purchase the goods will *not* have to be of a type ordinarily supplied for private use or consumption. (Required by SCGD) • Sales of second-hand goods by auction, where the consumer can be present, will not be subject to the absolute ban on contracting out. • Sellers by competitive tender will not be permitted to contract out. (Required by SCGD)

UCTA	UTCCR	Provisional proposals
Definition of business • "Business" includes a profession and the activities of any government department or local or public authority. • The party is acting in the "ordinary course of business".	• "Seller or supplier" means any natural or legal person who, in contracts covered by the regulations, is acting for purposes relating to his trade, business or profession, whether publicly owned or privately owned. • Refer to "relating to trade, business or profession".	• It should be made clear that "business" includes a profession and the activities of a government department or local or public authority. • A contract will be treated as a business transaction even if the item sold is not one normally sold or supplied.
Third party beneficiaries' rights • *England* A third party claiming rights under the Contracts (Rights of Third Parties) Act 1999 cannot challenge the validity of a clause, except under s 2(1) if it attempts to exclude liability for personal injury or death. • *Scotland* Third parties can challenge a clause if it attempts to exclude liability for death, personal injury, or other loss or damage caused by breach of duty. They may not be able to challenge clauses under section 17.	• Unclear, but it would appear that the regulations only apply to the rights of the consumer and not the rights of a third party beneficiary.	• For both England and Scotland, the present position under UCTA should be maintained.

UCTA	UTCCR	Provisional proposals
Application outside contract • Does not apply to the provision of gratuitous services or where there is a statutory duty to provide a service (eg an agreement for the supply of water). • Applies to notices excluding liability in tort [delict] for negligence [breach of duty].	• Unclear whether applicable to provision of gratuitous services or where there is a statutory duty to supply goods or services. Suggestion that ECJ might adopt view of contract that includes these agreements. • Do not appear to apply to notices; but suggestion that the ECJ might interpret "contract" within the meaning of the Directive to include circumstances where such notices are used.	• The new legislation should refer simply to consumer "contracts" so that the legislation could be interpreted in line with any future European legislation. • Should apply to notices excluding liability in tort [delict] for negligence [breach of duty].
Effect if term is held invalid • The term is of no effect and the parties' relationship continues as if the term had not been included in the contract.	• The term is not binding on the consumer, and the contract continues to bind the parties if it is capable of continuing in existence without the unfair term.	• The term should be of no effect to the extent that it is detrimental to the consumer, and the contract should continue to bind the parties if it is capable of continuing in existence without the unfair term.
Evasion of legislation *"Secondary contracts"* • A person is not bound by a term which seeks to prejudice or take away rights under another contract if they relate to liabilities of which the Act prevents exclusion. • The position on settlements in England is unclear; in Scotland they are exempt.	• The second contract would be equally subject to the legislation, unless it had no other subject matter so that the relevant term was a "core" term.	• There should be a provision subjecting terms in "secondary contracts" to the same controls as if they appeared in the main contract. Genuine agreements to settle a dispute should be exempted.

UCTA	UTCCR	Provisional proposals
Evasion by choice of law • UCTA applies irrespective of terms applying the law of a country outside the UK, if the contract would otherwise be subject to the laws of the UK.	• The regulations apply irrespective of any terms applying the law of a non-Member State in place of a Member State, if the contract has a close connection with the territory of the Member States.	• In consumer contracts, it should be made clear that, if the contract has a close connection with the UK, the new legislation will apply irrespective of a choice of another system of law.
Prevention • Nothing to prevent continued use of terms that are invalid. • The use of terms falling under section 6 is an offence under orders made under the Fair Trading Act 1973, Part II.	• The DGFT and certain "qualifying bodies" can bring proceedings for an injunction [interdict] against persons appearing to use or promote the use of unfair terms in consumer contracts. • Unclear whether these powers extend to terms that are not effectively incorporated into the agreement.	• The DGFT and certain "qualifying bodies" will be empowered to bring proceedings for an injunction [interdict] against persons appearing to use or promote the use of unfair terms in consumer contracts. (Required by Directive 93/13/EEC) • These bodies should be able to prevent the use of ineffectively incorporated contract terms, and of any term which is unfair because it is not transparent. • We invite views as to whether these bodies should have powers to act against practices of *negotiating* terms which are nonetheless unfair. • We ask whether the preventive controls should be extended to unfair terms in business-to-business contracts.